PENGUIN CLASSICS 🐧 DELUXE EDITION

TRAVELS WITH CHARLEY
IN SEARCH OF AMERICA

Born in Salinas, California, in 1902, John Steinbeck grew up in a fertile agricultural valley about twenty-five miles from the Pacific Coast—and both valley and coast would serve as settings for some of his best fiction. In 1919 he went to Stanford University, where he intermittently enrolled in literature and writing courses until he left in 1925 without taking a degree. During the next five years he supported himself as a laborer and journalist in New York City, all the time working on his first novel, *Cup of Gold* (1929). After marriage and a move to Pacific Grove, he published two California fictions, *The Pastures of Heaven* (1932) and *To a God Unknown* (1933), and worked on short stories later collected in *The Long Valley* (1938). Popular success and financial security came only with *Tortilla Flat* (1935), stories about Monterey's paisanos. A ceaseless experimenter throughout his career, Steinbeck changed courses regularly. Three powerful novels of the late 1930s focused on the California laboring class: *In Dubious Battle* (1936), *Of Mice and Men* (1937), and the book considered by many his finest, *The Grapes of Wrath* (1939). Early in the 1940s, Steinbeck became a filmmaker with *The Forgotten Village* (1941) and a serious student of marine biology with *Sea of Cortez* (1941). He devoted his services to the war, writing *Bombs Away* (1942) and the controversial play-novelette *The Moon Is Down* (1942). *Cannery Row* (1945), *The Wayward Bus* (1947), *The Pearl* (1947), *A Russian Journal* (1948), another experimental drama, *Burning Bright* (1950), and *The Log from the* Sea of Cortez (1951) preceded publication of the monumental *East of Eden* (1952), an ambitious saga of the Salinas Valley and his own family's history. The last decades of his life were spent in New York City and Sag Harbor with his third wife, with whom he traveled widely. Later books include *Sweet Thursday* (1954), *The Short Reign of Pippin IV: A Fabrication* (1957), *Once There Was a War* (1958), *The Winter of Our Discontent* (1961), *Travels with Charley in Search of America* (1962), *America and Americans* (1966), and the posthumously published *Journal of a Novel: The* East of Eden *Letters* (1969), *Viva Zapata!* (1975), *The Acts of King Arthur and His Noble Knights* (1976), and *Working Days: The Journal of* The Grapes of Wrath (1989). He died in 1968, having won a Nobel Prize in 1962.

Throughout his life Steinbeck signed his letters with his personal "Pigasus" logo, symbolizing himself "a lumbering soul but trying to fly." The Latin motto *Ad Astra Per Alia Porci* translates "To the stars on the wings of a pig."

JAY PARINI is a poet and novelist who teaches at Middlebury College in Vermont. His most recent volume of poems is *The Art of Subtraction: New and Selected Poems*. His novels include *The Last Station*, *Benjamin's Crossing*, and *The Passages of H.M.* He has also written biographies of John Steinbeck, Robert Frost, and William Faulkner. His other books include *Promised Land: Thirteen Books that Changed America* and *Why Poetry Matters*.

Publisher's note: The images printed below represent the original photographs as they were taken in 1961. With permission of the copyright holder, these photographs appear as original scans of a vintage edition jacket on the back cover and inside flap of our 50th-Anniversary Edition.

John Steinbeck and Charley, 1961 (detail) by Hans Namuth © 1991 Hans Namuth Estate

John Steinbeck, 1961 (detail) by Hans Namuth © 1991 Hans Namuth Estate

BY JOHN STEINBECK

FICTION

Cup of Gold   The Moon Is Down
The Pastures of Heaven   Cannery Row
To a God Unknown   The Wayward Bus
Tortilla Flat   The Pearl
In Dubious Battle   Burning Bright
Saint Katy the Virgin   East of Eden
Of Mice and Men   Sweet Thursday
The Red Pony   The Winter of Our Discontent
The Long Valley   The Short Reign of Pippin IV
The Grapes of Wrath
Las uvas de la ira (*Spanish-language edition of* The Grapes of Wrath)
The Acts of King Arthur and His Noble Knights

NONFICTION

Sea of Cortez: A Leisurely Journal of Travel and Research
(*in collaboration with Edward F. Ricketts*)
Bombs Away: The Story of a Bomber Team
A Russian Journal (*with pictures by Robert Capa*)
The Log from the *Sea of Cortez*
Once There Was a War
Travels with Charley in Search of America
America and Americans
America and Americans and Selected Nonfiction
Journal of a Novel: The *East of Eden* Letters
Working Days: The Journals of *The Grapes of Wrath*

PLAYS

Of Mice and Men
The Moon Is Down

COLLECTIONS

The Portable Steinbeck
The Short Novels of John Steinbeck
Steinbeck: A Life in Letters

OTHER WORKS

The Forgotten Village (*documentary*)
Viva Zapata! (screenplay)
Zapata (*includes the screenplay of* Viva Zapata!)

CRITICAL LIBRARY EDITION

The Grapes of Wrath (*edited by Peter Lisca*)

JOHN STEINBECK

Travels with Charley in Search of America

50TH-ANNIVERSARY EDITION

Introduction by
JAY PARINI

PENGUIN BOOKS

PENGUIN BOOKS
Published by the Penguin Group
Penguin Group (USA) Inc., 375 Hudson Street, New York, New York 10014, U.S.A. •
Penguin Group (Canada), 90 Eglinton Avenue East, Suite 700, Toronto, Ontario, Canada M4P 2Y3
(a division of Pearson Penguin Canada Inc.) • Penguin Books Ltd, 80 Strand, London WC2R 0RL,
England • Penguin Ireland, 25 St Stephen's Green, Dublin 2, Ireland (a division of Penguin
Books Ltd) • Penguin Group (Australia), 250 Camberwell Road, Camberwell, Victoria 3124, Australia
(a division of Pearson Australia Group Pty Ltd) • Penguin Books India Pvt Ltd, 11 Community Centre,
Panchsheel Park, New Delhi – 110 017, India • Penguin Group (NZ), 67 Apollo Drive, Rosedale,
Auckland 0632, New Zealand (a division of Pearson New Zealand Ltd) • Penguin Books (South Africa)
(Pty) Ltd, 24 Sturdee Avenue, Rosebank, Johannesburg 2196, South Africa

Penguin Books Ltd, Registered Offices: 80 Strand, London WC2R 0RL, England

First published in the United States of America by The Viking Press 1962
Published in Penguin Books 1980
Edition with an introduction by Jay Parini published 1997
This edition with a revised introduction by Jay Parini published 2012

13 15 17 19 20 18 16 14 12

Portions of this book appeared serially in *Holiday* under the title "In Quest for America."

LIBRARY OF CONGRESS CATALOGING-IN-PUBLICATION DATA
Steinbeck, John, 1902–1968.
Travels with Charley ; in search of America / John Steinbeck ; introduction
by Jay Parini.—50th-anniversary ed., Penguin Classics deluxe ed.
p. cm.
Originally published: New York : Viking Press, 1962.
Includes bibliographical references.
ISBN 978-0-14-310700-2
1. United States—Description and travel.   2. Steinbeck, John, 1902–1968—Travel—United States.
3. Authors, American—20th century—Biography.   I. Title.
E169.Z8S83 2012
917.3—dc23   2012028431

Printed in the United States of America
Set in Stempel Garamond
Designed by Virginia Norey

Contents

Introduction

Few writers in the history of American literature have thought more doggedly about the nature and fate of their own country than John Steinbeck. As Walt Whitman said in his preface to *Leaves of Grass*, "The United States themselves are essentially the greatest poem." Steinbeck certainly believed this; in book after book, beginning with *The Pastures of Heaven* (1932), his first collection of stories, he summoned a memorable vision of his people in their natural and human habitat. He is, of course, most famous as a writer of fiction. Novels such as *Tortilla Flat* (1935), *In Dubious Battle* (1936), *Of Mice and Men* (1937), *The Grapes of Wrath* (1939), *Cannery Row* (1945), *East of Eden* (1952), and *The Winter of Our Discontent* (1961) have long since been absorbed into the collective memory of this nation.

Beginning with major film versions of Steinbeck novels in the late 1930s—such as John Ford's classic production of *The Grapes of Wrath*—there has been a steady stream of theatrical adaptations, including a Broadway musical by Rodgers and Hammerstein called *Pipe Dream*, based on *Sweet Thursday* (1954), and an award-winning adaptation of *The Grapes of Wrath* by Frank Galati, which appeared on Broadway in 1990, winning a Tony Award for Best Play. When Steinbeck received the Nobel Prize for Literature in 1962, only five Americans before him had previously been so honored. Accepting the prize in Stockholm, he gave an impassioned speech in which he argued that "the ancient commission of the writer has not changed. He is charged with exposing our many grievous faults and failures, with dredging up to the light our dark and dangerous dreams for the purpose of improvement."

From the outset of his career as a novelist, he had accepted this commission without flinching, exposing the dangerous faults and failures of a nation while managing to celebrate what was good and noble in its citizens. This is also true of his nonfiction, although much less attention has been paid to this aspect of Steinbeck's work. Yet he wrote beautifully in this mode, often with the same passion for social justice that he brought to his novels. Even *The Grapes of Wrath*—certainly the most widely admired of his novels—began as a series of sketches for the *San Francisco News*. In his journalist mode, Steinbeck went off with a notebook in hand to record the plight of migrant workers from the dust bowl region of the Southwest. These unfortunate men and women had come by the thousands to California, dreaming of a better life, only to find themselves marooned in unsanitary, overcrowded camps and reviled by local residents.

In another piece of nonfiction from this period, Steinbeck wrote an absorbing account of life in a poor Mexican village. It was published as *The Forgotten Village* in 1941, based on a documentary film that Steinbeck scripted and produced under the same title. This research would feed into his later novella, *The Pearl* (1947), which remains an enduring and popular story. As usual for this productive writer, one project fed another, and he moved on several fronts at once.

Countless travel essays and opinion pieces appeared over several decades in periodicals such as *The Saturday Review* and *Newsday*. From an early age, Steinbeck had a thirst for travel, and at twenty (having temporarily dropped out of Stanford because of poor grades), he contemplated sailing across the Pacific on a freighter like his hero, Jack London. This fantastic scheme came to nothing, but when he finally left Stanford three years later (in 1925) without a degree, he hopped a freighter that took him through the Panama Canal to New York City. As his third wife, Elaine Steinbeck, said, "John would have gone to Paris, like Hemingway and Fitzgerald, but he didn't have the price of a ticket."

In his mid-twenties, Steinbeck worked in construction, did carpentry, and took odd jobs wherever he could find them. For the most part, he stayed in central California, near Salinas—where he was born in 1902 and grew up as the son of middle-class parents. Gradually, he began to piece together a living from his fiction, publishing a first novel called *Cup of Gold* in 1929 and placing various stories in such important national magazines as *Collier's* and *The Saturday Evening Post*. But it wasn't until the publication of his fourth novel, *Tortilla Flat*, that he found a sizable audience for his work. After selling this story to Hollywood, he suddenly had some money, or at least enough to afford the price of a ticket to anywhere he wished to go.

One generally associates Steinbeck with Monterey and the Salinas Valley—the lush settings for most of his novels and stories. But in fact Steinbeck spent the last half of his life with New York City as his primary residence, traveling abroad frequently. Mexico, France, and England were favorite destinations. A number of his books in the forties and fifties record his various journeys. The *Sea of Cortez* (1941), for instance, is a striking account of his journey by ship along the southern coastline of California into Mexico. In 1943, Steinbeck worked as a war correspondent in North Africa and Italy for the *New York Herald Tribune*, writing dispatches from the front that were ultimately published in *Once There Was a War* (1958). In *A Russian Journal* (1948), he describes a visit into the heart of the Soviet Union with Robert Capa, the photographer.

Travels with Charley in Search of America, originally published in 1962, is the final and most satisfying of his travelogues, summoning a complex vision of the United States at the beginning of a tumultuous decade, when race relations, in particular, had reached a point where the old ways could no longer remain in place. It is the work of a mature writer at the end of a long writing life, and it serves as a kind of elegy for a world that had already been lost. It is also a fascinating memoir, the self-portrait of a private man who did not much take to explicit autobiography. Indeed, it would be a mistake to take this travelogue too literally, as Steinbeck was at heart a novelist, and he added countless touches—changing the sequence of events, elaborating on scenes, inventing dialogue—that one associates more with fiction than nonfiction. (A mild controversy erupted, in the spring of 2011, when a former reporter for the *Pittsburgh Post-Gazette* did some fact-checking and noticed that Steinbeck's itinerary didn't exactly fit that described in the book, and that some of the people he supposedly interviewed, such as an actor at a campsite in North Dakota, never existed.)

It should be kept in mind, when reading this travelogue, that Steinbeck took liberties with the facts, inventing freely when it served his purposes, using everything in the arsenal of the novelist to make this book a readable, vivid narrative. The book remains "true" in the way all good novels or narratives are true. That is, it provides an authentic vision of America at a certain time. The evocation of its people and places stay forever in the mind, and Steinbeck's understanding of his country at this tipping point in its history was nothing short of extraordinary. It reflects his decades of observation and the years spent in honing his craft.

It must be said that by 1960, if not earlier, Steinbeck had grown fairly disenchanted with his country; he thought that consumerism and selfishness had begun to run rampant, destroying the community values he regarded as vital to the nation's moral health. In a letter to Adlai Stevenson (whose two unsuccessful presidential bids had frustrated Steinbeck), he complained about the "cynical immorality" of the United States. "Having too many THINGS," he says, "[Americans] spend their hours and money on the couch searching for a soul. A strange species we are. We can stand anything God and Nature throw at us save only plenty. If I wanted to destroy a nation, I would give it too much and I would have it on its knees, miserable, greedy and sick."

In 1960, he completed his last novel, *The Winter of Our Discontent*. A fair portion of the past decade had been spent abroad, in France and England, and it felt to him as though he had somehow lost touch with America and Americans. In a letter to his close friend Frank Loesser, he wrote:

> In the fall—right after Labor Day—I'm going to learn about my own country. I've lost the flavor and taste and sound of it. It's been years since I have seen it. Soooo! I'm buying a pick-up truck with a small apartment on it, kind of like the cabin of a small boat, bed, stove, desk, ice-box, toilet—not a trailer—what's called a coach. I'm going alone, out toward the West by the northern way but zigzagging through the Middle West and the mountain states. I'll avoid cities, hit small towns and farms and ranches, sit in bars and hamburger stands and on Sunday go to church. I'll go down the coast from Washington and Oregon and then back through the Southwest and South and up the East Coast but always zigzagging. Elaine will join me occasionally

but mostly I have to go alone, and I shall go unknown. I just want to look and listen. What I'll get I need badly—a re-knowledge of my own country, of its speeches, its views, its attitudes and its changes. It's long overdue—very long.

Part of what makes Steinbeck's best fiction so compelling is the author's intimate sense of landscape, both natural and human, and the crucial knit of people with their setting. It has been argued by critics that his powers of creativity dwindled to some extent after the 1930s, and that his physical removal from California had something to do with this diminishment. "Steinbeck should never have left California," mused his friend Elia Kazan some years after his death. "That was the source of his energy." Steinbeck himself felt that contact with the land and its people was important to him as a writer; he wanted to see the natural landscape, to hear the voices of ordinary men and women at work and play. These experiences were a kind of fuel to his imagination, and without them he felt abstracted, detached, impoverished. Having just finished what would prove to be his last novel, Steinbeck badly needed rejuvenation. As Elaine Steinbeck put it: "This trip across America was just something John had to do. And he had to go alone. He wanted to prove to himself that he was not an old man, that he could take control of his life, could drive himself, and could learn things again."

It was difficult for Elaine to let her husband go by himself on such a journey (and, in fact, she apparently did visit him along the way, although he never mentions this in the book). She was worried about him, with good reason, as she had recently witnessed episodes in Italy and France where Steinbeck passed out without obvious cause. He had also suffered several attacks of what appear in retrospect to have been small strokes. His fingers would go numb, and he would have difficulty grabbing objects; his speech would slur. The robust good health that had been part of his persona through middle age was waning, even though in 1960 he was only fifty-eight.

As he would, Steinbeck prepared carefully for the journey, outfitting this truck with a camper on its back as comfortably as possible. He christened his impressive new vehicle "Rocinante," after the hero's horse in Cervantes's *Don Quixote*. "I was advised that the name Rocinante painted on the side of my truck in sixteenth-century Spanish script would cause curiosity and inquiry in some places," wrote Steinbeck. "I do not know how many people recognized the name, but surely no one ever asked about it." Perhaps the people who noticed the name were simply being polite!

Steinbeck's trip was delayed by hurricane Donna, which swept the Atlantic coast late in the summer, wreaking havoc. He describes the storm evocatively in one of the opening passages of *Travels with Charley*: "The wind struck on the moment we were told it would, and ripped the water like a black sheet. It hammered like a fist. The whole top of an oak tree crashed down, grazing the cottage where we watched. The next gust stove one of the big windows in." He watched helplessly as the wind ripped "at earth and sea."

In his later years, Steinbeck spent the summer in Sag Harbor, New York, which in those days was an idyllic fishing village on Long Island. The proximity of the sea reminded him of Monterey, where he had spent his summers as a boy, and he spent a good deal of time on his motor launch, which he called the *Fayre Eleyne*—a double allusion to his wife, Elaine, and to a character in Sir Thomas Malory's *Le Morte d'Arthur*—a book that Steinbeck had recently translated into modern English. As Steinbeck tells the story, the hurricane suddenly tore his beloved boat from its moorings: "She was dragged fighting and protesting downwind and forced against a neighboring pier, and we could hear her hull crying against the oaken piles." By this time, the wind exceeded ninety-five miles per hour, and even the houses near the shoreline were severely threatened. Steinbeck insisted on going out into the storm to rescue his boat, ignoring his wife's protests.

She followed him into the wet, lashing wind and watched in disbelief as he plunged into the water toward the boat, fighting his way through crashing waves—no small feat for a man in his uncertain health. Working on pure adrenaline, Steinbeck managed to cut the *Fayre Eleyne* loose and jump into it. Luckily, the engine started at once, and he was able to steer the boat safely into the bay, where he dropped anchor. "Well, there I was," Steinbeck writes, "a hundred yards offshore with Donna baying over me like a pack of white-whiskered hounds." It was clear that no skiff could possibly make it across the roiling sea to bring him back, so he had no choice but to swim ashore.

A branch floated by in the water, and Steinbeck jumped in after it. The wind happened to be driving toward the shore, so all he had to do was hang onto the branch and let it pull him in. Before long, Elaine saw his head bobbing in the water. Soon he was back at the kitchen table, a whisky between his palms, with a towel around his head.

This little adventure before setting out is fetchingly told by Steinbeck, and it forms a paradigmatic moment in the larger arc of the story. Here is the weakened but still-courageous hero-narrator caught in a storm yet plunging forward to rescue something that is dear to him. The sheer abandon—and slight madness—involved in just plunging ahead into turbulent waters is crucial to the tone of the book. The writer has complete faith in his ability to enter a scene, to figure out what is going on, and to do the right thing. He also believes that, finally, he will return to his own fair Elaine, and that the storm will pass.

The journey described in *Travels with Charley* might be considered a classic example of the heroic journey, the archetypal myth that lends an essential structure to so much narrative literature. In the traditional myth, a hero—whoever he might be—abandons his safe haven and pushes forward into the wilderness (or depths) in order to test himself against the odds; in the course of this testing, he either discovers his own rich resources or comes into contact with higher powers that assist him. The story inevitably involves a returning, which completes the cycle: the point being that, upon returning, the hero has been immeasurably strengthened by the knowledge gained in the course of his difficult journey.

Steinbeck set off from Sag Harbor on the morning of September 23, 1960, with Charley, his tall and gregarious French poodle, for company. "I remember when he asked to take Charley Dog," his wife later recalled. "He said rather meekly, 'This is a big favor I'm going to ask, Elaine. Can I take Charley?' 'What a good idea,'

I said, 'if you get into any kind of trouble, Charley can go get help.' John looked at me sternly and said, 'Elaine, Charley isn't Lassie.'" He drove north toward Massachusetts, stopping by to visit John, the youngest of his two sons, at the Eaglebrook School in Deerfield. From there, he moved north through Vermont and east through the White Mountains of New Hampshire. Steinbeck writes: "The climate changed quickly to cold and the trees burst into color, the reds and yellows you can't believe. It isn't only color but a glowing, as though the leaves gobbled the light of the autumn sun and then released it slowly."

D. H. Lawrence once observed that greatness in literature is often connected to a particular author's feeling for the natural world in his or her native region; he pointed to Shakespeare, Tolstoy, and Hardy as good examples of writers with a highly particularized sense of nature. The same is true of Steinbeck. What makes his California novels so compelling is their attention to a specific, highly concrete environment; the lives of his characters are intimately bound to the rhythms of nature: weather, geography, cycles of planting and harvesting. What makes *Travels with Charley* so readily accessible to even the most casual reader is the deft evocation of the natural world, the colors and textures of leaves on the trees, the rich smells of earth, the slur of rain on pavement, the sharp rays of the sun as they pillar through a scud of clouds. Indeed, one can hardly open a page of this book without stumbling upon some bright image from nature.

Steinbeck's first major destination was Maine. Its rough and dense woods, thick with tall Norway pines and feathery spruce, reminded him of northern California. He drove north toward the Canadian border: "I wanted to go to the rooftree of Maine," he says, "to start my trip before turning west. It seemed to give the journey a design, and everything in the world must have design or the human mind rejects it." This is clearly the novelist talking, the man in search of narrative coherence; it's also a signal to readers, a way of saying that what lies before them is a shaped work, a kind of fiction (from the Latin *fictio*, which means "shaping"). In other words, this story has an elaborate design.

A stranger passing through an organic community quite

naturally has some difficulty in coming into contact with the people who actually live and work there, and Steinbeck was no exception. "I soon discovered," he writes, "that if a wayfaring stranger wishes to eavesdrop on a local population the places for him to slip in and hold his peace are bars and churches. But some New England towns don't have bars, and church is only on Sunday. A good alternative is the roadside restaurant where men gather for breakfast before going to work or going hunting." It so happens that laconic New Englanders were often unwilling to offer much of themselves over coffee and pancakes, as Steinbeck soon discovered. He came to rely on local radio stations for a feeling of human community: "Every town of a few thousand people has its station, and it takes the place of the old local newspapers. Bargains and trades are announced, social doings, prices of commodities, messages."

As ever, Steinbeck has a keen eye for transactions among people, and *Travels with Charley* is full of them. Every few days or so, Steinbeck would stop at a motel, not for the bed but for "the sake of hot, luxurious bathing." In this regard, *Travels with Charley* has something in common with *Lolita*, Vladimir Nabokov's classic novel of the mid-1950s. That novel had at its center a journey, with Humbert Humbert swooping across America from motel to motel with his beautiful nymphet, Lolita, in tow. Nabokov held up to the light the gaudy particulars of American lower middle-class life: the details like butterflies caught in the pincers of a sharp-eyed lepidopterist. Similarly in Steinbeck, the *kitsch* of contemporary America is savored: Swiss Cheese Candy, seashell emporia, and Dairy Queen roadside stands with huge bathtubs parked in front.

The sleazy human landscape of this country is also subjected to Steinbeck's rueful gaze. Writing home to Elaine in early October, Steinbeck said he was full of "impressions." "One is of our wastes," he says. "We can put chemical wastes in the rivers, and dispose of bowel wastes, but every town is ringed with automobiles, machines, wrecks of houses. It's exactly like the Christmas Eves I described—opened and thrown away for the next package." No wonder environmentalists have seized on Steinbeck as an early advocate of their cause; years before it was popular to do so, Steinbeck argued that the trashing of America was suicidal. He urged restraint and conservation of natural resources. He considered the wastefulness he saw everywhere around him and lack of caring for the environment as part of a greater malaise that seemed to have overwhelmed America.

With horror, he noted that trailer parks were cropping up at the edge of most towns. The people inhabiting these rootless buildings, which were propped on wheels or temporary foundations, seemed to him like alien creatures. "These are Martians," he writes home to Elaine, "and I wanted to ask them to take me to their leader. They have no humor, no past, and their future is new models." He added: "If I ever am looking for a theme—this mobility is a good one."

Indeed, the theme of rootlessness became integral to *Travels with Charley*. Past and present play against each other in the traveler's mind as he proceeds. There are frequent flashbacks, often to his childhood or young adulthood in California, as when he writes: "Long ago I owned a little ranch in the Santa Cruz mountains in California. In one place a forest of giant madrone trees joined their tops over a true tarn, a black, spring-fed lake. If there is such a thing as a haunted place, that one was haunted, made so by dim light strained through the leaves and various tricks of perspective." By contrast, of course, the new American "finds his challenge and his love in traffic-choked streets, skies nested in smog, choking with the acids of industry, the screech of rubber and houses leashed in against one another while the townlets wither a time and die."

This is, indeed, a terrible indictment of so-called progress. The fictional aspects of *Travels with Charley* are noticeable on most pages, the chief of these being the use of dialogue—perhaps the most obvious of fictional techniques employed by this master novelist. Steinbeck offers a sequence of human encounters, creating characters and dialogue as a true novelist would. For instance, when he crosses the Canadian border near Niagara Falls, he has a lovely, amusing exchange with the customs officer that could easily sit in the text of a short story. Steinbeck had no tape recorder, so it's made-up speech, based on real conversation. Nevertheless the dialogue goes on for pages, and there is a beginning, a middle, and an end. Discrete scene gives way to discrete scene in the mode of picaresque fiction invented by Cervantes, and it seems fitting that the driver of a truck called Rocinante should inhabit a similarly shaped narrative.

From the beginning of his journey, Steinbeck avoided big highways, "the great high-speed slashes of concrete and tar" that crisscross the nation. Perhaps for that reason, he dawdled in New England, where the turnpike is alien territory. Back roads, even dirt roads, were infinitely preferable to him: more scenic, reminiscent of a bygone era. But the American continent is vast, and Steinbeck finally had little option but to seek out a superhighway, where he could make time. He eventually turned onto U.S. 90, moving at high speed through Ohio, Michigan, and Illinois, where he noticed at once a shift in human attitudes. "I don't think for a second that the people I had seen and talked to in New England were either unfriendly or discourteous," he writes, "but they spoke tersely and usually waited for a newcomer to open communication."

In the Midwest, strangers seemed to talk to each other freely, without the reserve he had noticed in the Northeast. With a touch of alarm, Steinbeck noted that the rich differences in local speech patterns he remembered from his own youthful travels across America in the 1920s and 1930s were disappearing or already gone. "Forty years of radio and twenty years of television must have this impact," he concludes. A national speech was, perhaps inevitably, replacing the nuanced inflection of local dialects. "I who love words and the endless possibility of words am saddened by this inevitability," he says. The loss of colorful idioms, local conversational rhythms, and idiosyncratic figures of speech offended him deeply. He hated the notion of "a national speech, wrapped and packaged, standard and tasteless."

After a brief visit to Chicago, where he reunited with Elaine (who had flown in from the East to meet him), he set off by himself again, heading west through Wisconsin ("the prettiest state I ever saw") and Minnesota. Everywhere he went he listened, asked questions when he found an opening, then listened again. Every night, in a motel (or sometimes a nice hotel, though he does not mention this in the book) or huddled in Rocinante, he would reconstruct his day's journey, the landscapes witnessed, the people met, the incidents along the way. From these diary-like notes, he created the book, which had no title until he called home one night from a pay phone and Elaine suggested *Travels with Charley* on the model of Robert Louis Stevenson's *Travels with a Donkey*, one of Steinbeck's favorite books. Steinbeck avoided the most obvious tourist sites along the way, with Niagara Falls an exception. Who could bypass this miracle of nature?

Sometimes he would seek out a place of private interest, such as the birthplace of Sinclair Lewis—a novelist whose journalistic approach to fiction interested him greatly—in Sauk Centre, Minnesota. Wherever he paused to look around, he made some effort to meet the people who lived there. He wanted to experience for himself the emotional lay of the land. He wanted to know what America was thinking, although he soon enough came to believe that very little was on the mind of the average U.S. citizen. East of the Mississippi, the conversations he overheard usually revolved around baseball; west of the Mississippi, the topic was hunting. Even though this was the autumn of an election year—Kennedy versus Nixon—there was no rigorous political debate to be heard anywhere.

As Steinbeck moved slowly toward California, he grew steadily more disenchanted with everything but the natural world. In fact, he grows increasingly lyrical in writing about the sublime aspects of nature as he moves westward. "I drove across the upraised thumb of Idaho and through real mountains that climbed straight up, tufted with pines and deep-dusted with snow," he writes. The prose gets increasingly lush and cadenced as he reaches Oregon and heads southward into redwood country. "I stayed two days close to the bodies of the giants," he says, referring to the massive trees of his childhood:

> There's a cathedral hush here. Perhaps the thick soft bark absorbs sound and creates a silence. The trees rise straight up to zenith; there is no horizon. The dawn comes early and remains dawn until the sun is high. Then the green fernlike foliage so far up strains the sunlight to a green gold and distributes it in shafts or

rather in stripes of light and shade. After the sun passes zenith it is afternoon and quickly evening with a whispering dusk as long as was the morning.

The arrival in California brought with it problems he might have anticipated. The coastal area he knew so well as a young man seemed warped by recollections of what it used to be like, and with what happened to him there. Memories distorted the present scene, and every image that cropped up became a palimpsest: a picture drawn over a picture. He was dismayed by the clear lack of architectural distinction and differentiation, seeing little boxy houses, all too much alike, in row after row. It upset him that wild hilltops where coyotes sang all night had been razed, and that television stations now beamed their nervous pictures to thousands of tiny houses "clustered like aphids beside the roads." The overall picture was distressing, to say the least.

The situation worsened when he arrived in Monterey County, the landscape of his dreams. He visited his sisters, who began to argue with him about politics in a way that was only upsetting. Indeed, dinner conversation degenerated into silly arguments about the personalities and moral irregularities of Kennedy and Nixon. "You talk like a Communist," cried one of his sisters. "Well, you sound suspiciously like Genghis Khan," he fired back. When he entered Monterey itself, he was startled to discover that one of the movie theaters had been renamed the John Steinbeck Theater. He had become, in effect, his own theme park, and this was upsetting. "Tom Wolfe was right," he reflected. "You can't go home again because home has ceased to exist except in the mothballs of memory."

Wisely, Steinbeck quickly fled his native region, leaving behind "the permanent and changeless past where my mother is always shooting a wildcat and my father is always burning his name with his love." In a poignant moment, in flight from Monterey, Steinbeck says that he wished he could say that he went out to find the truth about America and found it. But he knew better; he understood that no single "truth" can ever be found. "I discovered long ago in collecting and classifying marine animals that what I found was closely intermeshed with how I felt

at the moment. External reality has a way of being not so external after all." In this, Steinbeck sounds tremendously contemporary, almost poststructuralist. The idea that objectivity is
inevitably tainted by mere expression—and by the fact that a
single human being has but a single viewpoint—permeates this
travelogue, making all of Steinbeck's conclusions tentative, as
they should be. "This monster of a land," he writes, "this mightiest of nations, this spawn of the future, turns out to be the
macrocosm of microcosm me."

One of the contradictory elements of *Travels with Charley*
occurs at this point. "From start to finish I found no strangers,"
he writes. "If I had, I might be able to report them more objectively. But these are my people and this my country. If I found
matters to criticize and to deplore, they were tendencies equally
present in myself." Given the comments to Elaine about "Martians" who lived in trailer parks, and given his fierce critique of
the ruined, industrialized landscape seen from coast to coast,
one must take this urge to identify and celebrate "his people"
with a grain of salt. This is the soft side of Steinbeck, a sentimen-
tality that crops up here and there.

He might, I think, have done better to stand apart, saying, "I
don't know these people." He pretty much did this in Texas,
where he headed in the book's final section. Because his wife,
Elaine, was Texan bred, Steinbeck understood that he could not
avoid that massive, complicated state, even had he wished to do
so. He arrived there in time for Thanksgiving with his wife's
family, near Amarillo, and well understood the difficulties facing
him in this part of his travelogue: "Writers facing the problem of
Texas find themselves floundering in generalities, and I am no
exception. Texas is a state of mind. Texas is an obsession. Above
all, Texas is a nation in every sense of the word." Despite his awe
and hesitance before a difficult task, Steinbeck writes beautifully
about Texas, in fact, characterizing its people and their setting
with typical lyricism and imagistic precision. He defines the
state by its stark contrasts:

> The stern horizon-fenced plains of the Panhandle are foreign
> to the little wooded hills and sweet streams in the Davis

Mountains. The rich citrus orchards of the Rio Grande valley do not relate to the sagebrush grazing of South Texas. The hot and humid air of the Gulf Coast has no likeness in the cool crystal in the north-west of the Panhandle. And Austin on its hills among the bordered lakes might be across the world from Dallas.

It was in Texas that Charley's prostate problems, which had been surfacing periodically throughout the journey, reached a crisis point, and he was tended to by a pleasant young vet. This problem solved, the newly risen poodle and his owner headed off for the last major stop on their visit, New Orleans. Steinbeck writes:

> While I was still in Texas, late in 1960, the incident most reported and pictured in the newspapers was the matriculation of a couple of tiny Negro children in a New Orleans school. Behind these small dark mites were the law's majesty and the law's power to enforce—both the scales and the sword were allied with the infants—while against them were three hundred years of fear and anger and terror of change in a changing world.

A group of appalling women—white "mothers," if that word may be used in this context—gathered each day to jeer at the black children as they entered or left school. They were known in the press, ironically, as the Cheerleaders, and Steinbeck wanted to see them for himself. It was somehow incomprehensible to him that human beings could act like this. Pretending to be an Englishman, from Liverpool, he joined the throng outside the school one day. A taxi driver explained to him that it was the New York Jews who were causing all of this trouble. "Jews— what? How do they cause trouble?" he asked the man, who said, "Them goddamn New York Jews come in and stir the niggers up." The man actually proposed lynching these trouble-causing Jews, much to Steinbeck's amazement and disgust.

Asked later the same day if he is traveling for pleasure, Steinbeck replied: "I was until today." The naked face of racism and prejudice, witnessed in the Cheerleaders and their hate-fueled behavior, filled him with a "weary nausea." His own childhood experience of black people in Salinas was so very different from this; he had, as he recalls, known only kind, considerate people, not the "lazy" ones derided by the racists he encountered on this final, unhappy leg of his journey. The contrast was difficult to accept.

In a moving little vignette on his rush homeward to Sag Harbor, in Alabama Steinbeck picked up a black hitchhiker. He and the young man fell into a conversation about Martin Luther King, Jr., and his "teaching of passive but unrelenting resistance." Steinbeck was obviously in favor of King's approach, and he found himself shocked by the response: "It's too slow," the young man told Steinbeck, ruefully. "It will take too long."

This was, in fact, a uniquely pivotal year for Steinbeck to set out upon such a journey, with the whole country poised on the edge of some extraordinary shift of consciousness. The Civil Rights movement wished to transform America's way of looking at itself, and even Steinbeck—in his role as Wise Man—was unprepared to deal with the consequences of these changes. He understood that the innocence of the 1950s was based on fixed notions of class and racial boundaries, but he did not dare to look too far ahead. He refused, at last, the prophetic note that might have lifted *Travels with Charley* above the level of a merely charming and absorbing travelogue, a well-shaped narrative that seeks to portray the United States at a particular moment in history.

Steinbeck rushed home to Sag Harbor now, exhausted by his nearly four months on the road. He had hoped to emulate Don Quixote, "who thought it fit and proper, both in order to increase his renown and to serve the state, to turn knight-errant and travel through the world with horse and armour in search of adventures, following in every way the practice of the knights-errant he had read of, redressing all manner of wrongs, and exposing himself to chances and dangers, by the overcoming of which he might win eternal honour and renown." Alas, Steinbeck had not really done much of this, although the book was warmly received by reviewers and became a huge bestseller. It certainly increased the renown of its author.

Travels with Charley offered the reading public a fairly intimate acquaintance with John Steinbeck, one of its favorite writers. Indeed, after more than eleven weeks on the road with this curmudgeonly author and his sprightly poodle, one feels very much at home in his company and sorry that the journey is coming to an end. Ideally, this travelogue should be read alongside Steinbeck's letters home to his wife and friends while on the road—a decent selection is available in *Steinbeck: A Life in Letters*, edited by Elaine Steinbeck and Robert Wallsten (1975).

Reflecting on his journey in search of America in a letter to Pat Covici, his editor, Steinbeck says:

> In all my travels I saw very little real poverty, I mean the grinding terrifying poorness of the Thirties. That at least was real and tangible. No, it was a sickness, a kind of wasting disease. There were wishes but no wants. And underneath it all the building energy like gases in a corpse. When that explodes, I tremble to think what will be the result. Over and over I thought we lack the pressures that make men strong and the anguish that makes men great. The pressures are debts, the desires are for more material toys and the anguish is boredom. Through time, the nation has become a discontented land.

And he reflects that discontent in his narrative, barely disguising his irritation.

Although *Travels with Charley* is replete with whimsical vignettes, charming dialogue, and lyrical descriptions of the natural landscape that often rise to the level of poetry, there is beneath its surface a sense of disenchantment that turns, eventually, into barely suppressed anger. Steinbeck seems never quite able to bring himself to say that he was truly and often disgusted by what he saw on his journey, but the reader is left with that impression. One puts down this book aware of how remarkably prophetic it really was, and how America continues to wrestle with the problems raised in its pages.

JAY PARINI

Suggestions for Further Reading

Astro, Richard. "Travels with Steinbeck: The Laws of Thought and the Law of Things." *Steinbeck Quarterly* 8 (1975): 35–44.

Benson, Jackson J. *The True Adventures of John Steinbeck, Writer.* New York: Viking, 1984.

Distky, John. "Steinbeck's Travels with Charley: The Quest that Failed." *Steinbeck Quarterly* 8 (1975): 45–50.

Ferrell, Keith. *John Steinbeck: The Voice of the Land.* New York: M. Evans, 1986.

French, Warren. *John Steinbeck.* Boston: Twayne, 1975.

George, Stephen K., ed. *The Moral Philosophy of John Steinbeck.* Lanham, MD: Scarecrow, 2005.

Hayashi, Tetsumaro, ed. *A Study Guide to Steinbeck: A Handbook to His Major Works.* Metuchen, NJ: The Scarecrow Press, 1974.

Levant, Howard. *The Novels of John Steinbeck: A Critical Study.* Columbia: University of Missouri Press, 1974.

Lisca, Peter. *The Wide World of John Steinbeck.* New York: Gordian Press, 1981.

McCarthy, Paul. *John Steinbeck.* New York: Frederick Ungar, 1980.

McGrath, Charles. "A Reality Check for Steinbeck and Charley." *The New York Times,* April 3, 2011.

Owens, Louis. *John Steinbeck's Re-Vision of America.* Athens: University of Georgia Press, 1985.

Parini, Jay. *John Steinbeck: A Biography.* New York: Holt, 1995.

Schultz, Jeffrey and Luchen Li. *A Critical Companion to John Steinbeck.* New York: Checkmark, 2005.

Simmons, Roy S. *A Biographical and Critical Introduction of John Steinbeck.* New York: Edwin Mellen Press, 2000.

Steinbeck, Elaine, and Robert Wallsten, eds. *Steinbeck: A Life in Letters.* New York: Viking, 1975.

Timmerman, John H. *John Steinbeck's Fiction: The Aesthetics of the Road Taken.* Norman: University of Oklahoma Press, 1986.

Travels with Charley in
Search of America

This book is dedicated to
Harold Guinzburg
with respect born of an association and
affection that just growed.

—JOHN STEINBECK

PART ONE

When I was very young and the urge to be someplace else was on me, I was assured by mature people that maturity would cure this itch. When years described me as mature, the remedy prescribed was middle age. In middle age I was assured that greater age would calm my fever and now that I am fifty-eight perhaps senility will do the job. Nothing has worked. Four hoarse blasts of a ship's whistle still raise the hair on my neck and set my feet to tapping. The sound of a jet, an engine warming up, even the clopping of shod hooves on pavement brings on the ancient shudder, the dry mouth and vacant eye, the hot palms and the churn of stomach high up under the rib cage. In other words, I don't improve; in further words, once a bum always a bum. I fear the disease is incurable. I set this matter down not to instruct others but to inform myself.

When the virus of restlessness begins to take possession of a wayward man, and the road away from Here seems broad and straight and sweet, the victim must first find in himself a good and sufficient reason for going. This to the practical bum is not difficult. He has a built-in garden of reasons to choose from. Next he must plan his trip in time and space, choose a direction and a destination. And last he must implement the journey. How to go, what to take, how long to stay. This part of the process is invariable and immortal. I set it down only so that newcomers to bumdom, like teen-agers in new-hatched sin, will not think they invented it.

Once a journey is designed, equipped, and put in process; a new factor enters and takes over. A trip, a safari, an exploration, is an entity, different from all other journeys. It has personality, temperament, individuality, uniqueness. A journey is a person in itself; no two are alike. And all plans, safeguards, policing, and coercion are fruitless. We find after years of struggle that we do not take a trip; a trip takes us. Tour masters, schedules, reservations, brass-bound and inevitable, dash themselves to wreckage on the personality of the trip. Only when this is recognized can the blown-in-the-glass bum relax and go along with it. Only then do the frustrations fall away. In this a journey is like marriage. The certain way to be wrong is to think you control it. I feel better now, having said this, although only those who have experienced it will understand it.

My plan was clear, concise, and reasonable, I think. For many years I have traveled in many parts of the world. In America I live in New York, or dip into Chicago or San Francisco. But New York is no more America than Paris is France or London is England. Thus I discovered that I did not know my own country. I, an American writer, writing about America, was working from memory, and the memory is at best a faulty, warpy reservoir. I had not heard the speech of America, smelled the grass and trees and sewage, seen its hills and water, its color and quality of light. I knew the changes only from books and newspapers. But more than this, I had not felt the country for twenty-five years. In short, I was writing of something I did not know about, and it seems to me that in a so-called writer this is criminal. My memories were distorted by twenty-five intervening years.

Once I traveled about in an old bakery wagon, double-doored rattler with a mattress on its floor. I stopped where people stopped or gathered, I listened and looked and felt, and in the process had a picture of my country the accuracy of which was impaired only by my own shortcomings.

So it was that I determined to look again, to try to rediscover this monster land. Otherwise, in writing, I could not tell the small diagnostic truths which are the foundations of the larger truth. One sharp difficulty presented itself. In the intervening twenty-five years my name had become reasonably well known. And it has been my experience that when people have heard of you, favorably or not, they change; they become, through shyness or the other qualities that publicity inspires, something they are not under ordinary circumstances. This being so, my trip demanded that I leave my name and my identity at home. I had to be peripatetic eyes and ears, a kind of moving gelatin plate. I could not sign hotel registers, meet people I knew, interview others, or even ask searching questions. Furthermore, two or more people disturb the ecologic complex of an area. I had to go alone and I had to be self-contained, a kind of casual turtle carrying his house on his back.

With all this in mind I wrote to the head office of a great corporation which manufactures trucks. I specified my purpose and my needs. I wanted a three-quarter-ton pick-up truck, capable of going anywhere under possibly rigorous conditions, and on this truck I wanted a little house built like the cabin of a small boat. A trailer is difficult to maneuver on mountain roads, is impossible and often illegal to park, and is subject to many restrictions. In due time, specifications came through, for a tough, fast, comfortable vehicle, mounting a camper top—a little house with double bed, a four-burner stove, a heater, refrigerator and lights operating on butane, a chemical toilet, closet space, storage space, windows screened against insects—exactly what I wanted. It was delivered in the summer to my little fishing place at Sag Harbor near the end of Long Island. Although I didn't want to start before Labor Day, when the nation settles back to normal living, I did want to get used to my turtle shell, to equip it and learn it. It arrived in August, a beautiful thing, powerful and yet lithe. It was almost as easy to handle as a passenger car. And because my planned trip had aroused some satiric remarks among my friends, I named it Rocinante, which you will remember was the name of Don Quixote's horse.

Since I made no secret of my project, a number of controversies arose among my friends and advisers. (A projected journey spawns advisers in schools.) I was told that since my photograph was as widely distributed as my publisher could make it, I would find it impossible to move about without being recognized. Let me say in advance that in over ten thousand miles, in thirty-four states, I was not recognized even once. I believe that people identify things only in context. Even those people who might have known me against a background I am supposed to have, in no case identified me in Rocinante.

I was advised that the name Rocinante painted on the side of my truck in sixteenth-century Spanish script would cause curiosity and inquiry in some places. I do not know how many people recognized the name, but surely no one ever asked about it.

Next, I was told that a stranger's purpose in moving about the country might cause inquiry or even suspicion. For this reason I racked a shotgun, two rifles, and a couple of fishing rods in my truck, for it is my experience that if a man is going hunting or fishing his purpose is understood and even applauded. Actually, my hunting days are over. I no longer kill or catch anything I cannot get into a frying pan; I am too old for sport killing. This stage setting turned out to be unnecessary.

It was said that my New York license plates would arouse interest and perhaps questions, since they were the only outward identifying marks I had. And so they did—perhaps twenty or thirty times in the whole trip. But such contacts followed an invariable pattern, somewhat as follows:

LOCAL MAN: "New York, huh?"

ME: "Yep."

LOCAL MAN: "I was there in nineteen thirty-eight—or was it thirty-nine? Alice, was it thirty-eight or thirty-nine we went to New York?"

ALICE: "It was thirty-six. I remember because it was the year Alfred died."

LOCAL MAN: "Anyway, I hated it. Wouldn't live there if you paid me."

There was some genuine worry about my traveling alone, open to attack, robbery, assault. It is well known that our roads are dangerous. And here I admit I had senseless qualms. It is some years since I have been alone, nameless, friendless, without any of the safety one gets from family, friends, and accomplices. There is no reality in the danger. It's just a very lonely, helpless feeling at first—a kind of desolate feeling. For this reason I took one companion on my journey—an old French gentleman poodle known as Charley. Actually his name is Charles le Chien. He was born in Bercy on the outskirts of Paris and trained in France, and while he knows a little poodle-English, he responds quickly only to commands in French. Otherwise he has to translate, and that slows him down. He is a very big poodle, of a color called *bleu*, and he is blue when he is clean. Charley is a born diplomat. He prefers negotiation to fighting, and properly so, since he is very bad at fighting. Only once in his ten years has he been in trouble—when he met a dog who refused to negotiate. Charley lost a piece of his right ear that time. But he is a good watch dog—has a roar like a lion, designed to conceal from night-wandering strangers the fact that he couldn't bite his way out of a *cornet de papier.* He is a good friend and traveling companion, and would rather travel about than anything he can imagine. If he occurs at length in this account, it is because he contributed much to the trip. A dog, particularly an exotic like Charley, is a bond between strangers. Many conversations en route began with "What degree of a dog is that?"

The techniques of opening conversation are universal. I knew long ago and rediscovered that the best way to attract attention, help, and conversation is to be lost. A man who seeing his mother starving to death on a path kicks her in the stomach to clear the way, will cheerfully devote several hours of his time giving wrong directions to a total stranger who claims to be lost.

Under the big oak trees of my place at Sag Harbor sat Rocinante, handsome and self-contained, and neighbors came to visit, some neighbors we didn't even know we had. I saw in their eyes something I was to see over and over in every part of the nation—a burning desire to go, to move, to get under way, anyplace, away from any Here. They spoke quietly of how they wanted to go someday, to move about, free and unanchored, not toward something but away from something. I saw this look and heard this yearning everywhere in every state I visited. Nearly every American hungers to move. One small boy about thirteen years old came back every day. He stood apart shyly and looked at Rocinante; he peered in the door, even lay on the ground and studied the heavy-duty springs. He was a silent, ubiquitous small boy. He even came at night to stare at Rocinante. After a week he could stand it no longer. His words wrestled their way hell-bent through his shyness. He said, "If you'll take me with you, why, I'll do anything. I'll cook, I'll wash all the dishes, and do all the work and I'll take care of you."

Unfortunately for me I knew his longing. "I wish I could," I said. "But the school board and your parents and lots of others say I can't."

"I'll do anything," he said. And I believe he would. I don't think he ever gave up until I drove away without him. He had the dream I've had all my life, and there is no cure.

Equipping Rocinante was a long and pleasant process. I took far too many things, but I didn't know what I would find. Tools for emergency, tow lines, a small block and tackle, a trenching tool and crowbar, tools for making and fixing and improvising. Then there were emergency foods. I would be late in the northwest and caught by snow. I prepared for at least a week of emergency. Water was easy; Rocinante carried a thirty-gallon tank.

I thought I might do some writing along the way, perhaps essays, surely notes, certainly letters. I took paper, carbon, type-writer, pencils, notebooks, and not only those but dictionaries, a compact encyclopedia, and a dozen other reference books, heavy ones. I suppose our capacity for self-delusion is boundless. I knew very well that I rarely make notes, and if I do I either lose them or can't read them. I also knew from thirty years of my profession that I cannot write hot on an event. It has to ferment. I must do what a friend calls "mule it over" for a time before it goes down. And in spite of this self-knowledge I equipped Rocinante with enough writing material to take care of ten volumes. Also I laid in a hundred and fifty pounds of those books one hasn't got around to reading—and of course those are the books one isn't ever going to get around to reading. Canned goods, shotgun shells, rifle cartridges, tool boxes, and far too many clothes, blankets and pillows, and many too many shoes and boots, padded nylon sub-zero underwear, plastic dishes and cups and a plastic dishpan, a spare tank of bottled gas. The overloaded springs sighed and settled lower and lower. I judge now that I carried about four times too much of everything.

Now, Charley is a mind-reading dog. There have been many trips in his lifetime, and often he has to be left at home. He knows we are going long before the suitcases come out, and he paces and worries and whines and goes into a state of mild hysteria, old as he is. During the weeks of preparation he was underfoot the whole time and made a damned nuisance of himself. He took to hiding in the truck, creeping in and trying to make himself look small.

Labor Day approached, the day of truth when millions of kids would be back in school and tens of millions of parents would be off the highways. I was prepared to set out as soon after that as possible. And about that time hurricane Donna was reported tromping her way out of the Caribbean in our direction. On Long Island's tip, we have had enough of that to be highly respectful. With a hurricane approaching we prepare to stand a siege. Our little bay is fairly well protected, but not that well. As Donna crept toward us I filled the kerosene lamps, activated the hand pump to the well, and tied down everything movable. I have a twenty-two-foot cabin boat, the *Fayre Eleyne*. I battened her down and took her to the middle of the bay, put down a huge old-fashioned hook anchor and half-inch chain, and moored her with a long swing. With that rig she could ride a hundred-and-fifty-mile wind unless her bow pulled out.

Donna sneaked on. We brought out a battery radio for reports, since the power would go off if Donna struck. But there was one added worry—Rocinante, sitting among the trees. In a waking nightmare I saw a tree crash down on the truck and crush her like a bug. I placed her away from a possible direct fall, but that didn't mean that the whole top of a tree might not fly fifty feet through the air and smash her.

By early morning we knew by radio that we were going to get it, and by ten o'clock we heard that the eye would pass over us and that it would reach us at 1:07—some exact time like that. Our bay was quiet, without a ripple, but the water was still dark and the *Fayre Eleyne* rode daintily slack against her mooring.

Our bay is better protected than most, so that many small craft came cruising in for mooring. And I saw with fear that many of their owners didn't know how to moor. Finally two boats, pretty things, came in, one towing the other. A light anchor went down and they were left, the bow of one tethered to the stern of the other and both within the swing of the *Fayre Eleyne*. I took a megaphone to the end of my pier and tried to protest against this foolishness, but the owners either did not hear or did not know or did not care.

The wind struck on the moment we were told it would, and ripped the water like a black sheet. It hammered like a fist. The whole top of an oak tree crashed down, grazing the cottage where we watched. The next gust stove one of the big windows in. I forced it back and drove wedges in top and bottom with a hand ax. Electric power and telephones went out with the first blast, as we knew they must. And eight-foot tides were predicted. We watched the wind rip at earth and sea like a surging pack of terriers. The trees plunged and bent like grasses, and the whipped water raised a cream of foam. A boat broke loose and tobogganed up on the shore, and then another. Houses built in the benign spring and early summer took waves in their second-story windows. Our cottage is on a little hill thirty feet above sea level. But the rising tide washed over my high pier. As the wind changed direction I moved Rocinante to keep her always to leeward of our big oaks. The *Fayre Eleyne* rode gallantly, swinging like a weather vane away from the changing wind.

The boats which had been tethered one to the other had fouled up by now, the tow line under propeller and rudder and the two hulls bashing and scraping together. Another craft had dragged its anchor and gone ashore on a mud bank.

Charley dog has no nerves. Gunfire or thunder, explosions or high winds leave him utterly unconcerned. In the midst of the howling storm, he found a warm place under a table and went to sleep.

The wind stopped as suddenly as it had begun, and although the waves continued out of rhythm they were not wind-tattered, and the tide rose higher and higher. All the piers around our little bay had disappeared under water, and only their piles or hand rails showed. The silence was like a rushing sound. The radio told us we were in the eye of Donna, the still and frightening calm in the middle of the revolving storm. I don't know how long the calm lasted. It seemed a long time of waiting. And then the other side struck us, the wind from the opposite direction. The *Fayre Eleyne* swung sweetly around and put her bow into the wind. But the two lashed boats dragged anchor, swarmed down on *Fayre Eleyne*, and bracketed her. She was dragged fighting and protesting downwind and forced against a neighboring pier, and we could hear her hull crying against the oaken piles. The wind registered over ninety-five miles now.

I found myself running, fighting the wind around the head of the bay toward the pier where the boats were breaking up. I think my wife, for whom the *Fayre Eleyne* is named, ran after me, shouting orders for me to stop. The floor of the pier was four feet under water, but piles stuck up and offered hand-holds. I worked my way out little by little up to my breast pockets, the shore-driven wind slapping water in my mouth. My boat cried and whined against the piles, and plunged like a frightened calf. Then I jumped and fumbled my way aboard her. For the first time in my life I had a knife when I needed it. The bracketing wayward boats were pushing *Eleyne* against the pier. I cut anchor line and tow line and kicked them free, and they blew ashore on the mud bank. But *Eleyne's* anchor chain was intact, and that great old mud hook was still down, a hundred pounds of iron with spear-shaped flukes wide as a shovel.

Eleyne's engine is not always obedient, but this day it started at a touch. I hung on, standing on the deck, reaching inboard for wheel and throttle and clutch with my left hand. And that boat tried to help—I suppose she was that scared. I edged her out and worked up the anchor chain with my right hand. Under ordinary conditions I can barely pull that anchor with both hands in a calm. But everything went right this time. I edged over the hook and it tipped up and freed its spades. Then I lifted it clear of the bottom and nosed into the wind and gave it throttle and we headed into that goddamn wind and gained on it. It was as though we pushed our way through thick porridge. A hundred yards offshore I let the hook go and it plunged down and grabbed bottom, and the *Fayre Eleyne* straightened and raised her bow and seemed to sigh with relief.

Well, there I was, a hundred yards offshore with Donna baying over me like a pack of white-whiskered hounds. No skiff could possibly weather it for a minute. I saw a piece of branch go skidding by and simply jumped in after it. There was no danger. If I could keep my head up I had to blow ashore, but I admit the half-Wellington rubber boots I wore got pretty heavy. It couldn't have been more than three minutes before I grounded and that other Fayre Eleyne and a neighbor pulled me out. It was only then that I began to shake all over, but looking out and seeing our little boat riding well and safely was nice. I must have strained something pulling that anchor with one hand, because I needed a little help home; a tumbler of whisky on the kitchen table was some help too. I've tried since to raise that anchor with one hand and I can't do it.

The wind died quickly and left us to wreckage—power lines down, and no telephone for a week. But Rocinante was not damaged at all.

PART TWO

In long-range planning for a trip, I think there is a private conviction that it won't happen. As the day approached, my warm bed and comfortable house grew increasingly desirable and my dear wife incalculably precious. To give these up for three months for the terrors of the uncomfortable and unknown seemed crazy. I didn't want to go. Something had to happen to forbid my going, but it didn't. I could get sick, of course, but that was one of my main but secret reasons for going at all. During the previous winter I had become rather seriously ill with one of those carefully named difficulties which are the whispers of approaching age. When I came out of it I received the usual lecture about slowing up, losing weight, limiting the cholesterol intake. It happens to many men, and I think doctors have memorized the litany. It had happened to so many of my friends. The lecture ends, "Slow down. You're not as young as you once were." And I had seen so many begin to pack their lives in cotton wool, smother their impulses, hood their passions, and gradually retire from their manhood into a kind of spiritual and physical semi-invalidism. In this they are encouraged by wives and relatives, and it's such a sweet trap.

Who doesn't like to be a center for concern? A kind of second childhood falls on so many men. They trade their violence for the promise of a small increase of life span. In effect, the head of the house becomes the youngest child. And I have searched myself for this possibility with a kind of horror. For I have always lived violently, drunk hugely, eaten too much or not at all, slept around the clock or missed two nights of sleeping, worked too hard and too long in glory, or slobbed for a time in utter laziness. I've lifted, pulled, chopped, climbed, made love with joy and taken my hangovers as a consequence, not as a punishment. I did not want to surrender fierceness for a small gain in yardage. My wife married a man; I saw no reason why she should inherit a baby. I knew that ten or twelve thousand

miles driving a truck, alone and unattended, over every kind of
road, would be hard work, but to me it represented the antidote
for the poison of the professional sick man. And in my own life
I am not willing to trade quality for quantity. If this projected
journey should prove too much then it was time to go anyway.
I see too many men delay their exits with a sickly, slow reluctance to leave the stage. It's bad theater as well as bad living. I
am very fortunate in having a wife who likes being a woman,
which means that she likes men, not elderly babies. Although
this last foundation for the journey was never discussed, I am
sure she understood it.

The morning came, a bright one with the tawny look of autumn in the sunlight. My wife and I parted very quickly, since
both of us hate good-bys, and neither one of us wanted to be
left when the other had gone. She gunned her motor and ex-
ploded away for New York and I, with Charley beside me,
drove Rocinante to the Shelter Island Ferry, and then to a second
ferry to Greenport and a third from Orient Point to the coast
of Connecticut, across Long Island Sound, for I wanted to avoid
New York traffic and get well on my way. And I confess to a
feeling of gray desolation.

On the ferry deck the sun was sharp and the coast of the
mainland only an hour away. A lovely sloop stood away from
us, her genoa set like a curving scarf, and all the coastal craft
trudged up the Sound or wallowed heavily toward New York.
Then a submarine slipped to the surface half a mile away, and
the day lost part of its brightness. Farther away another dark
creature slashed through the water, and another; of course they
are based in New London, and this is their home. And perhaps
they are keeping the world's peace with this venom. I wish I
could like submarines, for then I might find them beautiful, but
they are designed for destruction, and while they may explore
and chart the sea bottom, and draw new trade lines under the
Arctic ice, their main purpose is threat. And I remember too
well crossing the Atlantic on a troop ship and knowing that
somewhere on the way the dark things lurked searching for us
with their single-stalk eyes. Somehow the light goes bleak for
me when I see them and remember burned men pulled from the

oil-slicked sea. And now submarines are armed with mass murder, our silly, only way of deterring mass murder.

Only a few people stood in the wind on the top deck of the clanking iron ferry boat. A young man in a trench coat, with cornsilk hair and delphinium eyes red-edged by the dull wind, turned to me and then pointed. "That's the new one," he said. "She can stay down three months."

"How can you tell them?"

"I know them. I'm on them."

"Atomic?"

"Not yet, but I've got an uncle on one, and maybe pretty soon."

"You're not in uniform."

"Just had a leave."

"Do you like to serve on them?"

"Sure I do. The pay's good and there's all kinds of—future."

"Would you like to be down three months?"

"You'd get used to it. The food's good and there's movies and—I'd like to go under the Pole, wouldn't you?"

"I guess I would."

"And there's movies and all kinds of—future."

"Where are you from?"

"From over there—New London—born there. My uncle's in the service and two cousins. I guess we're a kind of submarine family."

"They worry me."

"Oh, you'd get over that, sir. Pretty soon you wouldn't even think you were submerged—that is, if you haven't got something wrong with you. Ever had claustrophobia?"

"No."

"Well, then. You soon get used to it. Care to go below for a cup of coffee? There's plenty of time."

"Sure I would."

And could be he's right and I'm wrong. It's his world, not mine any more. There's no anger in his delphinium eyes and no fear and no hatred either, so maybe it's all right. It's just a job with good pay and a future. I must not put my memories and my fear on him. Maybe it won't be true again, but that's his lookout. It's his world now. Perhaps he understands things I will never learn.

We drank our coffee out of paper cups, and through the square ferry windows he pointed out the dry docks and the skeletons of new submarines.

"Nice thing about it is if there's a storm you can submerge, and it's quiet. Sleep like a baby and all hell busting loose up above." He gave me directions for getting out of town, some of the few accurate ones I got on the whole trip.

"So long," I said. "I hope you have a good—future."

"It's not bad, you know. Good-by, sir."

And driving along a back Connecticut road, tree-bordered and gardened, I knew he had made me feel better and surer.

For weeks I had studied maps, large-scale and small, but maps are not reality at all—they can be tyrants. I know people who are so immersed in road maps that they never see the countryside they pass through, and others who, having traced a route, are held to it as though held by flanged wheels to rails. I pulled Rocinante into a small picnic area maintained by the state of Connecticut and got out my book of maps. And suddenly the United States became huge beyond belief and impossible ever to cross. I wondered how in hell I'd got myself mixed up in a project that couldn't be carried out. It was like starting to write a novel. When I face the desolate impossibility of writing five hundred pages a sick sense of failure falls on me and I know I can never do it. This happens every time. Then gradually I write one page and then another. One day's work is all I can permit myself to contemplate and I eliminate the possibility of ever finishing. So it was now, as I looked at the bright-colored projection of monster America. The leaves of the trees about the camp ground were thick and heavy, no longer growing but hanging limp and waiting for the first frost to whip them with color and the second to drive them to the earth and terminate their year.

Charley is a tall dog. As he sat in the seat beside me, his head was almost as high as mine. He put his nose close to my ear and said, "Ftt." He is the only dog I ever knew who could pronounce the consonant *F*. This is because his front teeth are crooked, a tragedy which keeps him out of dog shows; because his upper front teeth slightly engage his lower lip Charley can pronounce *F*. The word "Ftt" usually means he would like to salute a bush or a tree. I opened the cab door and let him out, and he went about his ceremony. He doesn't have to think about it to do it well. It is my experience that in some areas Charley is more intelligent than I am, but in others he is abysmally ignorant. He can't read, can't drive a car, and has no grasp of mathematics. But in his own field of endeavor, which he was now practicing, the slow, imperial smelling over and anointing of an area, he has no peer. Of course his horizons are limited, but how wide are mine?

We drove on in the autumn afternoon, heading north. Because I was self-contained, I thought it might be nice if I could invite people I met along the way to my home for a drink, but I had neglected to lay in liquor. But there are pretty little bottle stores on the back roads of this state. I knew there were some dry states but had forgotten which they were, and it was just as well to stock up. A small store was set well back from the road in a grove of sugar maples. It had a well-kept garden and flower boxes. The owner was a young-old man with a gray face, I suspect a teetotaller. He opened his order book and straightened the carbons with patient care. You never know what people will want to drink. I ordered bourbon, scotch, gin, vermouth, vodka, a medium good brandy, aged applejack, and a case of beer. It seemed to me that those might take care of most situations. It was a big order for a little store. The owner was impressed.

"Must be quite a party."

"No—it's just traveling supplies."

He helped me to carry the cartons out and I opened Rocinante's door.

"You going in that?"

"Sure."

"Where?"

"All over."

And then I saw what I was to see so many times on the journey—a look of longing. "Lord! I wish I could go."

"Don't you like it here?"

"Sure. It's all right, but I wish I could go."

"You don't even know where I'm going."

"I don't care. I'd like to go anywhere."

Eventually I had to come out of the tree-hidden roads and do my best to bypass the cities. Hartford and Providence and such are big cities, bustling with manufacturing, lousy with traffic. It takes far longer to go through cities than to drive several hundred miles. And in the intricate traffic pattern, as you try to find your way through, there's no possibility of seeing anything. But now I have been through hundreds of towns and cities in every climate and against every kind of scenery, and of course they are all different, and, the people have points of difference, but in some ways they are alike. American cities are like badger holes, ringed with trash—all of them—surrounded by piles of wrecked and rusting automobiles, and almost smothered with rubbish. Everything we use comes in boxes, cartons, bins, the so-called packaging we love so much. The mountains of things we throw away are much greater than the things we use. In this, if in no other way, we can see the wild and reckless exuberance of our production, and waste seems to be the index. Driving along I thought how in France or Italy every item of these thrown-out things would have been saved and used for something. This is not said in criticism of one system or the other but I do wonder whether there will come a time when we can no longer afford our wastefulness—chemical wastes in the rivers, metal wastes everywhere, and atomic wastes buried deep in the earth or sunk in the sea. When an Indian village became too deep in its own filth, the inhabitants moved. And we have no place to which to move.

I had promised my youngest son to say good-by in passing his school at Deerfield, Massachusetts, but I got there too late to arouse him, so I drove up the mountain and found a dairy, bought some milk, and asked permission to camp under an apple tree. The dairy man had a Ph.D. in mathematics, and he must have had some training in philosophy. He liked what he was doing and he didn't want to be somewhere else—one of the very few contented people I met in my whole journey.

I prefer to draw a curtain over my visit to Eaglebrook school. It can be imagined what effect Rocinante had on two hundred teen-age prisoners of education just settling down to serve their winter sentence. They visited my truck in droves, as many as fifteen at a time in the little cabin. And they looked courteous curses at me because I could go and they could not. My own son will probably never forgive me. Soon after I drove off, I stopped to make sure there were no stowaways.

My route went north in Vermont and then east in New Hampshire in the White Mountains. The roadside stands were piled with golden pumpkins and russet squashes and baskets of red apples so crisp and sweet that they seemed to explode with juice when I bit into them. I bought apples and a gallon jug of fresh-pressed cider. I believe that everyone along the highways sells moccasins and deerskin gloves. And those who don't sell goat-milk candy. Until then, I had not seen the factory-outlet stores in the open country selling shoes and clothes. The villages are the prettiest, I guess, in the whole nation, neat and white-painted, and—not counting the motels and tourist courts—unchanged for a hundred years except for traffic and paved streets.

The climate changed quickly to cold and the trees burst into color, the reds and yellows you can't believe. It isn't only color but a glowing, as though the leaves gobbled the light of the autumn sun and then released it slowly. There's a quality of fire in these colors. I got high in the mountains before dusk. A sign beside a stream offered fresh eggs for sale, and I drove up a farm road and bought some eggs and asked permission to camp beside the stream and offered to pay.

The farmer was a spare man, with what we think of as a Yankee face and the flat vowels we consider Yankee pronunciation. "No need to pay," he said. "The land's not working. But I would like to look at that rig you've got there."

I said, "Let me find a level place and put it in order, then come down for a cup of coffee—or something."

I backed and filled until I found a level place where I could hear the eager stream rattling; it was almost dark. Charley had said "Ftt" several times, meaning this time that he was hungry. I opened Rocinante's door, turned on the light, and found utter chaos inside. I have stowed a boat very often against roll and pitch, but the quick stops and starts of a truck are a different hazard. The floor was littered with books and papers. My type-writer roosted uncomfortably on a pile of plastic dishes, a rifle had fallen down and nudged itself against the stove, and one entire ream of paper, five hundred sheets, had drifted like snow to cover the whole place. I lighted the gas mantle lamp, stuffed the debris in a little closet, and put on water for coffee. In the morning I would have to reorganize my cargo. No one can tell how to do it. The technique must be learned the way I learned it, by failures. The moment it was dark it became bitterly cold, but the lamp and the gas burners of the stove warmed my little house cozily. Charley ate his supper, did his tour of duty, and retired into a carpeted corner under the table which was to be his for the next three months.

There are so many modern designs for easy living. On my boat I had discovered the aluminum, disposable cooking utensils, frying pans and deep dishes. You fry a fish and throw the pan overboard. I was well equipped with these things. I opened a can of corned-beef hash and patted it into a disposable dish and set it on an asbestos pad over a low flame, to heat very slowly. The coffee was barely ready when Charley let out his lion roar. I can't say how comforting it is to be told that someone is approaching in the dark. And if the approacher happened to have evil in his heart, that great voice would give him pause if he did not know Charley's basically pacific and diplomatic nature.

The farm owner knocked on my door and I invited him in. "You've got it nice in here," he said. "Yes, sir, you've got it nice."

He slipped in the seat beside the table. This table can be lowered at night and the cushions can be converted to make a double bed. "Nice," he said again.

I poured him a cup of coffee. It seems to me that coffee smells even better when the frost is in. "A little something on the side?" I asked. "Something to give it authority?"

"No—this is fine. This is nice."

"Not a touch of applejack? I'm tired from driving, I'd like a spot myself."

He looked at me with the contained amusement that is considered taciturnity by non-Yankees. "Would you have one if I didn't?"

"No, I guess not."

"I wouldn't rob you then—just a spoonful."

So I poured each of us a good dollop of twenty-one-year-old applejack and slipped in on my side of the table. Charley moved over to make room and put his chin down on my feet.

There's a gentility on the road. A direct or personal question is out of bounds. But this is simple good manners anywhere in the world. He did not ask my name nor I his, but I had seen his quick eyes go to the firearms in their rubber slings, to the fishing rods pinioned against the wall.

Khrushchev was at the United Nations, one of the few reasons I would have liked to be in New York. I asked, "Have you listened to the radio today?"

"Five-o'clock report."

"What happened at the U.N.? I forgot to listen."

"You wouldn't believe it," he said. "Mr. K. took off his shoe and pounded the table."

"What for?"

"Didn't like what was being said."

"Seems a strange way to protest."

"Well, it got attention. That's about all the news talked about."

"They should give him a gavel so he could keep his shoes on."

"That's a good idea. Maybe it could be in the shape of a shoe so he wouldn't be embarrassed." He sipped the applejack with a deep appreciation. "That's pretty nice," he said.

"How do folks around here feel about all this talking back to the Russians?"

"I don't know about other people. But I think if you're talking back it's kind of like a rear-guard action. I'd like to see us do something so they had to talk back to us."

"You've got something there."

"Seems to me we're always defending ourselves."

I refilled the coffee cups and poured a little more applejack for both of us. "You think we should attack?"

"I think we should at least take the ball sometimes."

"I'm not taking a poll, but how does the election seem to be going around here?"

"I wish I knew," he said. "People aren't talking. I think this might be the secretest election we ever had. People just won't put out an opinion."

"Could it be they haven't got one?"

"Maybe, or maybe they just don't want to tell. I remember other elections when there would be pretty peppery arguments. I haven't heard even one."

And that's what I found all over the country—no arguments, no discussion.

"Is it the same—other places?" He must have seen my license plates, but he would not mention that.

"That seems right to me. Do you think people are scared to have an opinion?"

"Maybe some. But I know some that don't scare, and they don't say, either."

"That's been my experience," I said. "But I don't know, really."

"I don't either. Maybe it's all part of the same thing. No thanks, no more. I can smell your supper's nearly ready. I'll step along."

"Part of what same thing?"

"Well, you take my grandfather and his father—he was still alive until I was twelve. They knew some things they were sure about. They were pretty sure give a little line and then what *might* happen. But now—what might happen?"

"I don't know."

"Nobody knows. What good's an opinion if you don't know? My grandfather knew the number of whiskers in the Almighty's beard. I don't even know what happened yesterday, let alone tomorrow. He knew what it was that makes a rock or a table. I don't even understand the formula that says nobody knows. We've got nothing to go on—got no way to think about things. I'll step along. Will I see you in the morning?"

"I don't know. I'm going to start early. I want to get clear across Maine to Deer Isle."

"Say, that's a pretty place isn't it?"

"I don't know yet. I haven't been there."

"Well, it's nice. You'll like it. Thanks for the—coffee. Good night."

Charley looked after him and sighed and went back to sleep. I ate my corned-beef hash, then made down my bed and dug out Shirer's *Rise and Fall of the Third Reich*. But I found I couldn't read, and when the light was off I couldn't sleep. The clattering stream on the rocks was a good reposeful sound, but the conversation of the farmer stayed with me—a thoughtful, articulate man he was. I couldn't hope to find many like him. And maybe he had put his finger on it. Humans had perhaps a million years to get used to fire as a thing and as an idea. Between the time a man got his fingers burned on a lightning-struck tree until another man carried some inside a cave and found it kept him warm, maybe a hundred thousand years, and from there to the blast furnaces of Detroit—how long?

And now a force was in hand how much more strong, and we hadn't had time to develop the means to think, for man has to have feelings and then words before he can come close to thought and, in the past at least, that has taken a long time.

Roosters were crowing before I went to sleep. And I felt at last that my journey was started. I think I hadn't really believed in it before.

Charley likes to get up early, and he likes me to get up early too. And why shouldn't he? Right after his breakfast he goes back to sleep. Over the years he has developed a number of innocent-appearing ways to get me up. He can shake himself and his collar loud enough to wake the dead. If that doesn't work he gets a sneezing fit. But perhaps his most irritating method is to sit quietly beside the bed and stare into my face with a sweet and forgiving look on his face; I come out of deep sleep with the feeling of being looked at. But I have learned to keep my eyes tight shut. If I even blink he sneezes and stretches, and that night's sleep is over for me. Often the war of wills goes on for quite a time, I squinching my eyes shut and he forgiving me, but he nearly always wins. He liked traveling so much he wanted to get started early, and early for Charley is the first tempering of darkness with the dawn.

I soon discovered that if a wayfaring stranger wishes to eavesdrop on a local population the places for him to slip in and hold his peace are bars and churches. But some New England towns

don't have bars, and church is only on Sunday. A good alternative is the roadside restaurant where men gather for breakfast
before going to work or going hunting. To find these places
inhabited, one must get up very early. And there is a drawback
even to this. Early-rising men not only do not talk much to
strangers, they barely talk to one another. Breakfast conversation
is limited to a series of laconic grunts. The natural New England
taciturnity reaches its glorious perfection at breakfast.

I fed Charley, gave him a limited promenade, and hit the road.
An icy mist covered the hills and froze on my windshield. I am
not normally a breakfast eater, but here I had to be or I wouldn't
see anybody unless I stopped for gas. At the first lighted roadside restaurant I pulled in and took my seat at a counter. The
customers were folded over their coffee cups like ferns. A normal
conversation is as follows:

WAITRESS: "Same?"

CUSTOMER: "Yep."

WAITRESS: "Cold enough for you?"

CUSTOMER: "Yep."

(Ten minutes.)

WAITRESS: "Refill?"

CUSTOMER: "Yep."

This is a really talkative customer. Some reduce it to "Burp"
and others do not answer at all. An early morning waitress in
New England leads a lonely life, but I soon learned that if I tried
to inject life and gaiety into her job with a blithe remark she
dropped her eyes and answered "Yep" or "Umph." Still, I did
feel that there was some kind of communication, but I can't say
what it was.

The best of learning came on the morning radio, which I
learned to love. Every town of a few thousand people has its
station, and it takes the place of the old local newspaper. Bargains and trades are announced, social doings, prices of commodities, messages. The records played are the same all over the
country. If "Teen-Age Angel" is top of the list in Maine, it is
top of the list in Montana. In the course of a day you may hear
"Teen-Age Angel" thirty or forty times. But in addition to local
news and chronicles, some foreign advertising creeps in. As I

went farther and farther north and it got colder I was aware of more and more advertising for Florida real estate and, with the approach of the long and bitter winter, I could see why Florida is a golden word. As I went along I found that more and more people lusted toward Florida and that thousands had moved there and more thousands wanted to and would. The advertising, with a side look at Federal Communications, made few claims except for the fact that the land they were selling was in Florida. Some of them went out on a limb and promised that it was above tide level. But that didn't matter; the very name Florida carried the message of warmth and ease and comfort. It was irresistible.

I've lived in good climate, and it bores the hell out of me. I like weather rather than climate. In Cuernavaca, Mexico, where I once lived, and where the climate is as near to perfect as is conceivable, I have found that when people leave there they usually go to Alaska. I'd like to see how long an Aroostook County man can stand Florida. The trouble is that with his savings moved and invested there, he can't very well go back. His dice are rolled and can't be picked up again. But I do wonder if a down-Easter, sitting on a nylon-and-aluminum chair out on a changelessly green lawn slapping mosquitoes in the evening of a Florida October—I do wonder if the stab of memory doesn't strike him high in the stomach just below the ribs where it hurts. And in the humid ever-summer I dare his picturing mind not to go back to the shout of color, to the clean rasp of frosty air, to the smell of pine wood burning and the caressing warmth of kitchens. For how can one know color in perpetual green, and what good is warmth without cold to give it sweetness?

I drove as slowly as custom and the impatient law permitted. That's the only way to see anything. Every few miles the states provided places of rest off the roads, sheltered places sometimes near dark streams. There were painted oil drums for garbage, and picnic tables, and sometimes fireplaces or barbecue pits. At intervals I drove Rocinante off the road and let Charley out to smell over the register of previous guests. Then I would heat my coffee and sit comfortably on my back step and contemplate wood and water and the quick-rising mountains with crowns of conifers and the fir trees high up, dusted with snow. Long ago

at Easter I had a looking-egg. Peering in a little porthole at the
end, I saw a lovely little farm, a kind of dream farm, and on the
farmhouse chimney a stork sitting on a nest. I regarded this as
a fairy-tale farm as surely imagined as gnomes sitting under toad-
stools. And then in Denmark I saw that farm or its brother, and
it was true, just as it had been in the looking-egg. And in Salinas,
California, where I grew up, although we had some frost the
climate was cool and foggy. When we saw colored pictures of a
Vermont autumn forest it was another fairy thing and we frankly
didn't believe it. In school we memorized "Snowbound" and
little poems about Old Jack Frost and his paintbrush, but the
only thing Jack Frost did for us was put a thin skin of ice on
the watering trough, and that rarely. To find not only that this
bedlam of color was true but that the pictures were pale and
inaccurate translations, was to me startling. I can't even imagine
the forest colors when I am not seeing them. I wondered
whether constant association could cause inattention, and asked
a native New Hampshire woman about it. She said the autumn
never failed to amaze her; to elate. "It is a glory," she said, "and
can't be remembered, so that it always comes as a surprise."

In the stream beside the resting place I saw a trout rise from
the dark water of a pool and make outflowing silver rings, and
Charley saw it too and waded in and got wet, the fool. He never
thinks of the future. I stepped into Rocinante to bring out my
poor mite of garbage for the oil drum, two empty cans; I had
eaten from one and Charley from the other. And among the
books I had brought along, I saw a well-remembered cover and
brought it out to the sunlight—a golden hand holding at once
a serpent and a mirror with wings, and below in scriptlike letters
"*The Spectator*, Edited by Henry Morley."

I seem to have had a fortunate childhood for a writer. My
grandfather, Sam'l Hamilton, loved good writing, and he knew
it too, and he had some bluestocking daughters, among them my
mother. Thus it was that in Salinas, in the great dark walnut
bookcase with the glass doors, there were strange and wonderful
things to be found. My parents never offered them, and the glass
doors obviously guarded them, and so I pilfered from that case.
It was neither forbidden nor discouraged. I think today if we

forbade our illiterate children to touch the wonderful things óf our literature, perhaps they might steal them and find secret joy. Very early I conceived a love for Joseph Addison which I have never lost. He plays the instrument of language as Casals plays a cello. I do not know whether he influenced my prose style, but I could hope he did. In the White Mountains in 1960, sitting in the sun, I opened the well-remembered first volume, printed in 1883. I turned to Number 1 of *The Spectator*—Thursday, March 1, 1711. It was headed:

"Non fumum ex fulgore, sed ex fumo dare lucem
Cogitat, et speciosa dehinc miracula promat."*—Horace.

I remember so well loving Addison's use of capital letters for nouns. He writes under this date:

"I have observed that a Reader seldom peruses a Book with Pleasure 'till he knows whether the Writer of it be a black or fair Man, of a mild or cholerick Disposition, Married or a Batchelor, with other Particulars of the like Nature, that conduce very much to the right Understanding of an Author. To gratify this Curiosity, which is so natural to a Reader, I design this Paper and my next, as Prefatory Discourses to my following Writings and shall give some Account in them of the several persons that are engaged in this Work. As the chief trouble of Compiling, Digesting and Correcting will fall to my Share, I must do myself the Justice to open the Work with my own History."

Sunday, January 29, 1961. Yes, Joseph Addison, I hear and I will obey within Reason, for it appears that the Curiosity you speak of has in no Way abated. I have found many Readers more interested in what I wear than in what I think, more avid to know how I do it than in what I do. In regarding my Work, some Readers profess greater Feeling for what it makes than for what it says. Since a Suggestion from the Master is a Command not unlike Holy Writ, I shall digress and comply at the same Time.

Among the generality of men I am tall—six feet even—although among the males of my family I am considered a dwarf. They range from six feet two inches to six feet five, and I know that both my sons, when they stretch their full height, will over-top me. I am very wide of shoulder and, in the condition I now find myself, narrow of hip. My legs are long in proportion to my trunk and are said to be shapely. My hair is a grizzled gray, my eyes blue and my cheeks ruddy, a complexion inherited from my Irish mother. My face has not ignored the passage of time, but recorded it with scars, lines, furrows, and erosions. I wear a beard and mustache but shave my cheeks; said beard, having a dark skunk stripe up the middle and white edges, commemorates certain relatives. I cultivate this beard not for the usual given reasons of skin trouble or pain of shaving, nor for the secret purpose of covering a weak chin, but as pure unblushing deco-ration, much as a peacock finds pleasure in his tail. And finally, in our time a beard is the one thing a woman cannot do better than a man, or if she can her success is assured only in a circus.

My costume for traveling was utilitarian if a trifle bizarre. Half-Wellington rubber boots with cork inner soles kept my feet warm and dry. Khaki cotton trousers, bought in an army-surplus store, covered my shanks, while my upper regions rejoiced in a hunting coat with corduroy cuffs and collar and a game pocket in the rear big enough to smuggle an Indian princess into a Y.M.C.A. My cap was one I have worn for many years, a blue serge British naval cap with a short visor and on its peak the royal lion and unicorn, as always fighting for the crown of En-gland. This cap is pretty ratty and salt-crusted, but it was given me by the skipper of a motor torpedo boat on which I sailed out of Dover during the war—a gentle gentleman and a mur-derer. After I left his command he attacked a German E-boat and held his fire trying to take it whole since none had ever been captured, and in the process he got himself sunk. I have worn his cap ever since in his honor and in his memory. Besides, I like it. It agrees with me. Down East this cap did not draw a second glance, but when later, in Wisconsin, North Dakota, Montana, I had left the sea far behind, I thought it drew atten-tion, and I bought what we used to call a stockman's hat, a Stetson, not too wide of brim, a rich but conservative western hat of the kind my cow-harrying uncles used to wear. Only when I came down to another sea in Seattle did I reassume the naval cap.

Thus far with Addison's injunction, but my Reader has me back in that New Hampshire picnic place. As I sat there fingering the first volume of *The Spectator* and considering how the mind usually does two things at once that it knows about and probably several it doesn't, a luxurious car drove in and a rather stout and bedizened woman released a rather stout and bedizened Pomeranian of the female persuasion. I would not have known this latter fact, but Charley knew. Emerging from behind the garbage can, he found her beautiful, his French blood flared up, and he proceeded to gallantries unmistakable even to the slack eyes of mademoiselle's mistress. This creature let out a shriek like a wounded rabbit, emerged from the car with an explosive ooze, and would have snatched her darling to her bosom if she could have bent down that far. The best she could do was to fetch a slap at tall Charley's head. He quite naturally and casually took a nip at her hand before proceeding toward romance. Until that moment I never quite knew the meaning of the phrase "to make the welkin ring." In the first place I didn't know what a welkin was. I looked it up later. And that bull bitch of a woman sure as hell made it ring. I grabbed her hand and saw that the skin wasn't even broken, so I grabbed her dog, which promptly bit me good and drew blood before I could get the little monster by the throat and gently throttle it.

Charley regarded the whole scene as nonsense. He wet on the garbage can for the twentieth time and called it a day.

It took time to calm the lady. I brought out the bottle of brandy, which might have killed her, and she took a slug that should have killed her.

After all I've done for him you'd think Charley would have come to my aid, but he dislikes neurotics and he detests drunks. He climbed in Rocinante, crawled under the table, and went to sleep. Sic semper cum Frogs.

At last milady flailed away with her hand brake on, and the kind of a day I had built lay in ruins. Addison had crashed in flames, the trout no longer ringed the pool, and a cloud covered the sun and put a chill in the air. I found myself driving faster than I wanted to and it began to rain, a cold steel rain. I didn't give the lovely villages the attention they deserved, and before long I had crossed into Maine and continued eastward.

I wish any two states could get together on a speed limit. Just about the time you get used to fifty miles an hour you cross a state line and it's sixty-five. I wonder why they can't settle down and agree. However, in one matter all states agree—each one admits it is the finest of all and announces that fact in huge letters as you cross the state line. Among nearly forty I didn't see a single state that hadn't a good word to say for itself. It seemed a little indelicate. It might be better to let visitors find out for themselves. But maybe we wouldn't if it weren't drawn to our attention.

Preparation for the winter in New England is drastic. The summer population must be large and the roads and highways gorged with refugees from the sticky heat of Boston and New York. Now the hot-dog stands, the ice-cream parlors, the curiosity shops, deerskin-moccasin-and-glove places, were all shuttered and closed, many of them with cards saying "Open Next Summer." I can never get used to the thousands of antique shops along the roads, all bulging with authentic and attested trash from an earlier time. I believe the population of the thirteen colonies was less than four million souls, and every one of them must have been frantically turning out tables, chairs, china, glass, candle molds, and oddly shaped bits of iron, copper, and brass for future sale to twentieth-century tourists. There are enough antiques for sale along the roads of New England alone to furnish the houses of a population of fifty million. If I were a good businessman, and cared a tittle for my unborn great grandchildren, which I do not, I would gather all the junk and the wrecked automobiles, comb the city dumps, and pile these gleanings in mountains and spray the whole thing with that stuff the Navy uses to mothball ships. At the end of a hundred years my descendants would be permitted to open this treasure trove and would be the antique kings of the world. If the battered, cracked, and broken stuff our ancestors tried to get rid of now brings so much money, think what a 1954 Oldsmobile, or a 1960 toastmaster will bring—and a vintage Waring Mixor—Lord, the possibilities are endless! Things we have to pay to have hauled away could bring fortunes.

If I seem to be over-interested in junk, it is because I am, and I have a lot of it, too—half a garage full of bits and broken pieces. I use these things for repairing other things. Recently I stopped my car in front of the display yard of a junk dealer near Sag Harbor. As I was looking courteously at the stock, it suddenly occurred to me that I had more than he had. But it can be seen that I do have a genuine and almost miserly interest in worthless objects. My excuse is that in this era of planned obsolescence, when a thing breaks down I can usually find something in my collection to repair it—a toilet, or a motor, or a lawn mower. But I guess the truth is that I simply like junk.

Before I started my tour, I had known that at intervals of every few days I would have to stop at auto courts or motels, not so much to sleep but for the sake of hot, luxurious bathing. In Rocinante I heated water in a tea kettle and took sponge baths, but bathing in a bucket delivers little cleanliness and no pleasure whatever. A deep-dish sit-down in a tub with scalding water is a pure joy. Quite early on my trip, however, I invented a method for washing clothes which you will go a long way to better. It came about this way. I had a large plastic garbage bucket with cover and bail. Since the normal movement of the truck tipped it over, I tethered it by a length of strong elastic rope of cotton-covered rubber to the clothes pole in my little closet, where it could jiggle to its heart's content without spilling. After a day of this, I opened it to dispose of the stuff at a roadside garbage can and found the most thoroughly mixed and kneaded garbage I have ever seen. I suppose all great inventions spring from some such experience. The next morning, I washed the plastic bucket, put in two shirts, underwear, and socks, added hot water and detergent, and hung it by its rubber rope to the clothes pole, where it jigged and danced crazily all day. That night I rinsed the clothes in a stream, and you've never seen clothes so clean. Inside Rocinante I strung a nylon line close to the window and hung the clothes to dry. From that time on, my clothing was washed on one day of driving and dried on the next. I even went overboard and washed sheets and pillow cases that way. So much for daintiness, but it didn't take care of hot baths.

Not far outside of Bangor I stopped at an auto court and rented a room. It wasn't expensive. The sign said "Greatly Reduced Winter Rates." It was immaculate; everything was done in plastics—the floors, the curtain, table tops of stainless burnless plastic, lamp shades of plastic. Only the bedding and the towels were of a natural material. I went to the small restaurant run in conjunction. It was all plastic too—the table linen, the butter dish. The sugar and crackers were wrapped in cellophane, the jelly in a small plastic coffin sealed with cellophane. It was early evening and I was the only customer. Even the waitress wore a sponge-off apron. She wasn't happy, but then she wasn't unhappy. She wasn't anything. But I don't believe anyone is a nothing. There has to be something inside, if only to keep the skin from collapsing. This vacant eye, listless hand, this damask cheek dusted like a doughnut with plastic powder, had to have a memory or a dream.

On a chance I asked, "How soon you going to Florida?"

"Nex' week," she said listlessly. Then something stirred in that aching void. "Say, how do you know I'm going?"

"Read your mind, I guess."

She looked at my beard. "You with a show?"

"No."

"Then how do you mean read my mind?"

"Maybe I guessed. Like it down there?"

"Oh, sure! I go every year. Lots of waitress jobs in the winter."

"What do you do down there, I mean for fun?"

"Oh, nothing. Just fool around."

"Do you fish or swim?"

"Not much. I just fool around. I don't like that sand, makes me itch."

"Make good money?"

"It's a cheap crowd."

"Cheap?"

"They rather spen' it on booze."

"Than what?"

"Than tips. Just the same here with the summer people. Cheap."

Strange how one person can saturate a room with vitality, with excitement. Then there are others, and this dame was one of them, who can drain off energy and joy, can suck pleasure dry and get no sustenance from it. Such people spread a grayness in the air about them. I'd been driving a long time, and perhaps my energy was low and my resistance down. She got me. I felt so blue and miserable I wanted to crawl into a plastic cover and die. What a date she must be, what a lover! I tried to imagine that last and couldn't. For a moment I considered giving her a five-dollar tip, but I knew what would happen. She wouldn't be glad. She'd just think I was crazy.

I went back to my clean little room. I don't ever drink alone. It's not much fun. And I don't think I will until I am an alcoholic. But this night I got a bottle of vodka from my stores and took it to my cell. In the bathroom two water tumblers were sealed in cellophane sacks with the words: "These glasses are sterilized for your protection." Across the toilet seat a strip of paper bore the message: "This seat has been sterilized with ultraviolet light for your protection." Everyone was protecting me and it was horrible. I tore the glasses from their covers. I violated the toilet-seat seal with my foot. I poured half a tumbler of vodka and drank it and then another. Then I lay deep in hot water in the tub and I was utterly miserable, and nothing was good anywhere.

Charley caught it from me, but he is a gallant dog. He came into the bathroom and that old fool played with the plastic bath mat like a puppy. What strength of character, what a friend! Then he rushed to the door and barked as though I were being invaded. And if it hadn't been for all that plastic he might have succeeded.

I remember an old Arab in North Africa, a man whose hands had never felt water. He gave me mint tea in a glass so coated with use that it was opaque, but he handed me companionship, and the tea was wonderful because of it. And without any protection my teeth didn't fall out, nor did running sores develop. I began to formulate a new law describing the relationship of protection to despondency. A sad soul can kill you quicker, far quicker, than a germ.

If Charley hadn't shaken and bounced and said "Ftt," I might have forgotten that every night he gets two dog biscuits and a walk to clear his head. I put on clean clothes and went out with him into the star-raddled night. And the Aurora Borealis was out. I've seen it only a few times in my life. It hung and moved with majesty in folds like an infinite traveler upstage in an infinite theater. In colors of rose and lavender and purple it moved and pulsed against the night, and the frost-sharpened stars shone through it. What a thing to see at a time when I needed it so badly! I wondered for a moment whether I should grab that waitress and kick her behind out to look at it, but I didn't dare. She could make eternity and infinity melt and run out through your fingers. The air had a sweet burn of frost, and Charley, moving ahead, saluted in detail a whole row of clipped privet, and he steamed as he went. When he came back, he was pleased and glad for me. I gave him three dog biscuits, rumpled up the sterile bed, and went out to sleep in Rocinante.

It is not unlike me that in heading toward the West I should travel east. That has always been my tendency. I was going to Deer Isle for a very good reason. My long-time friend and associate, Elizabeth Otis, has been going to Deer Isle every year. When she speaks of it, she gets an other-world look in her eyes and becomes completely inarticulate. When I planned my trip she said, "Of course you'll stop at Deer Isle."

"It's out of my way."

"Nonsense," she said in a tone I know very well. I gathered from her voice and manner that if I didn't go to Deer Isle I had better never show my face in New York again. She then telephoned Miss Eleanor Brace, with whom she always stays, and that was that. I was committed. All I knew about Deer Isle was that there was nothing you could say about it, but if I didn't go I was crazy. Also, Miss Brace was waiting for me.

I got thoroughly lost in Bangor, what with traffic and trucks, horns blaring and lights changing. I vaguely remembered that I should be on U.S. Highway 1, and I found it and drove ten miles in the wrong direction, back toward New York. I had been given written directions on how to go, detailed directions, but have you ever noticed that instructions from one who knows the country get you more lost than you are, even when they are accurate? I also got lost in Ellsworth, which I am told is impossible. Then the roads narrowed and the lumber trucks roared past me. I was lost almost all day, even though I found Blue Hill and Sedgwick. Late in the despairing afternoon I stopped

my truck and approached a majestic Maine state trooper. What
a man he was, granite as any quarried about Portland, a perfect
model for some future equestrian statue. I wonder if future he-
roes will be carved in marble jeeps or patrol cars?

"I seem to be lost, officer. I wonder if you could direct me?"

"Where is it you want to go?"

"I'm trying to get to Deer Isle."

He looked at me closely, and when he was satisfied that I
wasn't joking he swung on his hips and pointed across a small
stretch of open water, and he didn't bother to speak.

"Is that it?"

He nodded from up to down and left his head down.

"Well, how do I get there?"

I have always heard that Maine people are rather taciturn, but
for this candidate for Mount Rushmore to point twice in an
afternoon was to be unbearably talkative. He swung his chin in
a small arc in the direction I had been traveling. If the afternoon
had not been advancing I would have tried for another word
from him even if doomed to failure. "Thank you," I said, and
sounded to myself as though I rattled on forever.

First there was a very high iron bridge, as high-arched as a
rainbow, and after a bit of low stone bridge built in the shape
of an S-curve, and I was on Deer Isle. My written directions said
that I must take every road branch that turned right, and the
word "every" was underlined. I climbed a hill and turned right
into pine woods on a smaller road, and turned right on a very
narrow road and turned right again on wheel tracks on pine
needles. It is so easy once you have been over it. I couldn't
believe I would find the place, but in a hundred yards there was
the great old house of Miss Eleanor Brace, and there she was to
welcome me. I let Charley out, and suddenly an angry streak of
gray burned across the clearing in the pines and bucketed into
the house. That was George. He didn't welcome me and he particularly didn't welcome Charley. I never did rightly see George,
but his sulking presence was everywhere. For George is an old
gray cat who has accumulated a hatred of people and things so
intense that even hidden upstairs he communicates his prayer
that you will go away. If the bomb should fall and wipe out

every living thing except Miss Brace, George would be happy. That's the way he would design a world if it were up to him. And he could never know that Charley's interest in him was purely courteous; if he did, he would be hurt in his misanthropy, for Charley has no interest in cats whatever, even for chasing purposes.

We didn't give George any trouble because for two nights we stayed in Rocinante, but I am told that when guests sleep in the house George goes into the pine woods and watches from afar, grumbling his dissatisfaction and pouring out his dislike. Miss Brace admits that for the purposes of a cat, whatever they are, George is worthless. He isn't good company, he is not sympathetic, and he has little aesthetic value.

"Perhaps he catches mice and rats," I suggested helpfully.

"Never," said Miss Brace. "Wouldn't think of it. And do you want to know something? George is a girl."

I had to restrain Charley because the unseen presence of George was everywhere. In a more enlightened day when witches and familiars were better understood, George would have found his, or rather her, end in a bonfire, because if ever there was a familiar, an envoy of the devil, a consorter with evil spirits, George is it.

One doesn't have to be sensitive to feel the strangeness of Deer Isle. And if people who have been going there for many years cannot describe it, what can I do after two days? It is an island that nestles like a suckling against the breast of Maine, but there are many of those. The sheltered darkling water seems to suck up light, but I've seen that before. The pine woods rustle and the wind cries over open country that is like Dartmoor. Stonington, Deer Isle's chief town, does not look like an American town at all in place or in architecture. Its houses are layered down to the calm water of the bay. This town very closely resembles Lyme Regis on the coast of Dorset, and I would willingly bet that its founding settlers came from Dorset or Somerset or Cornwall. Maine speech is very like that in West Country England, the double vowels pronounced as they are in Anglo-Saxon, but the resemblance is doubly strong on Deer Isle. And the coastal people below the Bristol Channel are secret people, and perhaps magic people. There's aught behind their eyes, hidden away so deep that perhaps even they do not know they have it. And that same thing is so in Deer Islers. To put it plainly, this Isle is like Avalon; it must disappear when you are not there. Or take for example the mystery of the coon cats, huge tailless cats with gray coats barred with black, which is why they are called coon cats. They are wild; they live in the woods and are very fierce. Once in a while a native brings in a kitten and raises it, and it is a pleasure to him, almost an honor, but coon cats are rarely even approximately tame. You take a chance of being raked or bitten all the time. These cats are obviously of Manx origin, and even interbreeding with tame cats they contribute taillessness. The story is that the great ancestors of the coon cats were brought by some ship's captain and that they soon went wild. But I wonder where they get their size. They are twice as big as any Manx cat I ever saw. Could it be that they bred with bobcat or lynx? I don't know. Nobody knows.

Down by the Stonington Harbor the summer boats were being pulled up for storage. And not only here but in other inlets nearby are very large lobster pounds crawling with those dark-shelled Maine lobsters from the dark water which are the best lobsters in the world. Miss Brace ordered up three, not more than a pound and a half, she said, and that night their excellence was demonstrated beyond a doubt. There are no lobsters like these—simply boiled, with no fancy sauces, only melted butter and lemon, they have no equals anywhere. Even shipped or flown alive away from their dark homes, they lose something.

At a wonderful store in Stonington, half hardware store and half ship's chandler, I bought a kerosene lamp with a tin reflector for Rocinante. I had the fear that I might somewhere run out of butane gas, and how would I read in bed then? I screwed the lamp bracket to the wall over my bed and trimmed the wick to make a golden butterfly of flame. And often on my trip I used it for warmth and color as well as light. It was exactly the same lamp that was in all the rooms at the ranch when I was a child. And no pleasanter light was ever designed, although old timers say that whale oil makes a nicer flame.

I have demonstrated that I can't describe Deer Isle. There is

something about it that opens no door to words. But it stays
with you afterward, and, more than that, things you didn't know
you saw come back to you after you have left. One thing I
remember very clearly. It might have been caused by the season
with a quality of light, or the autumn clarity. Everything stood
out separate from everything else, a rock, a rounded lump of
sea-polished driftwood on a beach, a roof line. Each pine tree
was itself and separate even if it was a part of a forest. Drawing
a very long bow of relationships, could I say that the people
have that same quality? Surely I never met such ardent individuals. I would hate to try to force them to do anything they didn't
want to do. I heard many stories about the Isle—I remember it
is Isle and not Island—and was given much taciturn advice. I
will repeat only one admonishment from a native of Maine, and
I will not put a name to that person for fear of reprisal.

"Don't ever ask directions of a Maine native," I was told.

"Why ever not?"

"Somehow we think it is funny to misdirect people and we
don't smile when we do it, but we laugh inwardly. It is our
nature."

I wonder if that is true. I could never test it, because through
my own efforts I am lost most of the time without any help
from anyone.

I have spoken with approval, even affection, of Rocinante but
not of the pick-up truck on which the camper top rode. It was
a new model, with a powerful V-6 engine. It had automatic
transmission and an oversized generator to give me lights inside
the cabin if I should need them. The cooling system was so
loaded with antifreeze that it could have withstood polar
weather. I believe that American-made automobiles for passen-
gers are made to wear out so that they must be replaced. This
is not so with the trucks. A trucker requires many more
thousands of miles of good service than a passenger-car owner.
He is not to be dazzled with trimming or fins or doodads and
he is not required by his status to buy a new model every year
or so to maintain social face. Everything about my truck was
made to last. Its frame was heavy, the metal rigid, the engine big
and sturdy. Of course I treated it well in matters of oil changes

and greasing, and I did not drive it to its limit or force it to do
acrobatics required of sports cars. The cab was double-walled,
and a good heater had been installed. When I returned after more
than ten thousand miles the engine was only well broken in. And
it never failed or stuttered even once during the journey.

I moved up the coast of Maine, through Millbridge and Addison and Machias and Perry and South Robbinston, until there
was no more coast. I never knew or had forgotten how much
of Maine sticks up like a thumb into Canada with New Bruns-
wick on the east. We know so little of our own geography. Why,
Maine extends northward almost to the mouth of the St.
Lawrence, and its upper border is perhaps a hundred miles north
of Quebec. And another thing I had conveniently forgotten was
how incredibly huge America is. As I drove north through the
little towns and the increasing forest rolling away to the horizon,
the season changed quickly and out of all proportion. Perhaps
it was my getting away from the steadying hand of the sea, and
also perhaps I was getting very far north. The houses had a
snow-beaten look, and many were crushed and deserted, driven
to earth by the winters. Except in the towns there was evidence
of a population which had once lived here and farmed and had
its being and had then been driven out. The forests were marching back, and where farm wagons once had been only the big
logging trucks rumbled along. And the game had come back,
too; deer strayed on the roads and there were marks of bear.

There are customs, attitudes, myths and directions and
changes that seem to be part of the structure of America. And I
propose to discuss them as they were first thrust on my attention. While these discussions go on you are to imagine me bowl-
ing along on some little road or pulled up behind a bridge, or
cooking a big pot of lima beans and salt pork. And the first of
these has to do with hunting. I could not have escaped hunting
if I had wanted to, for open seasons spangle the autumn. We
have inherited many attitudes from our recent ancestors who
wrestled this continent as Jacob wrestled the angel, and the pioneers won. From them we take a belief that every American is
a natural-born hunter. And every fall a great number of men set
out to prove that without talent, training, knowledge, or practice

they are dead shots with rifle or shotgun. The results are horrid. From the moment I left Sag Harbor the guns were booming at the migrating ducks, and as I drove in Maine the rifle shots in the forests would have frightened off any number of redcoats so long as they didn't know what was happening. This is bound to get me a bad name as a sportsman, but let me say at once that I have nothing against the killing of animals. Something has to kill them, I suppose. In my youth I often crawled miles on my belly through freezing wind for the pure glory of blasting a mudhen which even soaked in salt water made poor eating. I don't greatly care for venison or bear or moose or elk except for the livers. The recipes, the herbs, the wine, the preparation that goes into a good venison dish would make an old shoe a gourmet's delight. If I were hungry, I would happily hunt anything that runs or crawls or flies, even relatives, and tear them down with my teeth. But it isn't hunger that drives millions of armed American males to forests and hills every autumn, as the high incidence of heart failure among the hunters will prove. Somehow the hunting process has to do with masculinity, but I don't quite know how. I know there are any number of good and efficient hunters who know what they are doing; but many more are overweight gentlemen, primed with whisky and armed with high-powered rifles. They shoot at anything that moves or looks as though it might, and their success in killing one another may well prevent a population explosion. If the casualties were limited to their own kind there would be no problem, but the slaughter of cows, pigs, farmers, dogs, and highway signs makes autumn a dangerous season in which to travel. A farmer in upper New York State painted the word cow in big black letters on both sides of his white bossy, but the hunters shot it anyway. In Wisconsin, as I was driving through, a hunter shot his own guide between the shoulder blades. The coroner questioning this nimrod asked, "Did you think he was a deer?"

"Yes, sir, I did."

"But you weren't sure he was a deer."

"Well, no sir. I guess not."

With the rolling barrage going on in Maine, of course I was afraid for myself. Four automobiles were hit on opening day, but mainly I was afraid for Charley. I know that a poodle looks very like a buck deer to one of these hunters, and I had to find some way of protecting him. In Rocinante there was a box of red Kleenex that someone had given me as a present. I wrapped Charley's tail in red Kleenex and fastened it with rubber bands. Every morning I renewed his flag, and he wore it all the way west while bullets whined and whistled around us. This is not intended to be funny. The radios warned against carrying a white handkerchief. Too many hunters seeing a flash of white have taken it for the tail of a running deer and cured a head cold with a single shot.

But this legacy of the frontiersman is not a new thing. When I was a child on the ranch near Salinas, California, we had a Chinese cook who regularly made a modest good thing of it. On a ridge not far away, a sycamore log lay on its side supported by two of its broken branches. Lee's attention was drawn to this speckled fawn-colored chunk of wood by the bullet holes in it. He nailed a pair of horns to one end and then retired to his cabin until deer season was over. Then he harvested the lead from the old tree trunk. Some seasons he got fifty or sixty pounds of it. It wasn't a fortune but it was wages. After a couple of years, when the tree was completely shot away, Lee replaced it with four gunny sacks of sand and the same antlers. Then it was even easier to harvest his crop. If he had put out fifty of them it would have been a fortune, but Lee was a humble man who didn't care for mass production.

Maine seemed to stretch on endlessly. I felt as Peary must have when he approached what he thought was the North Pole. But I wanted to see Aroostook County, the big northern county of Maine. There are three great potato-raising sections—Idaho, Suffolk County on Long Island, and Aroostook, Maine. Lots of people had talked of Aroostook County, but I had never met anyone who had actually been there. I had been told that the crop is harvested by Canucks from Canada who flood over the border at harvest time. My way went endlessly through forest country and past many lakes, not yet frozen. As often as I could I chose the small wood roads, and they are not conducive to speed. The temperature lifted and it rained endlessly and the forests wept. Charley never got dry, and smelled as though he were mildewed. The sky was the color of wet gray aluminum and there was no indication on the translucent shield where the sun might be, so I couldn't tell direction. On a curving road I might have been traveling east or south or west instead of the north I wanted. That old fake about the moss growing on the north sides of trees lied to me when I was a Boy Scout. Moss grows on the shady side, and that may be any side. I determined to buy a compass in the next town, but there wasn't any next town on the road I was traveling. The darkness crept down and the rain drummed on the steel roof of the cab and the windshield wipers sobbed their arcs. Tall dark trees lined the road, crowding the gravel. It seemed hours since I had passed a car or a house or a store, for this was the country gone back to forest. A desolate loneliness settled on me—almost a frightening loneliness. Charley, wet and shivering, curled up in his corner of the seat and offered no companionship. I pulled in behind the approach to a concrete bridge, but couldn't find a level place on the sloping roadside.

Even the cabin was dismal and damp. I turned the gas mantle high, lit the kerosene lamp, and lighted two burners of my stove to drive the loneliness away. The rain drummed on the metal roof. Nothing in my stock of foods looked edible. The darkness fell and the trees moved closer. Over the rain drums I seemed to hear voices, as though a crowd of people muttered and mumbled offstage. Charley was restless. He didn't bark an alarm, but he growled and whined uneasily, which is very unlike him, and he didn't eat his supper and he left his water dish untouched—and that by a dog who drinks his weight in water every day and needs to because of the outgo. I succumbed utterly to my desolation, made two peanut-butter sandwiches, and went to bed and wrote letters home, passing my loneliness around. Then the rain stopped falling and the trees dripped and I helped to spawn a school of secret dangers. Oh, we can populate the dark with horrors, even we who think ourselves informed and sure, believing nothing we cannot measure or weigh. I knew beyond all doubt that the dark things crowding in on me either did not exist or were not dangerous to me, and still I was afraid. I thought how terrible the nights must have been in a time when men knew the things were there and were deadly. But no, that's wrong. If I knew they were there, I would have weapons against them, charms, prayers, some kind of alliance with forces equally strong but on my side. Knowing they were not there made me defenseless against them and perhaps more afraid.

Long ago I owned a little ranch in the Santa Cruz mountains in California. In one place a forest of giant madrone trees joined their tops over a true tarn, a black, spring-fed lake. If there is such a thing as a haunted place, that one was haunted, made so by dim light strained through the leaves and various tricks of perspective. I had working for me a Filipino man, a hill man, short and dark and silent, of the Maori people perhaps. Once, thinking he must have come from a tribal system which recognizes the unseen as a part of reality, I asked this man if he was not afraid of the haunted place, particularly at night. He said he was not afraid because years before a witch doctor gave him a charm against evil spirits.

"Let me see that charm," I asked.

"It's words," he said. "It's a word charm."

"Can you say them to me?"

"Sure," he said and he droned, *"In nomine Patris et Fillii et Spiritus Sancti."*

"What does it mean?" I asked.

He raised his shoulders. "I don't know," he said. "It's a charm against evil spirits so I am not afraid of them."

I've dredged this conversation out of a strange-sounding Spanish but there is no doubt of his charm, and it worked for him.

Lying in my bed under the weeping night I did my best to read to take my mind out of misery, but while my eyes moved on the lines I listened to the night. On the edge of sleep a new sound jerked me awake, the sound of footsteps, I thought, moving stealthily on gravel. On the bed beside me I had a flashlight two feet long, made for coon hunters. It throws a powerful beam at least a mile. I got up from bed and lifted my 30/30 carbine from the wall and listened again near the door of Rocinante— and I heard the steps come closer. Then Charley roared his warning and I opened the door and sprayed the road with light. It was a man in boots and a yellow oilskin. The light pinned him still.

"What do you want?" I called.

He must have been startled. It took him a moment to answer. "I want to go home. I live up the road."

And now I felt the whole silly thing, the ridiculous pattern that had piled up layer on layer. "Would you like a cup of coffee, or a drink?"

"No, it's late. If you'll take that light out of my face I'll get along."

I snapped off the light and he disappeared but his voice in passing said, "Come to think of it, what are you doing here?"

"Camping," I said, "just camped for the night." And I went to sleep the moment I hit the bed.

The sun was up when I awakened and the world was remade and shining. There are as many worlds as there are kinds of days, and as an opal changes its colors and its fire to match the nature of a day, so do I. The night fears and loneliness were so far gone that I could hardly remember them.

Even Rocinante, dirty and pine-needle-covered as she was, seemed to leap over the road with joy. Now there were open fields among the lakes and forests, fields with the crumbly friable soil potatoes love. Trucks with flat beds loaded with empty potato barrels moved on the roads, and the mechanical potato digger turned up long windrows of pale-skinned tubers.

In Spanish there is a word for which I can't find a counterword in English. It is the verb *vacilar*, present participle *vacilando*. It does not mean vacillating at all. If one is vacilando, he is going somewhere but doesn't greatly care whether or not he gets there, although he has direction. My friend Jack Wagner has often, in Mexico, assumed this state of being. Let us say we wanted to walk in the streets of Mexico City but not at random. We would choose some article almost certain not to exist there and then diligently try to find it.

I wanted to go to the rooftree of Maine to start my trip before turning west. It seemed to give the journey a design, and everything in the world must have design or the human mind rejects it. But in addition it must have purpose or the human conscience shies away from it. Maine was my design, potatoes my purpose. If I had not seen a single potato my status as *vacilador* would not have been affected. As it turned out I saw almost more potatoes than I needed to see. I saw mountains of potatoes—oceans—more potatoes than you would think the world's population could consume in a hundred years.

I've seen many migrant crop-picking people about the country: Hindus, Filipinos, Mexicans, Okies away from their states. Here in Maine a great many were French Canadians who came over the border for the harvest season. It occurs to me that, just as the Carthaginians hired mercenaries to do their fighting for them, we Americans bring in mercenaries to do our hard and humble work. I hope we may not be overwhelmed one day by peoples not too proud or too lazy or too soft to bend to the earth and pick up the things we eat.

These Canucks were a hardy people. They traveled and camped by families and groups of families, perhaps even clans: men, women, boys, girls, and small children too. Only the nurslings did not work at picking up the potatoes and placing them in the barrels. Americans drove the trucks and used a windlass and a kind of davit to pull the filled barrels aboard. Then they drove away to deposit the crop in the potato barns with earth heaped high about their sides to prevent freezing.

My knowledge of Canuck French derives from motion pictures usually with Nelson Eddy and Jeanette MacDonald, and it consists largely of "By gar." It's odd, but I didn't hear a single one of the potato pickers say "By gar," and they must have seen the pictures and known what is right. The women and girls wore pants usually of corduroy and thick sweaters, and they covered their heads with bright-colored scarves to protect their hair from the dust that rises from the fields with the smallest wind. Most of these people traveled in big trucks covered with dark canvas tarpaulins, but there were some trailers and a few camper tops like Rocinante. At night some slept in the trucks and trailers, but also there were tents pitched in pleasant places, and the smells that came from their cooking fires indicated that they had not lost their French genius for making soup.

Fortunately the tents and trucks and two trailers were settled on the edge of a clear and lovely lake. I parked Rocinante about ninety-five yards away but also on the lake's edge. Then I put on coffee to boil and brought out my garbage-bucket laundry, which had been jouncing for two days, and rinsed the detergent out at the edge of the lake. Attitudes toward strangers crop up mysteriously. I was downwind from the camp and the odor of their soup drifted to me. Those people might have been murderers, sadists, brutes, ugly apish subhumans for all I knew, but I found myself thinking, "What charming people, what flair, how beautiful they are. How I wish I knew them." And all based on the delicious smell of soup.

In establishing contact with strange people, Charley is my ambassador. I release him, and he drifts toward the objective, or rather to whatever the objective may be preparing for dinner. I retrieve him so that he will not be a nuisance to my neighbors —*et voilà!* A child can do the same thing, but a dog is better.

The incident came off as smoothly as one might expect of a tested and well-rehearsed script. I sent out my ambassador and drank a cup of coffee while I gave him time to operate. Then I strolled to the camp to relieve my neighbors of the inconvenience of my miserable cur. They were nice-looking people, a dozen of them, not counting children, three of the girls pretty and given to giggling, two of the wives buxom and a third even buxomer with child, a patriarch, two brothers-in-law, and a couple of young men who were working toward being brothers-in-law. But the operating chieftain, with deference of course to the patriarch, was a fine-looking man of about thirty-five, broad-shouldered and lithe, with the cream-and-berries complexion of a girl and crisp black curling hair.

The dog had caused no trouble, he said. The truth was that they had remarked that he was a handsome dog. I of course found myself prejudiced in spite of his deficiencies, being his owner, but the dog had one advantage over most dogs. He was born and raised in France.

The group closed ranks. The three pretty girls giggled and were instantly smothered by the navy-blue eye of the chieftain, backed by a hiss from the patriarch.

Was that the truth? Where in France?

In Bercy, on the outskirts of Paris, did they know it?

No, unfortunately they had never been to the fatherland.

I hoped they might remedy that.

They should have known Charley for a French national by his manners. They had observed my *roulotte* with admiration.

It was simple but comfortable. If they found it convenient, I should be pleased to show it to them.

I was very kind. It would give them pleasure.

If the elevated tone indicates to you that it was carried on in French, you are wrong. The chieftain spoke a very pure and careful English. The one French word used was *roulotte*. The asides among themselves were in Canuck. My French is ridiculous, anyway. No, the elevated tone was a part and parcel of the pageantry of establishing a rapport. I gathered Charley to me. Might I expect them after their supper, which I smelled on the fire?

They would be honored.

I set my cabin in order, heated and ate a can of chili con carne, made sure the beer was cold, and even picked a bouquet of autumn leaves and put them in a milk bottle on the table. The roll of paper cups laid in for just such an occasion had got squashed flat by a flying dictionary my first day out, but I made coasters from folded paper towels. It's amazing what trouble you will go to for a party. Then Charley barked them in and I was host in my own house. Six people can squeeze in behind my table, and they did. Two others beside me stood up, and the back door was wreathed with children's faces. They were very nice people but quite formal. I opened beer for the big ones and pop for the outsiders.

In due course these people told me quite a bit about themselves. They came over the border every year for the potato harvest. With everyone working, it made a nice little pool against the winter. Did they have any trouble with immigration people at the border? Well, no. The rules seemed to relax during the harvest season, and besides, the way was smoothed by a contractor to whom they paid a small percentage of their pay. But they didn't really pay him. He collected directly from the farmers. I've known quite a few migrant people over the years— Okies and Mexican wetbacks, and the Negroes who move into New Jersey and Long Island. And wherever I've seen them there has always been a contractor in the background to smooth the way for them for a consideration. Years ago the farmers tried to draw more labor than they needed so that they could lower wages. This seems to be no longer true, for government agencies channel only as many laborers as are needed, and some kind of minimum wage is maintained. In other cases the migrants have been driven to movement and seasonal work by poverty and terrible need.

Surely my guests for the evening were neither mistreated nor driven. This clan, having put their own small farm to bed for the winter in the Province of Quebec, came over the line to make a small nest egg. They even carried a little feeling of holiday with them almost like the hops- and strawberry-pickers from London and the Midland cities of England. These were a hardy and self-sufficient people, quite capable of taking care of themselves.

I opened more beer. After the night of desolate loneliness I felt very good to be surrounded by warm and friendly but cautious people. I tapped an artesian well of good feeling and made a small speech in my pidgin type of French. It began: "Messy dam. *Je vous porte un cher souvenir de la belle France—en particulier du Departement de Charente."*

They looked startled but interested. Then John the chieftain slowly translated my speech into high-school English and put it back into Canadian French. "Charente?" he asked. "Why Charente?" I leaned down and opened a compartment under my sink and lifted out a bottle of very old and reverend brandy brought along for weddings, frost bite, and heart attacks. John studied the label with the devout attention a good Christian might give to the holy sacrament. And his words were reverent: "Jesus Christ," he said. "I forgot. Charente—that's where Cognac is." Then he read the purported year of the bottle's nativity and softly repeated his first words.

He passed the bottle to the patriarch in his corner, and the old man smiled so sweetly that for the first time I could see he lacked front teeth. The brother-in-law growled in his throat like a happy tomcat and the pregnant ladies twittered like *alouettes* singing to the sun. I handed John a corkscrew while I laid out the crystal—three plastic coffee cups, a jelly glass, a shaving mug, and several wide-mouthed pill bottles. I emptied their capsules into a saucepan and rinsed out the odor of wheat germ with water from the tap. The cognac was very, very good, and from the first muttered *"Santé"* and the first clicking sip you could feel the Brotherhood of Man growing until it filled Rocinante full—and the sisterhood also.

They refused seconds and I insisted. And the division of thirds was put on the basis that there wasn't enough to save. And with the few divided drops of that third there came into Rocinante a triumphant human magic that can bless a house, or a truck for that matter—nine people gathered in complete silence and the nine making a whole as surely as my arms and legs are part of me, separate and inseparable. Rocinante took on a glow it never quite lost.

Such a fabric cannot be prolonged and should not be. The patriarch gave some kind of signal. My guests squirmed out of their squeezed-up seats behind the table and the adieux, as they should be, were short and formal. Then they went into the night, their way home lighted by the chieftain John carrying a tin kerosene lantern. They walked in silence among sleepy stumbling children and I never saw them again. But I like them.

I didn't make down my bed because I wanted to start very early. I curled up behind the table and slept a little while until in the dim false dawn Charley looked into my face and said "Ftt." While I heated my coffee, I made a little sign on card-board and stuck it in the neck of the empty brandy bottle, then passing the sleeping camp I stopped and stood the bottle where they would see it. The sign read: *"Enfant de France, Mort pour la Patrie."* And I drove as quietly as I could, for on this day I intended to drive a little west and then take the long road south down the long reach of Maine. There are times that one treasures for all one's life, and such times are burned clearly and sharply on the material of total recall. I felt very fortunate that morning.

On such a trip as mine, so much there is to see and to think about that event and thought set down as they occurred would roil and stir like a slow-cooking *minestrone.* There are map people whose joy is to lavish more attention on the sheets of colored paper than on the colored land rolling by. I have listened to accounts by such travelers in which every road number was re-membered, every mileage recalled, and every little countryside discovered. Another kind of traveler requires to know in terms of maps exactly where he is pin-pointed every moment, as though there were some kind of safety in black and red lines, in dotted indications and squirming blue of lakes and the shadings that indicate mountains. It is not so with me. I was born lost and take no pleasure in being found, nor much identification from shapes which symbolize continents and states. Besides, roads change, increase, are widened or abandoned so often in our country that one must buy road maps like daily newspapers. But since I know the passions of the mapifiers I can report that I moved north in Maine roughly or parallel to U.S. Highway 1 through Houlton, Mars Hill, Presque Isle, Caribou, Van Buren, turned westward, still on U.S. 1, past Madawaska, Upper Frenchville, and Fort Kent, then went due south on State High-way 11 past Eagle Lake, Winterville, Portage, Squa Pan, Masar-dis, Knowles Corner, Patten, Sherman, Grindstone, and so to Millinocket.

I can report this because I have a map before me, but what I remember has no reference to the numbers and colored lines and squiggles. I have thrown this routing in as a sop and shall not make a habit of it. What I remember are the long avenues in the frost, the farms and houses braced against the winter, the flat, laconic Maine speech in crossroads stores where I stopped to buy supplies. The many deer that crossed the road on nimbling hooves and leaped like bounding rubber away from the passing Rocinante. The roaring lumber trucks. And always I remember that this huge area had once been much more settled and was now abandoned to the creeping forest, the animals, the lumber camps and the cold. The big towns are getting bigger and the villages smaller. The hamlet store, whether grocery, general, hardware, clothing, cannot compete with the supermarket and the chain organization. Our treasured and nostalgic picture of the village general store, the cracker-barrel store where an informed yeomanry gather to express opinions and formulate the national character, is very rapidly disappearing. People who once held family fortresses against wind and weather, against scourges of frost and drought and insect enemies, now cluster against the busy breast of the big town.

The new American finds his challenge and his love in traffic-choked streets, skies nested in smog, choking with the acids of industry, the screech of rubber and houses leashed in against one another while the townlets wither a time and die. And this, as I found, is as true in Texas as in Maine. Clarendon yields to Amarillo just as surely as Stacyville, Maine, bleeds its substance into Millinocket, where the logs are ground up, the air smells of chemicals, the rivers are choked and poisoned, and the streets swarm with this happy, hurrying breed. This is not offered in criticism but only as observation. And I am sure that, as all pendulums reverse their swing, so eventually will the swollen cities rupture like dehiscent wombs and disperse their children back to the countryside. This prophecy is underwritten by the tendency of the rich to do this already. Where the rich lead, the poor will follow, or try to.

Some years ago at Abercrombie and Fitch I bought a cattle caller, an automobile horn manipulated by a lever with which nearly all cow emotions can be imitated, from the sweet lowing of a romantic heifer to the growling roar of a bull in the prime and lust of his bullhood. I had this contraption on Rocinante, and it was most effective. When its call goes out, every bovine within hearing distance raises its head from grazing and moves toward the sound.

In the silver chill of the Maine afternoon, as I bucketed and lumbered over the pitted surface of a wood road, I saw four lady mooses moving with stately heaviness across my bow. As I came near they broke into a heavy-cushioned trot. On an impulse I pressed down the lever of the cattle caller and a bellow came out like that of a Miura bull as he poises before firing himself at the butterfly sweep of his first veronica. The ladies, who were on the point of disappearing into the forest, heard the sound, stopped, turned, and then came for me with gathering speed and with what looked to me like romance in their eyes—but four romances, each weighing well over a thousand pounds! And much as I favor love in all its aspects, I trod my accelerator and got the hell out of there fast. And I remembered a story of the great Fred Allen. His character was a Maine man telling of a moose hunt. "I sat on a log and blew my moose call and waited. Then suddenly I felt something like a warm bath mat on my neck and head. Well sir, it was a moosess licking me and there was a light of passion in her eyes."

"Did you shoot her?" he was asked.

"No, sir. I went away from there fast, but I have often thought that somewhere in Maine there's a moose with a broken heart."

Maine is just as long coming down as it is going up, maybe longer. I could and should have gone to Baxter State Park, but I didn't. I had dawdled too long and it was getting cold and I had visions of Napoleon at Moscow and the Germans at Stalingrad. So I retreated smartly—Brownville Junction, Milo, Dover-Foxcroft, Guilford, Bingham, Skowhegan, Mexico, Rumford, where I joined a road I had already traveled through the White Mountains. Perhaps this was weak of me, but I wanted to get on with it. The rivers were full of logs, bank to bank for miles, waiting their turn at the abbatoir to give their woody hearts so that the bulwarks of our civilization such as *Time* magazine and the *Daily News* can survive, to defend us against ignorance. The mill towns, with all respect, are knots of worms. You come out of serene country and suddenly you are tossed and battered by a howling hurricane of traffic. For a time you fight your way blindly in the mad crush of hurtling metal and then suddenly it dies away and you are in serene and quiet countryside again. And there is no margin or overlap. It is a mystery but a happy one.

In the short time since I had passed, the foliage of the White Mountains had changed and tattered. The leaves were falling, rolling in dusky clouds, and the conifers on the slopes were crusted with snow. I drove long and furiously, to Charley's great disgust. Any number of times he said "Ftt" to me and I ignored him, and barreled on across the upraised thumb of New Hampshire. I wanted a bath and a new bed and a drink and a little human commerce, and I thought to find it on the Connecticut River. It is very strange that when you set a goal for yourself, it is hard not to hold toward it even if it is inconvenient and not even desirable. The way was longer than I had thought and I was very tired. My years spoke for my attention with aching shoulders but I was aimed at the Connecticut River and I ignored the weariness, and this was utter nonsense. It was nearly dark when I found the place I wanted, not far from Lancaster, New Hampshire. The river was wide and pleasant, bordered with trees and edged with a pleasant meadow. And near the bank there stood what I was lusting for—a row of neat little white houses on the green meadow by the river, and a small, compactly housed office and lunch room with a sign on the roadside that bore the welcome words "Open" and "Vacancy." I swung Rocinante off the road and opened the cab door to let Charley out.

The afternoon light made mirrors of the windows of the office and lunch room. My whole body ached from the road as I opened the door and went in. Not a soul was there. The register was on the desk, stools at the lunch counter, pies and cakes under plastic covers; the refrigerator hummed; a few dirty dishes soaked in soapy water in the stainless-steel sink, and a faucet dripped slowly into it.

I banged the little bell on the desk, then called out, "Anybody here?" No answer, nothing. I sat down on a stool to await the return of the management. The numbered keys to the little white houses hung on a board. The daylight slipped away and the place darkened. I went outside to collect Charley and to verify my impression that the sign said "Open" and "Vacancy." By now it was getting dark. I brought out a flashlight and looked through the office for a note saying "Back in ten minutes," but there was none. I felt strangely like a Peeping Tom; I didn't belong there. Then I went outside and moved Rocinante out of the driveway, fed Charley, made some coffee, and waited.

It would have been simple to take a key, leave a note on the desk saying that I had done so, and open one of the little houses. It wasn't right. I couldn't do it. On the highway a few cars went by and crossed the bridge over the river, but none turned in. The windows of the office and grill flashed under approaching headlights and then blacked out again. I had planned to eat a light supper and then to fall dog-weary into bed. I made my bed, found I wasn't hungry after all, and lay down. But sleep would not come to me. I listened for the return of the management. At last I lighted my gas mantle and tried to read, but with listening I could not follow the words. At last I dozed, awakened in the dark, looked out—nothing, nobody. My little sleep was troubled and uneasy.

At dawn I arose and created a long, slow, time-wasting breakfast. The sun came up, searching out the windows. I walked down to the river to keep Charley company, returned, even shaved and took a sponge bath in a bucket. The sun was well up by now. I went to the office and entered. The refrigerator hummed, the faucet dripped into the cold soapy water of the sink. A new-born, heavy-winged fat fly crawled fretfully over a plastic pie cover. At nine-thirty I drove away and no one had come, nothing had moved. The sign still read "Open" and "Vacancy." I drove across the iron bridge, rattling the steel-tread plates. The empty place disturbed me deeply, and, come to think of it, it still does.

On the long journey doubts were often my companions. I've always admired those reporters who can descend on an area, talk to key people, ask key questions, take samplings of opinions, and then set down an orderly report very like a road map. I envy this technique and at the same time do not trust it as a mirror of reality. I feel that there are too many realities. What I set down here is true until someone else passes that way and rearranges the world in his own style. In literary criticism the critic has no choice but to make over the victim of his attention into something the size and shape of himself.

And in this report I do not fool myself into thinking I am dealing with constants. A long time ago I was in the ancient city of Prague and at the same time Joseph Alsop, the justly famous critic of places and events, was there. He talked to informed people, officials, ambassadors; he read reports, even the fine print and figures, while I in my slipshod manner roved about with actors, gypsies, vagabonds. Joe and I flew home to America in the same plane, and on the way he told me about Prague, and his Prague had no relation to the city I had seen and heard. It just wasn't the same place, and yet each of us was honest, neither one a liar, both pretty good observers by any standard, and we brought home two cities, two truths. For this reason I cannot commend this account as an America that you will find. So much there is to see, but our morning eyes describe a different world than do our afternoon eyes, and surely our wearied evening eyes can report only a weary evening world.

Sunday morning, in a Vermont town, my last day in New England, I shaved, dressed in a suit, polished my shoes, whited my sepulcher, and looked for a church to attend. Several I eliminated for reasons I do not now remember, but on seeing a John Knox church I drove into a side street and parked Rocinante out of sight, gave Charley his instructions about watching the truck, and took my way with dignity to a church of blindingly white ship lap. I took my seat in the rear of the spotless, polished place of worship. The prayers were to the point, directing the attention of the Almighty to certain weaknesses and undivine tendencies I know to be mine and could only suppose were shared by others gathered there.

The service did my heart and I hope my soul some good. It had been long since I had heard such an approach. It is our practice now, at least in the large cities, to find from our psychiatric priesthood that our sins aren't really sins at all but accidents that are set in motion by forces beyond our control. There was no such nonsense in this church. The minister, a man of iron with tool-steel eyes and a delivery like a pneumatic drill, opened up with prayer and reassured us that we were a pretty sorry lot. And he was right. We didn't amount to much to start with, and due to our own tawdry efforts we had been slipping ever since. Then, having softened us up, he went into a glorious sermon, a fire-and-brimstone sermon. Having proved that we, or perhaps only I, were no damn good, he painted with cool certainty what was likely to happen to us if we didn't make some basic reorganizations for which he didn't hold out much hope. He spoke of hell as an expert, not the mush-mush hell of these soft days, but a well-stoked, white-hot hell served by technicians of the first order. This reverend brought it to a point where we could understand it, a good hard coal fire, plenty of draft, and a squad of open-hearth devils who put their hearts into their work, and their work was me. I began to feel good all over. For some years now God has been a pal to us, practicing togetherness, and that causes the same emptiness a father does playing softball with his son. But this Vermont God cared enough about me to go to a lot of trouble kicking the hell out of me. He put my sins in a new perspective. Whereas they had been small and mean and nasty and best forgotten, this minister gave them some size and bloom and dignity. I hadn't been thinking very well of myself for some years, but if my sins had this dimension there was some pride left. I wasn't a naughty child but a first rate sinner, and I was going to catch it.

I felt so revived in spirit that I put five dollars in the plate, and afterward, in front of the church, shook hands warmly with the minister and as many of the congregation as I could. It gave me a lovely sense of evil-doing that lasted clear through till Tuesday. I even considered beating Charley to give him some satisfaction too, because Charley is only a little less sinful than I am. All across the country I went to church on Sundays, a different denomination every week, but nowhere did I find the quality of that Vermont preacher. He forged a religion designed to last, not predigested obsolescence.

I crossed into New York State at Rouses Point and stayed as near to Lake Ontario as I could because it was my intention to look at Niagara Falls, which I had never seen, and then to slip into Canada, from Hamilton to Windsor, keeping Lake Erie on the south, and to emerge at Detroit—a kind of end run, a small triumph over geography. We know, of course, that each of our states is an individual and proud of it. Not content with their names, they take descriptive titles also—the Empire State, the Garden State, the Granite State—titles proudly borne and little given to understatement. But now for the first time I became aware that each state had also its individual prose style, made sharply evident in its highway signs. Crossing state lines one is aware of this change of language. The New England states use a terse form of instruction, a tight-lipped, laconic style sheet, wasting no words and few letters. New York State shouts at you the whole time. Do this. Do that. Squeeze left. Squeeze right. Every few feet an imperious command. In Ohio the signs are more benign. They offer friendly advice, and are more like suggestions. Some states use a turgid style which can get you lost with the greatest ease. There are states which tell you what you may expect to find in the way of road conditions ahead, while others let you find out for yourself. Nearly all have abandoned the adverb for the adjective. Drive Slow. Drive Safe.

I am an avid reader of all signs, and I find that in the historical markers the prose of statehood reaches its glorious best, and most lyric. I have further established, at least to my own satisfaction, that those states with the shortest histories and the least world-shaking events have the most historical markers. Some Western states even find glory in half-forgotten murders and bank robberies. The towns not to be left behind proudly announce their celebrated sons, so the traveler is informed by signs and banners—Birthplace of Elvis Presley, of Cole Porter, of Alan P. Huggins. This is no new thing, of course. I seem to remember that small cities in ancient Greece quarreled bitterly over which was the birthplace of Homer. Within my memory an outraged home-town citizenry wanted Red Lewis back for tarring and feathering after he wrote *Main Street*. And today Sauk Centre celebrates itself for having produced him. We, as a nation, are as hungry for history as was England when Geoffrey of Monmouth concocted his History of British Kings, many of whom he manufactured to meet a growing demand. And as in states and communities, so in individual Americans this hunger for decent association with the past. Genealogists are worked to death winnowing the debris of ancestry for grains of greatness. Not long ago it was proved that Dwight D. Eisenhower was descended from the royal line of Britain, a proof if one were needed that everyone is descended from everyone. The then little town where I was born, which within my grandfather's memory was a blacksmith shop in a swamp, recalls with yearly pageantry a glowing past of Spanish dons and rose-eating senoritas who have in public memory wiped out the small, desolate tribe of grub- and grasshopper-eating Indians who were our true first settlers.

I find this interesting, but it does make for suspicion of history as a record of reality. I thought of these things as I read the historical markers across the country, thought how the myth wipes out the fact. On a very low level the following is the process of a myth. Visiting in the town where I was born, I talked with a very old man who had known me as a child. He remembered vividly seeing me, a peaked, shivering child walking past his house one freezing morning, my inadequate overcoat fastened across my little chest with horse-blanket pins. This in its small way is the very stuff of myths—the poor and suffering child who rises to glory, on a limited scale of course. Even though I didn't remember the episode, I knew it could not be true. My mother was a passionate sewer-on of buttons. A button off was more than sloppiness; it was a sin. If I had pinned my coat, my mother would have whaled me. The story could not be true, but this old gentleman so loved it that I could never convince him of its falsity, so I didn't try. If my home town wants me in horse-blanket pins, nothing I can do is likely to change it, particularly the truth.

It rained in New York State, the Empire State, rained cold and pitiless, as the highway-sign writers would put it. Indeed the dismal downpour made my intended visit to Niagara Falls seem redundant. I was then hopelessly lost in the streets of a small but endless town in the neighborhood of Medina, I think. I pulled to the side of the street and got out my book of road maps. But to find where you are going, you must know where you are, and I didn't. The windows of the cab were tightly closed and opaque with streaming rain. My car radio played softly. Suddenly there was a knock on the window, the door was wrenched open, and a man slipped into the seat beside me. The man was quite red of face, quite whisky of breath. His trousers were held up by red braces over the long gray underwear that covered his chest.

"Turn that damn thing off," he said, and then turned off my radio himself. "My daughter saw you out the window," he continued. "Thought you was in trouble." He looked at my maps. "Throw those things away. Now, where is it you want to go?"

I don't know why it is a man can't answer such a question with the truth. The truth was that I had turned off the big highway 104 and into the smaller roads because the traffic was heavy and passing vehicles threw sheets of water on my windshield. I wanted to go to Niagara Falls. Why couldn't I have admitted it? I looked down at my map and said, "I'm trying to get to Erie, Pennsylvania."

"Good," he said. "Now, throw those maps away. Now you turn around, go two traffic lights, that'll bring you to Egg Street. Turn left there and about two hundred yards on Egg turn right at an angle. That's a twisty kind of street and you'll come to an overpass, but don't take it. You turn left there and it will curve around like this—see? Like this." His hand made a curving motion. "Now, when the curve straightens out you'll come to three branching roads. There's a big red house on the left-hand branch so you don't take that, you take the right-hand branch. Now, have you got that so far?"

"Sure," I said. "That's easy."

"Well repeat it back so I'll know you're going right."

I had stopped listening at the curving road. I said, "Maybe you better tell me again."

"I thought so. Turn around and go two traffic lights to Egg Street, turn left for two hundred yards and turn right at an angle on a twisty street till you come to an overpass but don't take it."

"That clears it up for me," I said quickly. "I sure do thank you for helping me out."

"Hell," he said, "I ain't even got you out of town yet."

Well, he got me out of town by a route which, if I could have remembered it, let alone followed it, would have made the path into the Labyrinth at Knossos seem like a throughway. When he was finally satisfied and thanked, he got out and slammed the door, but such is my social cowardice that I actually did turn around, knowing he would be watching out the window. I drove around two blocks and blundered my way back to 104, traffic or not.

Niagara Falls is very nice. It's like a large version of the old Bond sign on Times Square. I'm very glad I saw it, because from now on if I am asked whether I have seen Niagara Falls I can say yes, and be telling the truth for once.

When I told my adviser that I was going to Erie, Pennsylvania, I had no idea of going there, but as it turned out, I was. My intention was to creep across the neck of Ontario, bypassing not only Erie but Cleveland and Toledo.

I find out of long experience that I admire all nations and hate all governments, and nowhere is my natural anarchism more aroused than at national borders where patient and efficient public servants carry out their duties in matters of immigration and customs. I have never smuggled anything in my life. Why, then, do I feel an uneasy sense of guilt on approaching a customs barrier? I crossed a high toll bridge and negotiated a no man's land and came to the place where the Stars and Stripes stood shoulder to shoulder with the Union Jack. The Canadians were very kind. They asked where I was going and for how long, gave Rocinante a cursory inspection, and came at last to Charley.

"Do you have a certificate of rabies vaccination on the dog?"

"No, I haven't. You see he's an old dog. He was vaccinated long ago."

Another official came out. "We advise you not to cross the border with him, then."

"But I'm just crossing a small part of Canada and reentering the U.S."

"We understand," they said kindly. "You can take him into Canada but the U.S. won't let him back."

"But technically I am still in the U.S. and there's no complaint."

"There will be if he crosses the line and tries to get back."

"Well, where can I get him vaccinated?"

They didn't know. I would have to retrace my way at least

twenty miles, find a vet, have Charley vaccinated, and then return. I was crossing only to save a little time, and this would
wipe out the time saved and much more.

"Please understand, it is your own government, not ours. We
are simply advising you. It's the rule."

I guess this is why I hate governments, all governments. It is
always the rule, the fine print, carried out by fine-print men.
There's nothing to fight, no wall to hammer with frustrated fists.
I highly approve of vaccination, feel it should be compulsory;
rabies is a dreadful thing. And yet I found myself hating the rule
and all governments that made rules. It was not the shots but
the certificate that was important. And it is usually so with
governments—not a fact but a small slip of paper. These were
such nice men, friendly and helpful. It was a slow time at the
border. They gave me a cup of tea and Charley half a dozen
cookies. And they seemed genuinely sorry that I had to go to
Erie, Pennsylvania, for the lack of a paper. And so I turned about
and proceeded toward the Stars and Stripes and another government. Exiting I had not been required to stop, but now the barrier was down.

"Are you an American citizen?"

"Yes, sir, here's my passport."

"Do you have anything to declare?"

"I haven't been away."

"Have you a rabies vaccination certificate for your dog?"

"He hasn't been away either."

"But you are coming from Canada."

"I have not been in Canada."

I saw the steel come into eyes, the brows lower to a level of
suspicion. Far from saving time, it looked as though I might lose
much more than even Erie, Pennsylvania.

"Will you step into the office?"

This request had the effect on me a Gestapo knock on the
door might have. It raises panic, anger, and guilty feelings
whether or not I have done wrong. My voice took on the stri-
dent tone of virtuous outrage which automatically arouses
suspicion.

"Please step into the office."

"I tell you I have not been in Canada. If you were watching, you would have seen that I turned back."

"Step this way, please, sir."

Then into the telephone: "New York license so-and-so. Yes. Pick-up truck with camper top. Yes—a dog." And to me: "What kind of dog is it?"

"Poodle."

"Poodle—I said poodle. Light brown."

"Blue," I said.

"Light brown. Okay. Thanks."

I do hope I did not sense a certain sadness at my innocence.

"They say you didn't cross the line."

"That's what I told you."

"May I see your passport?"

"Why? I haven't left the country. I'm not about to leave the country." But I handed over my passport just the same. He leafed through it, pausing at the entry-and-exit stamps of other journeys. He inspected my photograph, opened the yellow smallpox vaccination certificate stapled to the back cover. At the bottom of the last page he saw pencilled in a faint set of letters and figures. "What is this?"

"I don't know. Let me see. Oh, that! Why, it's a telephone number."

"What's it doing in your passport?"

"I guess I didn't have a slip of paper. I don't even remember whose number it is."

By now he had me on the run and he knew it. "Don't you know it is against the law to deface a passport?"

"I'll erase it."

"You should not write anything in your passport. That's the regulation."

"I won't ever do it again. I promise." And I wanted to promise him I wouldn't lie or steal or associate with persons of loose morals, or covet my neighbor's wife, or anything. He closed my passport firmly and handed it back to me. I'm sure he felt better having found that telephone number. Suppose after all his trouble he hadn't found me guilty of anything, and on a slow day.

"Thank you, sir," I said. "May I proceed now?"

He waved his hand kindly. "Go ahead," he said.

And that's why I went toward Erie, Pennsylvania, and it was Charley's fault. I crossed the high iron bridge and stopped to pay toll. The man leaned out the window. "Go on," he said, "it's on the house."

"How do you mean?"

"I seen you go through the other way a little while ago. I seen the dog. I knew you'd be back."

"Why didn't you tell me?"

"Nobody believes it. Go ahead. You get a free ride one way."

He wasn't government, you see. But government can make you feel so small and mean that it takes some doing to build back a sense of self-importance. Charley and I stayed at the grandest auto court we could find that night, a place only the rich could afford, a pleasure dome of ivory and apes and peacocks and moreover with a restaurant, and room service. I ordered ice and soda and made a scotch and soda and then another. Then I had a waiter in and bespoke soup and a steak and a pound of raw hamburger for Charley, and I overtipped mercilessly. Before I went to sleep I went over all the things I wished I had said to that immigration man, and some of them were incredibly clever and cutting.

From the beginning of my journey, I had avoided the great high-speed slashes of concrete and tar called "thruways," or "super-highways." Various states have different names for them, but I had dawdled in New England, the winter grew apace, and I had visions of being snowbound in North Dakota. I sought out U.S. 90, a wide gash of a super-highway, multiple-lane carrier of the nation's goods. Rocinante bucketed along. The minimum speed on this road was greater than any I had previously driven. I drove into a wind quartering in from my starboard bow and felt the buffeting, sometimes staggering blows of the gale I helped to make. I could hear the sough of it on the square surfaces of my camper top. Instructions screamed at me from the road once: "Do not stop! No stopping. Maintain speed." Trucks as long as freighters went roaring by, delivering a wind like the blow of a fist. These great roads are wonderful for moving goods but not for inspection of a countryside. You are bound to the wheel and your eyes to the car ahead and to the rear-view mirror for the car behind and the side mirror for the car or truck about to pass, and at the same time you must read all the signs for fear you may miss some instructions or orders. No roadside stands selling squash juice, no antique stores, no farm products or factory outlets. When we get these thruways across the whole country, as we will and must, it will be possible to drive from New York to California without seeing a single thing.

At intervals there are places of rest and recreation, food, fuel and oil, postcards, steam-table food, picnic tables, garbage cans all fresh and newly painted, rest rooms and lavatories so spotless, so incensed with deodorants and with detergents that it takes a time to get your sense of smell back. For deodorants are not quite correctly named; they substitute one smell for another, and the substitute must be much stronger and more penetrating than the odor it conquers. I had neglected my own country too long. Civilization had made great strides in my absence. I remember when a coin in a slot would get you a stick of gum or a candy bar, but in these dining palaces were vending machines where various coins could deliver handkerchiefs, comb-and-nail-file sets, hair conditioners and cosmetics, first-aid kits, minor drugs such as aspirin, mild physics, pills to keep you awake. I found myself entranced with these gadgets. Suppose you want a soft drink; you pick your kind—Sungrape or Cooly Cola—press a button, insert the coin, and stand back. A paper cup drops into place, the drink pours out and stops a quarter of an inch from the brim—a cold, refreshing drink guaranteed synthetic. Coffee is even more interesting, for when the hot black fluid has ceased, a squirt of milk comes down and an envelope of sugar drops beside the cup. But of all, the hot-soup machine is the triumph. Choose among ten—pea, chicken noodle, beef and veg., insert the coin. A rumbling hum comes from the giant and a sign lights up that reads "Heating." After a minute a red light flashes on and off until you open a little door and remove the paper cup of boiling-hot soup.

It is life at a peak of some kind of civilization. The restaurant accommodations, great scallops of counters with simulated leather stools, are as spotless as and not unlike the lavatories. Everything that can be captured and held down is sealed in clear plastic. The food is oven-fresh, spotless and tasteless; untouched by human hands. I remembered with an ache certain dishes in France and Italy touched by innumerable human hands.

These centers for rest, food, and replenishment are kept beautiful with lawns and flowers. At the front, nearest the highway, are parking places for passenger automobiles together with regiments of gasoline pumps. At the rear the trucks draw up, and there they have their services—the huge overland caravans. Being technically a truck, Rocinante took her place in the rear, and I soon made acquaintance with the truckers. They are a breed set apart from the life around them, the long-distance truckers. In some town or city somewhere their wives and children live while the husbands traverse the nation carrying every kind of food and product and machine. They are clannish and they stick together, speaking a specialized language. And although I was a small craft among monsters of transportation they were kind to me and helpful.

I learned that in the truck parks there are showers and soap and towels—that I could park and sleep the night if I wished. The men had little commerce with local people, but being avid radio listeners they could report news and politics from all parts of the nation. The food and fuel centers on the parkways or thruways are leased by the various states, but on other highways private enterprise has truckers' stations that offer discounts on fuel, beds, baths, and places to sit and shoot the breeze. But being a specialized group, leading special lives, associating only with their own kind, they would have made it possible for me to cross the country without talking to a local town-bound man. For the truckers cruise over the surface of the nation without being a part of it. Of course in the towns where their families live they have whatever roots are possible—clubs, dances, love affairs, and murders.

I liked the truckers very much, as I always like specialists. By listening to them talk I accumulated a vocabulary of the road, of tires and springs, of overweight. The truckers over long distances have stations along their routes where they know the service men and the waitresses behind the counters, and where occasionally they meet their opposite numbers in other trucks. The great get-together symbol is the cup of coffee. I found I often stopped for coffee, not because I wanted it but for a rest and a change from the unrolling highway. It takes strength and control and attention to drive a truck long distances, no matter how much the effort is made easier by air brakes and power-assisted steering. It would be interesting to know and easy to establish with modern testing methods how much energy in foot pounds is expended in driving a truck for six hours. Once Ed Ricketts and I, collecting marine animals, turning over rocks in an area, tried to estimate how much weight we lifted in an average collecting day. The stones we turned over were not large —weighing from three to fifty pounds. We estimated that on a rich day, when we had little sense of energy expended, each of us had lifted four to ten tons of rock. Consider then the small, unnoticed turning of the steering wheel, perhaps the exertion of only one pound for each motion, the varying pressure of foot on accelerator, not more than half a pound perhaps but an enormous total over a period of six hours. Then there are the muscles of shoulders and neck, constantly if unconsciously flexed for emergency, the eyes darting from road to rear-view mirror, the thousand decisions so deep that the conscious mind is not aware of them. The output of energy, nervous and muscular, is enormous. Thus the coffee break is a rest in many senses.

Quite often I sat with these men and listened to their talk and now and then asked questions. I soon learned not to expect knowledge of the country they passed through. Except for the truck stops, they had no contact with it. It was driven home to me how like sailors they were. I remember when I first went to sea being astonished that the men who sailed over the world and touched the ports to the strange and exotic had little contact with that world. Some of the truckers on long hauls traveled in pairs and took their turns. The one off duty slept or read paperbacks. But on the roads their interests were engines, and weather, and maintaining the speed that makes a predictable schedule possible. Some of them were on regular runs back and forth while others moved over single operations. It is a whole pattern of life, little known to the settled people along the routes of the great trucks. I learned only enough about these men to be sure I would like to know much more.

If one has driven a car over many years, as I have, nearly all reactions have become automatic. One does not think about what to do. Nearly all the driving technique is deeply buried in a machine-like unconscious. This being so, a large area of the conscious mind is left free for thinking. And what do people think of when they drive? On short trips perhaps of arrival at a destination or memory of events at the place of departure. But there is left, particularly on very long trips, a large area for daydreaming or even, God help us, for thought. No one can know what another does in that area. I myself have planned houses I will never build, have made gardens I will never plant, have designed a method for pumping the soft silt and decayed shells from the bottom of my bay up to my point of land at Sag Harbor, of leeching out the salt, thus making a rich and productive soil. I don't know whether or not I will do this, but driving along I have planned it in detail even to the kind of pump, the leeching bins, the tests to determine disappearance of salinity. Driving, I have created turtle traps in my mind, have written long, detailed letters never to be put to paper, much less sent. When the radio was on, music has stimulated memory of times and places, complete with characters and stage sets, memories so exact that every word of dialogue is recreated. And I have projected future scenes, just as complete and convincing—scenes that will never take place. I've written short stories in my mind, chuckling at my own humor, saddened or stimulated by structure or content.

I can only suspect that the lonely man peoples his driving dreams with friends, that the loveless man surrounds himself with lovely loving women, and that children climb through the dreaming of the childless driver. And how about the areas of regrets? If only I had done so-and-so, or had not said such-and-such—my God, the damn thing might not have happened. Finding this potential in my own mind, I can suspect it in others, but I will never know, for no one ever tells. And this is why, on my journey which was designed for observation, I stayed as much as possible on secondary roads where there was much to see and hear and smell, and avoided the great wide traffic slashes which promote the self by fostering daydreams. I drove this wide, eventless way called U.S. 90 which bypassed Buffalo and Erie to Madison, Ohio, and then found the equally wide and fast U.S. 20 past Cleveland and Toledo, and so into Michigan.

On these roads out of the manufacturing centers there moved many mobile homes, pulled by specially designed trucks, and since these mobile homes comprise one of my generalities, I may as well get to them now. Early in my travels I had become aware of these new things under the sun, of their great numbers, and since they occur in increasing numbers all over the nation, observation of them and perhaps some speculation is in order. They are not trailers to be pulled by one's own car but shining cars long as pullmans. From the beginning of my travels I had noticed the sale lots where they were sold and traded, but then I began to be aware of the parks where they sit down in uneasy permanence. In Maine I took to stopping the night in these parks, talking to the managers and to the dwellers in this new kind of housing, for they gather in groups of like to like.

They are wonderfully built homes, aluminum skins, double-walled, with insulation, and often paneled with veneer of hardwood. Sometimes as much as forty feet long, they have two to five rooms, and are complete with air-conditioners, toilets, baths, and invariably television. The parks where they sit are sometimes landscaped and equipped with every facility. I talked with the park men, who were enthusiastic. A mobile home is drawn to the trailer park and installed on a ramp, a heavy rubber sewer pipe is bolted underneath, water and electric power connected, the television antenna raised, and the family is in residence. Several park managers agreed that last year one in four new housing units in the whole country was a mobile home. The park men charge a small ground rent plus fees for water and electricity. Telephones are connected in nearly all of them simply by plugging in a jack. Sometimes the park has a general store for supplies, but if not the supermarkets which dot the countryside are available. Parking difficulties in the towns have caused these markets to move to the open country where they are immune from town taxes. This is also true of the trailer parks. The fact that these homes can be moved does not mean that they do move. Sometimes their owners stay for years in one place, plant gardens, build little walls of cinder blocks, put out awnings and garden furniture. It is a whole way of life that was new to me. These homes are never cheap and often are quite expensive and lavish. I have seen some that cost $20,000 and contained all the thousand appliances we live by—dishwashers, automatic clothes washers and driers, refrigerators and deep freezes.

The owners were not only willing but glad and proud to show their homes to me. The rooms, while small, were well proportioned. Every conceivable unit was built in. Wide windows, some even called picture windows, destroyed any sense of being closed in; the bedrooms and beds were spacious and the storage space unbelievable. It seemed to me a revolution in living and on a rapid increase. Why did a family choose to live in such a home? Well, it was comfortable, compact, easy to keep clean, easy to heat.

In Maine: "I'm tired of living in a cold barn with the wind whistling through, tired of the torment of little taxes and payments for this and that. It's warm and cozy and in the summer the air-conditioner keeps us cool."

"What is the usual income bracket of the mobiles?"

"That is variable but a goodly number are in the ten-thousand- to twenty-thousand-dollar class."

"Has job uncertainty anything to do with the rapid increase of these units?"

"Well perhaps there may be some of that. Who knows what is in store tomorrow? Mechanics, plant engineers, architects, accountants, and even here and there a doctor or a dentist live in the mobile. If a plant or a factory closes down, you're not trapped with property you can't sell. Suppose the husband has a job and is buying a house and there's a layoff. The value goes out of his house. But if he has a mobile home he rents a trucking service and moves on and he hasn't lost anything. He may never have to do it, but the fact that he can is a comfort to him."

"How are they purchased?"

"On time, just like an automobile. It's like paying rent."

And then I discovered the greatest selling appeal of all—one that crawls through nearly all American life. Improvements are made on these mobile homes every year. If you are doing well you turn yours in on a new model just as you do with an automobile if you can possibly afford to. There's status to that. And the turn-in value is higher than that of automobiles because there's a ready market for used homes. And after a few years the once expensive home may have a poorer family. They are easy to maintain, need no paint since they are usually of aluminum, and are not tied to fluctuating land values.

"How about schools?"

The school buses pick the children up right at the park and bring them back. The family car takes the head of the house to work and the family to a drive-in movie at night. It's a healthy life out in the country air. The payments, even if high and festooned with interest, are no worse than renting an apartment and fighting the owner for heat. And where could you rent such a comfortable ground-floor apartment with a place for your car outside the door? Where else could the kids have a dog? Nearly every mobile home has a dog, as Charley discovered to his delight. Twice I was invited to dinner in a mobile home and several times watched a football game on television. A manager told me that one of the first considerations in his business was to find and buy a place where television reception is good. Since I did not require any facilities, sewer, water, or electricity, the price to me for stopping the night was one dollar.

The first impression forced on me was that permanence is neither achieved nor desired by mobile people. They do not buy for the generations, but only until a new model they can afford comes out. The mobile units are by no means limited to the park communities. Hundreds of them will be found sitting beside a farm house, and this was explained to me. There was a time when, on the occasion of a son's marriage and the addition of a wife and later of children to the farm, it was customary to add a wing or at least a lean-to on the home place. Now in many cases a mobile unit takes the place of additional building. A farmer from whom I bought eggs and home-smoked bacon told me of the advantages. Each family has a privacy it never had before. The old folks are not irritated by crying babies. The mother-in-law problem is abated because the new daughter has a privacy she never had and a place of her own in which to build the structure of a family. When they move away, and nearly all Americans move away, or want to, they do not leave unused and therefore useless rooms. Relations between the generations are greatly improved. The son is a guest when he visits the parents' house, and the parents are guests in the son's house.

Then there are the loners, and I have talked with them also. Driving along, you see high on a hill a single mobile home placed to command a great view. Others nestle under trees fringing a river or a lake. These loners have rented a tiny piece of land from the owner. They need only enough for the unit and the right of passage to get to it. Sometimes the loner digs a well and a cesspool, and plants a small garden, but others transport their water in fifty-gallon oil drums. Enormous ingenuity is apparent with some of the loners in placing the water supply higher than the unit and connecting it with plastic pipe so that a gravity flow is insured.

One of the dinners that I shared in a mobile home was cooked in an immaculate kitchen, walled in plastic tile, with stainless-steel sinks and ovens and stoves flush with the wall. The fuel is butane or some other bottled gas which can be picked up anywhere. We ate in a dining alcove paneled in mahogany veneer. I've never had a better or a more comfortable dinner. I had brought a bottle of whisky as my contribution, and afterward we sat in deep comfortable chairs cushioned in foam rubber. This family liked the way they lived and wouldn't think of going back to the old way. The husband worked as a garage mechanic about four miles away and made good pay. Two children walked to the highway every morning and were picked up by a yellow school bus.

Sipping a highball after dinner, hearing the rushing of water in the electric dishwasher in the kitchen, I brought up a question that had puzzled me. These were good, thoughtful, intelligent people. I said, "One of our most treasured feelings concerns roots, growing up rooted in some soil or some community." How did they feel about raising their children without roots? Was it good or bad? Would they miss it or not?

The father, a good-looking, fair-skinned man with dark eyes, answered me. "How many people today have what you are talking about? What roots are there in an apartment twelve floors up? What roots are in a housing development of hundreds and thousands of small dwellings almost exactly alike? My father came from Italy," he said. "He grew up in Tuscany in a house where his family had lived maybe a thousand years. That's roots for you, no running water, no toilet, and they cooked with charcoal or vine clippings. They had just two rooms, a kitchen and a bedroom where everybody slept, grandpa, father and all the kids, no place to read, no place to be alone, and never had had. Was that better? I bet if you gave my old man the choice he'd cut his roots and live like this." He waved his hands at the comfortable room. "Fact is, he cut his roots away and came to America. Then he lived in a tenement in New York—just one room, walk-up, cold water and no heat. That's where I was born and I lived in the streets as a kid until my old man got a job upstate in New York in the grape country. You see, he knew about vines, that's about all he knew. Now you take my wife. She's Irish descent. Her people had roots too."

"In a peat bog," the wife said. "And lived on potatoes." She gazed fondly through the door at her fine kitchen.

"Don't you miss some kind of permanence?"

"Who's got permanence? Factory closes down, you move on. Good times and things opening up, you move on where it's better. You got roots you sit and starve. You take the pioneers in the history books. They were movers. Take up land, sell it, move on. I read in a book how Lincoln's family came to Illinois on a raft. They had some barrels of whisky for a bank account. How many kids in America stay in the place where they were born, if they can get out?"

"You've thought about it a lot."

"Don't have to think about it. There it is. I've got a good trade. Long as there's automobiles I can get work, but suppose the place I work goes broke. I got to move where there's a job. I get to my job in three minutes. You want I should drive twenty miles because I got roots?"

Later they showed me magazines designed exclusively for mobile dwellers, stories and poems and hints for successful mobile living. How to stop a leak. How to choose a place for sun or coolness. And there were advertisements for gadgets, fascinating things, for cooking, cleaning, washing clothes, furniture and beds and cribs. Also there were full-page pictures of new models, each one grander and more shiny than the next.

"There's thousands of them," said the father, "and there's going to be millions."

"Joe's quite a dreamer," the wife said. "He's always figuring something out. Tell him your ideas, Joe."

"Maybe he wouldn't be interested."

"Sure I would."

"Well, it's not a dream like she said, it's for real, and I'm going to do it pretty soon now. Take a little capital, but it would pay off. I been looking around the used lots for the unit I want at the price I want to pay. Going to rip out the guts and set it up for a repair shop. I got enough tools nearly already, and I'll stock little things like windshield wipers and fan belts and cylinder rings and inner tubes, stuff like that. You take these courts are getting bigger and bigger. Some of the mobile people got two cars. I'll rent me a hundred feet of ground right near and I'll be in business. There's one thing you can say about cars, there's nearly always something wrong with them that's got to be fixed. And I'll have my house, this here one right beside my shop. That way I would have a bell and give twenty-four-hour service."

"Sounds like a good deal," I said. And it does.

"Best thing about it," Joe went on, "if business fell off, why, I'd just move on where it was good."

His wife said, "Joe's got it all worked out on paper where everything's going to go, every wrench and drill, even an electric welder. Joe's a wonderful welder."

I said, "I take back what I said, Joe. I guess you've got your roots in a grease pit."

"You could do worse. I even worked that out. And you know, when the kids grow up, we could even work our way south in the winter and north in the summer."

"Joe does good work," said his wife. "He's got his own steady customers where he works. Some men come fifty miles to get Joe to work on their cars because he does good work."

"I'm a real good mechanic," said Joe.

Driving the big highway near Toledo I had a conversation with Charley on the subject of roots. He listened but he didn't reply. In the pattern-thinking about roots I and most other people have left two things out of consideration. Could it be that Americans are a restless people, a mobile people, never satisfied with where they are as a matter of selection? The pioneers, the immigrants who peopled the continent, were the restless ones in Europe. The steady rooted ones stayed home and are still there. But every one of us, except the Negroes forced here as slaves, are descended from the restless ones, the wayward ones who were not content to stay at home. Wouldn't it be unusual if we had not inherited this tendency? And the fact is that we have. But that's the short view. What are roots and how long have we had them? If our species has existed for a couple of million years, what is its history? Our remote ancestors followed the game, moved with the food supply, and fled from evil weather, from ice and the changing seasons. Then after millennia beyond thinking they domesticated some animals so that they lived with their food supply. Then of necessity they followed the grass that fed their flocks in endless wanderings. Only when agriculture came into practice—and that's not very long ago in terms of the whole history—did a place achieve meaning and value and permanence. But land is a tangible, and tangibles have a way of getting into few hands. Thus it was that one man wanted ownership of land and at the same time wanted servitude because someone had to work it. Roots were in ownership of land, in tangible and immovable possessions. In this view we are a restless species with a very short history of roots, and those not widely distributed. Perhaps we have overrated roots as a psychic need. Maybe the greater the urge, the deeper and more ancient is the need, the will, the hunger to be somewhere else.

Charley had no answer to my premise. Also, he was a mess. I had promised myself to keep him combed and clipped and beautiful, and I hadn't done it. His fur was balled and dirty. Poodles do not shed any more than sheep do. At night, when I had planned this virtuous grooming, I was always too busy with something else. Also I discovered a dangerous allergy I didn't know he had. One night I had pulled up at a trucker's park where huge cattle trucks put up and cleaned their beds; around the park there was a mountain of manure and a fog of flies. Although Rocinante was screened the flies got in in their millions and hid in corners and would not be dislodged. For the first time I got out the bug bomb and sprayed heavily, and Charley broke into a sneezing attack so violent and prolonged that I had finally to carry him out in my arms. In the morning the cab was full of sleepy flies and I sprayed it and Charley had another attack. After that, whenever flying visitors invaded I had to close Charley out and air out the house or cab after the pests were dead. I never saw such a severe allergy.

Since I hadn't seen the Middle West for a long time many impressions crowded in on me as I drove through Ohio and Michigan and Illinois. The first was the enormous increase in population. Villages had become towns and towns had grown to cities. The roads squirmed with traffic; the cities were so dense with people that all attention had to be devoted to not hitting anyone or not being hit. The next impression was of an electric energy, a force, almost a fluid of energy so powerful as to be stunning in its impact. No matter what the direction, whether for good or for bad, the vitality was everywhere. I don't think for a second that the people I had seen and talked to in New England were either unfriendly or discourteous, but they spoke tersely and usually waited for the newcomer to open communication. Almost on crossing the Ohio line it seemed to me that people were more open and more outgoing. The waitress in a roadside stand said good morning before I had a chance to, discussed breakfast as though she liked the idea, spoke with enthusiasm about the weather, sometimes even offered some information about herself without my delving. Strangers talked freely to one another without caution. I had forgotten how rich and beautiful is the countryside—the deep topsoil, the wealth of great trees, the lake country of Michigan handsome as a well-made woman, and dressed and jeweled. It seemed to me that the earth was generous and outgoing here in the heartland, and perhaps the people took a cue from it.

One of my purposes was to listen, to hear speech, accent, speech rhythms, overtones and emphasis. For speech is so much more than words and sentences. I did listen everywhere. It seemed to me that regional speech is in the process of disappearing, not gone but going. Forty years of radio and twenty years of television must have this impact. Communications must destroy localness, by a slow, inevitable process. I can remember a time when I could almost pinpoint a man's place of origin by his speech. That is growing more difficult now and will in some foreseeable future become impossible. It is a rare house or building that is not rigged with spiky combers of the air. Radio and television speech becomes standardized, perhaps better English than we have ever used. Just as our bread, mixed and baked, packaged and sold without benefit of accident or human frailty, is uniformly good and uniformly tasteless, so will our speech become one speech.

I who love words and the endless possibility of words am saddened by this inevitability. For with local accent will disappear local tempo. The idioms, the figures of speech that make language rich and full of the poetry of place and time must go.

And in their place will be a national speech, wrapped and packaged, standard and tasteless. Localness is not gone but it is going. In the many years since I have listened to the land the change is very great. Traveling west along the northern routes I did not hear a truly local speech until I reached Montana. That is one of the reasons I fell in love again with Montana. The West Coast went back to packaged English. The Southwest kept a grasp but a slipping grasp on localness. Of course the Deep South holds on by main strength to its regional expressions, just as it holds and treasures some other anachronisms, but no region can hold out for long against the highway, the high-tension line, and the national television. What I am mourning is perhaps not worth saving, but I regret its loss nevertheless.

Even while I protest the assembly-line production of our food, our songs, our language, and eventually our souls, I know that it was a rare home that baked good bread in the old days. Mother's cooking was with rare exceptions poor, that good unpasteurized milk touched only by flies and bits of manure crawled with bacteria, the healthy old-time life was riddled with aches, sudden death from unknown causes, and that sweet local speech I mourn was the child of illiteracy and ignorance. It is the nature of a man as he grows older, a small bridge in time, to protest against change, particularly change for the better. But it is true that we have exchanged corpulence for starvation, and either one will kill us. The lines of change are down. We, or at least I, can have no conception of human life and human thought in a hundred years or fifty years. Perhaps my greatest wisdom is the knowledge that I do not know. The sad ones are those who waste their energy in trying to hold it back, for they can only feel bitterness in loss and no joy in gain.

As I passed through or near the great hives of production—Youngstown, Cleveland, Akron, Toledo, Pontiac, Flint, and later South Bend and Gary—my eyes and mind were battered by the fantastic hugeness and energy of production, a complication that resembles chaos and cannot be. So might one look down on an ant hill and see no method or direction or purpose in the darting hurrying inhabitants. What was so wonderful was that I could come again to a quiet country road, tree-bordered, with fenced

fields and cows, could pull up Rocinante beside a lake of clear,
clean water and see high overhead the arrows of southing ducks
and geese. There Charley could with his delicate exploring nose
read his own particular literature on bushes and tree trunks and
leave his message there, perhaps as important in endless time as
these pen scratches I put down on perishable paper. There in the
quiet, with the wind flicking tree branches and distorting the
water's mirror, I cooked improbable dinners in my disposable
aluminum pans, made coffee so rich and sturdy it would float a
nail, and, sitting on my own back doorsteps, could finally come
to think about what I had seen and try to arrange some pattern
of thought to accommodate the teeming crowds of my seeing
and hearing.

I'll tell you what it was like. Go to the Ufizzi in Florence, the
Louvre in Paris, and you are so crushed with the numbers, once
the might of greatness, that you go away distressed, with a feeling like constipation. And then when you are alone and remembering, the canvases sort themselves out; some are eliminated by
your taste or your limitations, but others stand up clear and
clean. Then you can go back to look at one thing untroubled by
the shouts of the multitude. After confusion I can go into the
Prado in Madrid and pass unseeing the thousand pictures shouting for my attention and I can visit a friend—a not large Greco,
San Pablo con un Libro. St. Paul has just closed the book. His
finger marks the last page read and on his face are the wonder
and will to understand after the book is closed. Maybe understanding is possible only after. Years ago when I used to work
in the woods it was said of lumber men that they did their logging in the whorehouse and their sex in the woods. So I have to
find my way through the exploding production lines of the Middle West while sitting alone beside a lake in northern Michigan.

As I sat secure in the silence, a jeep scuffed to a stop on the
road and good Charley left his work and roared. A young man
in boots, corduroys, and a red and black checked mackinaw
climbed out and strode near. He spoke in the harsh unfriendly
tone a man uses when he doesn't much like what he has to do.

"Don't you know this land is posted? This is private
property."

Normally his tone would have sparked a tinder in me. I would

have flared an ugliness of anger and he would then have been
able to evict me with pleasure and good conscience. We might
even have edged into a quarrel with passion and violence. That
would be only normal, except that the beauty and the quiet made
me slow to respond with resentment, and in my hesitation I lost
it. I said, "I knew it must be private. I was about to look for
someone to ask permission or maybe pay to rest here."

"The owner don't want campers. They leave papers around
and build fires."

"I don't blame him. I know the mess they make."

"See that sign on that tree? No trespassing, hunting, fishing,
camping."

"Well," I said, "that sounds as if it means business. If it's your
job to throw me off, you've got to throw me off. I'll go peace-
fully. But I've just made a pot of coffee. Do you think your boss
would mind if I finished it? Would he mind if I offered you a
cup? Then you could kick me off quicker."

The young man grinned. "What the hell," he said. "You don't
build no fires and you don't throw out no trash."

"I'm doing worse than that. I'm trying to bribe you with a
cup of coffee. It's worse than that, too. I'm suggesting a dollop
of Old Granddad in the coffee."

He laughed then. "What the hell!" he said. "Let me get my
jeep off the road."

Well, the whole pattern was broken. He squatted cross-legged
in the pine needles on the ground and sipped his coffee. Charley
sniffed close and let himself be touched, and that's a rare thing
for Charley. He does not permit strangers to touch him, just
happens to be somewhere else. But this young man's fingers
found the place behind the ears Charley delights to have rubbed,
and he sighed contentedly and sat down.

"What you doing—going hunting? I see your guns in the
truck."

"Just driving through. You know how you see a place and it's
just right, and you're just tired enough, I guess you can't help
stopping."

"Yeah," he said. "I know what you mean. You got a nice
outfit."

"I like it and Charley likes it."

"Charley? Never heard of a dog named Charley. Hello, Charley."

"I wouldn't want to get you in trouble with your boss. Think I ought to drag ass now?"

"What the hell?" he said. "He ain't here. I'm in charge. You ain't doing no harm."

"I'm trespassing."

"Know something? Fella camped here, kind of a nut. So I came to kick him off. He said something funny. He says, 'Trespassing ain't a crime and ain't a misdemeanor.' He says it's a tort. Now what the hell does that mean? He was a kind of a nut."

"Search me," I said, "I'm not a nut. Let me warm up your coffee." I warmed it two ways.

"You make swell coffee," said my host.

"Before it gets too dark I've got to find a place to park. Know any place up the road where they'll let me stay the night?"

"If you pull over that way behind those pine trees nobody could see you from the road."

"But I'd be committing a tort."

"Yeah. I wish to Christ I knew what that meant."

He drove ahead of me in the jeep and helped me find a level place in the pine grove. And after dark he came into Rocinante and admired her facilities and we drank some whisky together and had a nice visit and told each other a few lies. I showed him some fancy jigs and poppers I'd bought at Abercrombie and Fitch, and gave him one, and I gave him some paperback thrillers I'd finished with, all loaded with sex and sadism, and also a copy of *Field and Stream*. In return he invited me to stay as long as I wished and said that he'd come by tomorrow and we'd do a little fishing, and I accepted for one day at least. It's nice to have friends, and besides I wanted a little time to think about the things I'd seen, the huge factories and plants and the scurry and production.

The guardian of the lake was a lonely man, the more so because he had a wife. He showed me her picture in a plastic shield in his wallet, a prettyish blonde girl trying her best to live up to the pictures in the magazines, a girl of products, home permanents, shampoos, rinses, skin conditioners. She hated being out in what she called the Sticks, longed for the great and gracious life in Toledo or South Bend. Her only company was found in the shiny pages of *Charm* and *Glamour*. Eventually she would sulk her way to success. Her husband would get a job in some great clanging organism of progress, and they would live happily ever after. All this came through in small, oblique spurts in his conversation. She knew exactly what she wanted and he didn't, but his want would ache in him all his life. After he drove away in his jeep I lived his life for him and it put a mist of despair on me. He wanted his pretty little wife and he wanted something else and he couldn't have both.

Charley had a dream so violent that he awakened me. His legs jerked in the motions of running and he made little yipping cries. Perhaps he dreamed he chased some gigantic rabbit and couldn't quite catch it. Or maybe in his dream something chased him. On the second supposition I put out my hand and awakened him, but the dream must have been strong. He muttered to himself and complained and drank half a bowl of water before he went back to sleep.

The guardian came back soon after sun-up. He brought a rod and I got out my own and rigged a spinning reel, and had to find my glasses to tie on the bright painted popper. The monofilament line is transparent, said to be invisible to fish, and is completely invisible to me without my glasses.

I said, "You know, I don't have a fishing license."

"What the hell," he said, "we probably won't catch anything anyway."

And he was right, we didn't.

We walked and cast and walked and did everything we knew to interest bass or pike. My friend kept saying, "They're right down there if we can just get the message through." But we never did. If they were down there, they still are. A remarkable amount of my fishing is like that, but I like it just the same. My wants are simple. I have no desire to latch onto a monster symbol of fate and prove my manhood in titanic piscine war. But sometimes I do like a couple of cooperative fish of frying size. At noon I refused an invitation to come to dinner and meet the wife. I was growing increasingly anxious to meet my own wife, so I hurried on.

There was a time not too long ago when a man put out to sea and ceased to exist for two or three years or forever. And when the covered wagons set out to cross the continent, friends and relations remaining at home might never hear from the wanderers again. Life went on, problems were settled, decisions were taken. Even I can remember when a telegram meant just one thing—a death in the family. In one short lifetime the telephone has changed all that. If in this wandering narrative I seem to have cut the cords of family joys and sorrows, of Junior's current delinquency and junior Junior's new tooth, of business triumph and agony, it is not so. Three times a week from some bar, supermarket, or tire-and-tool-cluttered service station, I put calls through to New York and reestablished my identity in time and space. For three or four minutes I had a name, and the duties and joys and frustrations a man carries with him like a comet's tail. It was like dodging back and forth from one dimension to another, a silent explosion of breaking through a sound barrier, a curious experience, like a quick dip into a known but alien water.

It was established that my wife was to fly out to meet me in Chicago for a short break in my journey. In two hours, in theory at least, she would slice through a segment of the earth it had taken me weeks to clamber over. I became impatient, stuck to the huge toll road that strings the northern border of Indiana, bypassed Elkhart and South Bend and Gary. The nature of the road describes the nature of the travel. The straightness of the way, the swish of traffic, the unbroken speed are hypnotic, and while the miles peel off an imperceptible exhaustion sets in. Day and night are one. The setting sun is neither an invitation nor a command to stop, for the traffic rolls constantly.

Late in the night I pulled into a rest area, had a hamburger at the great lunch counter that never closes, and walked Charley on the close-clipped grass. I slept an hour but awakened long before daylight. I had brought city suits and shirts and shoes, but had forgotten to bring a suitcase to transport them from truck to hotel room. Indeed, I don't know where I could have stored a suitcase. In a garbage can under an arc light I found a clean corrugated paper carton and packed my city clothes. I wrapped my clean white shirts in road maps and tied the carton with fishing line.

Knowing my tendency to panic in the roar and crush of traffic, I started into Chicago long before daylight. I wanted to end up at the Ambassador East, where I had reservations, and, true to form, ended up lost. Finally, in a burst of invention, I hired an all-night taxi to lead me, and sure enough I had passed very near my hotel. If the doorman and bellhops found my means of traveling unusual, they gave no sign. I handed out my suits on hangers, my shoes in the game pocket of a hunting coat, and my shirts in their neat wrapping of New England road maps. Rocinante was whisked away to a garage for storage. Charley had to go to a kennel to be stored, bathed, and Hollanderized. Even at his age he is a vain dog and loves to be beautified, but when he found he was to be left and in Chicago, his ordinary aplomb broke down and he cried out in rage and despair. I closed my ears and went away quickly to my hotel.

I think I am well and favorably known at the Ambassador East, but this need not apply when I arrive in wrinkled hunting clothes, unshaven and lightly crusted with the dirt of travel and bleary-eyed from driving most of the night. Certainly I had a reservation, but my room might not be vacated until noon. The hotel's position was explained to me carefully. I understood it and forgave the management. My own position was that I would like a bath and a bed, but since that was impossible I would simply pile up in a chair in the lobby and go to sleep until my room was ready.

I saw in the desk man's eyes his sense of uneasiness. Even I knew I would be no ornament to this elegant and expensive pleasure dome. He signaled an assistant manager, perhaps by telepathy, and all together we worked out a solution. A gentleman had just checked out to catch an early airplane. His room was not cleaned and prepared, but I was welcome to use it until mine was ready. Thus the problem was solved by intelligence and patience, and each got what he wanted—I had my chance at a hot bath and a sleep, and the hotel was spared the mischance of having me in the lobby.

The room had not been touched since its former occupant had

left. I sank into a comfortable chair to pull off my boots and even got one of them off before I began to notice things and then more things and more. In a surprisingly short time I forgot the bath and the sleep and found myself deeply involved with Lonesome Harry.

An animal resting or passing by leaves crushed grass, footprints, and perhaps droppings, but a human occupying a room for one night prints his character, his biography, his recent history, and sometimes his future plans and hopes. I further believe that personality seeps into walls and is slowly released. This might well be an explanation of ghosts and such manifestations. Although my conclusions may be wrong, I seem to be sensitive to the spoor of the human. Also, I am not shy about admitting that I am an incorrigible Peeping Tom. I have never passed an unshaded window without looking in, have never closed my ears to a conversation that was none of my business. I can justify or even dignify this by protesting that in my trade I must know about people, but I suspect that I am simply curious.

As I sat in this unmade room, Lonesome Harry began to take shape and dimension. I could feel that recently departed guest in the bits and pieces of himself he had left behind. Of course Charley, even with his imperfect nose, would have known more. But Charley was in a kennel preparing to be clipped. Even so, Harry is as real to me as anyone I ever met, and more real than many. He is not unique, in fact is a member of a fairly large group. Therefore he becomes of interest in any investigation of America. Before I begin to patch him together, lest a number of men grow nervous, let me declare that his name is not Harry. He lives in Westport, Connecticut. This information comes from the laundry strips from several shirts. A man usually lives where he has his shirts laundered. I only suspect that he commutes to work in New York. His trip to Chicago was primarily a business trip with some traditional pleasures thrown in. I know his name because he signed it a number of times on hotel stationery, each signature with a slightly different slant. This seems to indicate that he is not entirely sure of himself in the business world, but there were other signs of that.

He had started a letter to his wife which also ended in the wastebasket. "Darling: Everything is going OK. Tried to call your aunt but no answer. I wish you were here with me. This is a lonesome town. You forgot to put in my cuff links. I bought a cheap pair at Marshall Field. I'm writing this while I wait for C.E. to call. Hope he brings the cont . . ."

It's just as well that Darling didn't drop in to make Chicago less lonesome for Harry. His guest was not C.E. with a contract. She was a brunette and wore very pale lipstick—cigarette butts in the ash tray and the edge of a highball glass. They drank Jack Daniel's, a whole bottle—the empty bottle, six soda bottles, and a tub that had held ice cubes. She used a heavy perfume and did not stay the night—the second pillow used but not slept on, also no lipstick on discarded tissues. I like to think her name was Lucille—I don't know why. Maybe because it was and is. She was a nervous friend—smoked Harry's recessed, filtered cigarettes but stubbed each one out only one-third smoked and lighted another, and she didn't put them out, she crushed them, frayed the ends. Lucille wore one of those little smidgins of hats held on by inturned combs. One of the combs broke loose. That and a bobby pin beside the bed told me Lucille is a brunette. I don't know whether or not Lucille is professional, but at least she is practiced. There is a fine businesslike quality about her. She didn't leave too many things around, as an amateur might. Also she didn't get drunk. Her glass was empty but the vase of red roses—courtesy of the management—smelled of Jack Daniel's, and it didn't do them any good.

I wonder what Harry and Lucille talked about. I wonder whether she made him less lonesome. Somehow I doubt it. I think both of them were doing what was expected of them. Harry shouldn't have slugged his drinks. His stomach isn't up to it—Tums wrappers in the wastebasket. I guess his business is a sensitive one and hard on the stomach. Lonesome Harry must have finished the bottle after Lucille left. He had a hangover—two foil tubes of Bromo Seltzer in the bathroom.

Three things haunted me about Lonesome Harry. First, I don't think he had any fun; second, I think he was really lonesome, maybe in a chronic state; and third, he didn't do a single thing that couldn't be predicted—didn't break a glass or a mirror, committed no outrages, left no physical evidence of joy. I had been hobbling around with one boot off finding out about Harry. I even looked under the bed and in the closet. He hadn't even forgotten a tie. I felt sad about Harry.

PART THREE

Chicago was a break in my journey, a resumption of my name, identity, and happy marital status. My wife flew in from the East for her brief visit. I was delighted at the change, back to my known and trusted life—but here I run into a literary difficulty.

Chicago broke my continuity. This is permissible in life but not in writing. So I leave Chicago out, because it is off the line, out of drawing. In my travels, it was pleasant and good; in writing, it would contribute only a disunity.

When that time was over and the good-bys said, I had to go through the same lost loneliness all over again, and it was no less painful than at first. There seemed to be no cure for loneliness save only being alone.

Charley was torn three ways—with anger at me for leaving him, with gladness at the sight of Rocinante, and with pure pride in his appearance. For when Charley is groomed and clipped and washed he is as pleased with himself as is a man with a good tailor or a woman newly patinaed by a beauty parlor, all of whom can believe they are like that clear through. Charley's combed columns of legs were noble things, his cap of silver blue fur was rakish, and he carried the pompon of his tail like the baton of a bandmaster. A wealth of combed and clipped mustache gave him the appearance and attitude of a French rake of the nineteenth century, and incidentally concealed his crooked front teeth. I happen to know what he looks like without the tailoring. One summer when his fur grew matted and mildewed I clipped him to the skin. Under those sturdy towers of legs are spindly shanks, thin and not too straight; with his chest ruff removed one can see the sagging stomach of the middle-aged. But if Charley was aware of his deep-down inadequacy, he gave no sign. If manners maketh man, then manner and grooming maketh poodle. He sat straight and nobly in the seat of Rocinante and he gave me to understand that while forgiveness was not impossible, I would have to work for it.

He is a fraud and I know it. Once when our boys were little and in summer camp we paid them the deadly parents' visit. When we were about to depart, a lady parent told us she had to leave quickly to keep her child from going into hysterics. And with brave but trembling lips she fled blindly, masking her feeling to save her child. The boy watched her go and then with infinite relief went back to his gang and his business, knowing that he too had played the game. And I know for a fact that five minutes after I had left Charley he had found new friends and had made his arrangements for his comfort. But one thing Charley did not fake. He was delighted to be traveling again, and for a few days he was an ornament to the trip.

Illinois did a fair autumn day for us, crisp and clean. We moved quickly northward, heading for Wisconsin through a noble land of good fields and magnificent trees, a gentleman's countryside, neat and white-fenced and I would guess subsidized by outside income. It did not seem to me to have the thrust of land that supports itself and its owner. Rather it was like a beautiful woman who requires the support and help of many faceless ones just to keep going. But this fact does not make her less lovely —if you can afford her.

It is possible, even probable, to be told a truth about a place, to accept it, to know it and at the same time not to know anything about it. I had never been to Wisconsin, but all my life I had heard about it, had eaten its cheeses, some of them as good as any in the world. And I must have seen pictures. Everyone must have. Why then was I unprepared for the beauty of this region, for its variety of field and hill, forest, lake? I think now I must have considered it one big level cow pasture because of the state's enormous yield of milk products. I never saw a country that changed so rapidly, and because I had not expected it everything I saw brought a delight. I don't know how it is in other seasons, the summers may reek and rock with heat, the winters may groan with dismal cold, but when I saw it for the first and only time in early October, the air was rich with butter-colored sunlight, not fuzzy but crisp and clear so that every frost-gay tree was set off, the rising hills were not compounded, but alone and separate. There was a penetration of the light into solid substance so that I seemed to see into things, deep in, and I've seen that kind of light elsewhere only in Greece. I remembered now that I had been told Wisconsin is a lovely state, but the telling had not prepared me. It was a magic day. The land dripped with richness, the fat cows and pigs gleaming against green, and, in the smaller holdings, corn standing in little tents as corn should, and pumpkins all about.

I don't know whether or not Wisconsin has a cheese-tasting festival, but I who am a lover of cheese believe it should. Cheese was everywhere, cheese centers, cheese cooperatives, cheese stores and stands, perhaps even cheese ice cream. I can believe anything, since I saw a score of signs advertising Swiss Cheese Candy. It is sad that I didn't stop to sample Swiss Cheese Candy. Now I can't persuade anyone that it exists, that I did not make it up.

Beside the road I saw a very large establishment, the greatest distributor of sea shells in the world—and this in Wisconsin, which hasn't known a sea since pre-Cambrian times. But Wisconsin is loaded with surprises. I had heard of the Wisconsin Dells but was not prepared for the weird country sculptured by the Ice Age, a strange, gleaming country of water and carved rock, black and green. To awaken here might make one believe it a dream of some other planet, for it has a non-earthly quality, or else the engraved record of a time when the world was much younger and much different. Clinging to the sides of the dream-like waterways was the litter of our times, the motels, the hot-dog stands, the merchants of the cheap and mediocre and tawdry so loved by summer tourists, but these incrustations were closed and boarded against the winter and, even open, I doubt that they could dispel the enchantment of the Wisconsin Dells.

I stopped that night on a hilltop that was a truckers' place but of a special kind. Here the gigantic cattle trucks rested and scraped out the residue left by their recent cargoes. There were mountains of manure and over them mushroom clouds of flies. Charley moved about smiling and sniffing ecstatically like an American woman in a French perfume shop. I can't bring myself to criticize his taste. Some people like one thing and some another. The odors were rich and earthy, but not disgusting.

As the evening deepened, I walked with Charley among his mountains of delight to the brow of the hill and looked down on the little valley below. It was a disturbing sight. I thought too much driving had distorted my vision or addled my judgment, for the dark earth below seemed to move and pulse and breathe. It was not water but it rippled like a black liquid. I walked quickly down the hill to iron out the distortion. The valley floor was carpeted with turkeys, it seemed like millions of them, so densely packed that they covered the earth. It was a great relief. Of course, this was a reservoir for Thanksgiving.

To mill so close together is in the nature of turkeys in the evening. I remembered how on the ranch in my youth the turkeys gathered and roosted in clots in the cypress trees, out of reach of wildcats and coyotes, the only indication I know of that turkeys have any intelligence at all. To know them is not to admire them, for they are vain and hysterical. They gather in vulnerable groups and then panic at rumors. They are subject to all the sicknesses of other fowl, together with some they have invented. Turkeys seem to be manic-depressive types, gobbling with blushing wattles, spread tails, and scraping wings in amorous bravado at one moment and huddled in craven cowardice the next. It is hard to see how they can be related to their wild, clever, suspicious cousins. But here in their thousands they carpeted the earth waiting to lie on their backs on the platters of America.

I know it is a shame that I had never seen the noble twin cities of St. Paul and Minneapolis, but how much greater a disgrace that I still haven't, although I went through them. As I approached, a great surf of traffic engulfed me, waves of station wagons, rip tides of roaring trucks. I wonder why it is that when I plan a route too carefully it goes to pieces, whereas if I blunder along in blissful ignorance aimed in a fancied direction I get through with no trouble. In the early morning I had studied maps, drawn a careful line along the way I wished to go. I still have that arrogant plan—into St. Paul on Highway 10, then gently across the Mississippi. The S-curve in the Mississippi here would give me three crossings of the river. After this pleasant jaunt I meant to go through Golden Valley, drawn by its name. That seems simple enough, and perhaps it can be done, but not by me.

First the traffic struck me like a tidal wave and carried me along, a bit of shiny flotsam bounded in front by a gasoline truck half a block long. Behind me was an enormous cement mixer on wheels, its big howitzer revolving as it proceeded. On my right was what I judged to be an atomic cannon. As usual I panicked and got lost. Like a weakening swimmer I edged to the right into a pleasant street only to be stopped by a policeman, who informed me that trucks and such vermin were not permitted there. He thrust me back into the ravening stream.

I drove for hours, never able to take my eyes from the surrounding mammoths. I must have crossed the river but I couldn't see it. I never did see it. I never saw St. Paul or Minneapolis. All I saw was a river of trucks; all I heard was a roar of motors. The air saturated with Diesel fumes burned in my lungs. Charley got a coughing fit and I couldn't take time to pat him on the back. At a red light I saw that I was on an Evacuation Route. It took some time for that to penetrate. My head was spinning. I had lost all sense of direction. But the signs—"Evacuation Route"—continued. Of course, it is the planned escape route from the bomb that hasn't been dropped. Here in the middle of the Middle West an escape route, a road designed by fear. In my mind I could see it because I have seen people running away—the roads clogged to a standstill and the stampede over the cliff of our own designing. And suddenly I thought of that valley of the turkeys and wondered how I could have the gall to think turkeys stupid. Indeed, they have an advantage over us. They're good to eat.

It took me nearly four hours to get through the Twin Cities. I've heard that some parts of them are beautiful. And I never found Golden Valley. Charley was no help. He wasn't involved with a race that could build a thing it had to escape from. He didn't want to go to the moon just to get the hell away from it all. Confronted with our stupidities, Charley accepts them for what they are—stupidities.

Sometime in these bedlam hours I must have crossed the river again because I had got back on U.S. 10 and was moving north on the east side of the Mississippi. The country opened out and I stopped at a roadside restaurant, exhausted. It was a German restaurant complete with sausages, sauerkraut, and beer steins hanging in rows over the bar, shining but unused. I was the only customer at that time of day. The waitress was no Brunhild but a lean, dark-faced little thing, either a young and troubled girl or a very spry old woman, I couldn't tell which. I ordered bratwurst and sauerkraut and distinctly saw the cook unwrap a sausage from a cellophane slip cover and drop it in boiling water. The beer came in a can. The bratwurst was terrible and the kraut an insulting watery mess.

"I wonder if you can help me?" I asked the young-ancient waitress.

"What's your trouble?"

"I guess I'm a little lost."

"How do you mean lost?" she said.

The cook leaned through his window and rested bare elbows on the serving counter.

"I want to go to Sauk Centre and I don't seem to be getting there."

"Where'd you come from?"

"Minneapolis."

"Then what you doing this side of the river?"

"Well, I seem to have got lost in Minneapolis, too."

She looked at the cook. "He got lost in Minneapolis," she said.

"Nobody can get lost in Minneapolis," the cook said. "I was born there and I know."

The waitress said, "I come from St. Cloud and I can't get lost in Minneapolis."

"I guess I brought some new talent to it. But I want to go to Sauk Centre."

The cook said, "If he can stay on a road he can't get lost. You're on Fifty-two. Cross over at St. Cloud and stay on Fifty-two."

"Is Sauk Centre on Fifty-two?"

"Ain't no place else. You must be a stranger around here, getting lost in Minneapolis. I couldn't get lost blindfolded."

I said a little snappishly, "Could you get lost in Albany or San Francisco?"

"I never been there but I bet I wouldn't get lost."

"I been to Duluth," the waitress said. "And Christmas I'm going to Sioux Falls. I got a aunt there."

"Ain't you got relatives in Sauk Centre?" the cook asked.

"Sure, but that's not so far away—like he says San Francisco.

My brother's in the Navy. He's in San Diego. You got relations in Sauk Centre?"

"No, I just want to see it. Sinclair Lewis came from there."

"Oh! Yeah. They got a sign up. I guess quite a few folks come to see it. It does the town some good."

"He's the first man who told me about this part of the country."

"Who is?"

"Sinclair Lewis."

"Oh! Yeah. You know him?"

"No, I just read him."

I'm sure she was going to say "Who?" but I stopped her. "You say I cross at St. Cloud and stay on Fifty-two?"

The cook said, "I don't think what's-his-name is there any more."

"I know. He's dead."

"You don't say."

There was a sign in Sauk Centre all right: "Birthplace of Sinclair Lewis."

For some reason I went through there fast and turned north on 71 to Wadena and it got dark and I pounded on to Detroit Lakes. There was a face before me, a lean and shriveled face like an apple too long in the barrel, a lonely face and sick with loneliness.

I didn't know him well, never knew him in the boisterous days when he was called Red. Toward the end of his life he called me several times in New York and we would have lunch at the Algonquin. I called him Mr. Lewis—still do in my mind. He didn't drink any more and took no pleasure in his food, but now and then his eyes would glitter with steel.

I had read *Main Street* when I was in high school, and I remember the violent hatred it aroused in the countryside of his nativity.

Did he go back?

Just went through now and again. The only good writer was a dead writer. Then he couldn't surprise anyone any more, couldn't hurt anyone any more. And the last time I saw him he seemed to have shriveled even more. He said, "I'm cold. I seem to be always cold. I'm going to Italy."

And he did, and he died there, and I don't know whether or not it's true but I've heard he died alone. And now he's good for the town. Brings in some tourists. He's a good writer now.

If there had been room in Rocinante I would have packed the W.P.A. Guides to the States, all forty-eight volumes of them. I have all of them, and some are very rare. If I remember correctly, North Dakota printed only eight hundred copies and South Dakota about five hundred. The complete set comprises the most comprehensive account of the United States ever got together, and nothing since has even approached it. It was compiled during the depression by the best writers in America, who were, if that is possible, more depressed than any other group while maintaining their inalienable instinct for eating. But these books were detested by Mr. Roosevelt's opposition. If W.P.A. workers leaned on their shovels, the writers leaned on their pens. The result was that in some states the plates were broken up after a few copies were printed, and that is a shame because they were reservoirs of organized, documented, and well-written information, geological, historical, and economic. If I had carried my guides along, for example, I would have looked up Detroit Lakes, Minnesota, where I stopped, and would have known why it is called Detroit Lakes, who named it, when, and why. I stopped near there late at night and so did Charley, and I don't know any more about it than he does.

The next day a long-cultivated ambition was to blossom and fruit.

Curious how a place unvisited can take such hold on the mind so that the very name sets up a ringing. To me such a place was Fargo, North Dakota. Perhaps its first impact is in the name Wells-Fargo, but my interest certainly goes beyond that. If you will take a map of the United States and fold it in the middle, eastern edge against western, and crease it sharply, right in the crease will be Fargo. On double-page maps sometimes Fargo gets lost in the binding. That may not be a very scientific method for finding the east-west middle of the country, but it will do. But beyond this, Fargo to me is brother to the fabulous places of the earth, kin to those magically remote spots mentioned by Herodotus and Marco Polo and Mandeville. From my earliest memory, if it was a cold day, Fargo was the coldest place on the continent. If heat was the subject, then at that time the papers listed Fargo as hotter than any place else, or wetter or drier, or deeper in snow. That's my impression, anyway. But I know that a dozen or half a hundred towns will rise up in injured wrath to denounce me with claims and figures for having much more dreadful weather than Fargo. I apologize to them in advance. As a sop to hurt feelings, I must admit that when I passed through Moorhead, Minnesota, and rattled across the Red River into Fargo on the other side, it was a golden autumn day, the town as traffic-troubled, as neon-plastered, as cluttered and milling with activity as any other up-and-coming town of forty-six thousand souls. The countryside was no different from Minnesota over the river. I drove through the town as usual, seeing little but the truck ahead of me and the Thunderbird in my rearview mirror. It's bad to have one's myth shaken up like that. Would Samarkand or Cathay or Cipango have suffered the same fate if visited? As soon as I had cleared the outskirts, the broken-metal-and-glass outer ring, and moved through Mapleton I found a pleasant place to stop on the Maple River not far from Alice—what a wonderful name for a town, Alice. It had 162 inhabitants in 1950 and 124 at the last census—and so much for the population explosion at Alice. Anyway, on the Maple River I drew into a little copse, of sycamores I think, that overhung the stream, and paused to lick my mythological wounds. And I found with joy that the fact of Fargo had in no way disturbed my mind's picture of it. I could still think of Fargo as I always had—blizzard-riven, heat-blasted, dust-raddled. I am happy to report that in the war between reality and romance, reality is not the stronger.

Although it was only mid-morning, I cooked a sumptuous dinner for myself, but I don't remember what it was. And Charley, who still had vestiges of his Chicago grooming, waded in the water and became his old dirty self again.

After the comfort and the company of Chicago I had had to learn to be alone again. It takes a little time. But there on the Maple River, not far from Alice, the gift of it was coming back. Charley had forgiven me in a nauseatingly superior way, but now he had settled down to business also. The pull-out place beside the water was pleasant. I brought out my garbage-can washing machine and rinsed clothes that had been jiggling in detergent for two days. And then, because a pleasant breeze was blowing, I spread my sheets to dry on some low bushes. I don't know what kind of bushes they were, but the leaves had a rich smell like sandalwood, and there's nothing I like better than scented sheets. And I made some notes on a sheet of yellow paper on the nature and quality of being alone. These notes would in the normal course of events have been lost as notes are always lost, but these particular notes turned up long afterward wrapped around a bottle of ketchup and secured with a rubber band. The first note says: "Relationship Time to Aloneness." And I remember about that. Having a companion fixes you in time and that the present, but when the quality of aloneness settles down, past, present, and future all flow together. A memory, a present event, and a forecast all equally present.

The second note lies obscurely under a streak of ketchup, or catsup, but the third is electric. It says: "Reversion to pleasure-pain basis," and this is from some observation of another time.

A number of years ago I had some experience with being alone. For two succeeding years I was alone each winter for eight months at a stretch in the Sierra Nevada mountains on Lake Tahoe. I was a caretaker on a summer estate during the winter months when it was snowed in. And I made some observations then. As the time went on I found that my reactions thickened. Ordinarily I am a whistler. I stopped whistling. I stopped conversing with my dogs, and I believe that subtleties of feeling began to disappear until finally I was on a pleasure-pain basis. Then it occurred to me that the delicate shades of feeling, of reaction, are the result of communication, and without such communication they tend to disappear. A man with nothing to say has no words. Can its reverse be true—a man who has no one to say anything to has no words as he has no need for words? Now and then there appear accounts of babies raised by animals—wolves and such. It is usually reported that the youngster crawls on all fours, makes those sounds learned from his foster parents, and perhaps even thinks like a wolf. Only through imitation do we develop toward originality. Take Charley, for example. He has always associated with the learned, the gentle, the literate, and the reasonable both in France and in America. And Charley is no more like a dog dog than he is like a cat. His perceptions are sharp and delicate and he is a mind-reader. I don't know that he can read the thoughts of other dogs, but he can read mine. Before a plan is half formed in my mind, Charley knows about it, and he also knows whether he is to be included in it. There's no question about this. I know too well his look of despair and disapproval when I have just thought that he must be left at home. And so much for the three notes below the red stain on the ketchup bottle.

Soon Charley moved downstream and found some discarded bags of garbage, which he went through with discrimination. He nosed over an empty bean can, sniffed in its opening, and rejected it. Then he took up the paper bag in his teeth and gently shook it so that more treasures rolled out, among them a balled-up piece of heavy white paper.

I opened it and smoothed the angry creases from its surface. It was a court order addressed to Jack So-and-so, informing him that if he didn't pay his back alimony he would be in contempt and punishable. The court sat in an eastern state, and this was North Dakota. Some poor guy on the lam. He shouldn't have left this spoor around, in case anyone was looking for him. I snapped my Zippo lighter and burned the evidence with full knowledge that I compounded the contempt. Good Lord, the trails we leave! Suppose someone, finding the ketchup bottle, tried to reconstruct me from my notes. I helped Charley sort over the garbage, but there was no other written material, only the containers of prepared foods. The man was no cook. He lived out of cans, but then perhaps his former wife did also.

It was only shortly after noon but I was so relaxed and comfortable that I hated to move. "Should we stay the night, Charley?" He inspected me and wagged his tail as a professor wags a pencil—once to the left, once to the right, and return to center. I sat on the bank, took off socks and boots, and dipped my feet in water so cold it burned until the freezing went deep and deadened feeling. My mother believed that cold water on the feet forced the blood to your head so that you thought better. "Time for examination, *mon vieux Chamal*," I said aloud, "which is another way of saying I feel comfortingly lazy. I came out on this trip to try to learn something of America. Am I learning anything? If I am, I don't know what it is. So far can I go back with a bag full of conclusions, a cluster of answers to riddles? I doubt it, but maybe. When I go to Europe, when I am asked what America is like, what will I say? I don't know. Well, using your olfactory method of investigation, what have you learned, my friend?"

Two complete wags. At least he didn't leave the question open.

"Does all America so far smell alike? Or are there sectional smells?" Charley began to turn around and around to the left, and then he reversed and turned eight times to the right before he finally settled and put his nose on his paws and his head within reach of my hand. He has a hard time getting down. When he was young a car hit him and broke his hip. He wore a cast for a long time. Now in his golden age his hip troubles him when he is tired. After too long a run he limps on his right hind leg. But because of his long turning before lying down, we sometimes call him a whirl poodle—much to our shame. If my mother's rule was right I was thinking pretty well. But she also said, "Cold feet—warm heart." And that's a different matter.

I had parked well away from the road and from any traffic for my time of rest and recount. I am serious about this. I did not put aside my sloth for the sake of a few amusing anecdotes. I came with the wish to learn what America is like. And I wasn't sure I was learning anything. I found I was talking aloud to Charley. He likes the idea but the practice makes him sleepy.

"Just for ducks, let's try a little of what my boys would call this generality jazz. Under heads and subheads. Let's take food as we have found it. It is more than possible that in the cities we have passed through, traffic-harried, there are good and distinguished restaurants with menus of delight. But in the eating places along the roads the food has been clean, tasteless, colorless, and of a complete sameness. It is almost as though the customers had no interest in what they ate as long as it had no character to embarrass them. This is true of all but the breakfasts, which are uniformly wonderful if you stick to bacon and eggs and pan-fried potatoes. At the roadsides I never had a really good dinner or a really bad breakfast. The bacon or sausage was good and packaged at the factory, the eggs fresh or kept fresh by refrigeration, and refrigeration was universal." I might even say roadside America is the paradise of breakfast except for one thing. Now and then I would see a sign that said "home-made sausage" or "home-smoked bacons and hams" or "new-laid eggs" and I would stop and lay in supplies. Then, cooking my own breakfast and making my own coffee, I found that the difference was instantly apparent. A freshly laid egg does not taste remotely like the pale, battery-produced refrigerated egg. The sausage would be sweet and sharp and pungent with spices, and my coffee a wine-dark happiness. Can I then say that the America I saw has put cleanliness first, at the expense of taste? And —since all our perceptive nerve trunks including that of taste are not only perfectible but also capable of trauma—that the sense of taste tends to disappear and that strong, pungent, or exotic flavors arouse suspicion and dislike and so are eliminated?

"Let's go a little farther into other fields, Charley. Let's take the books, magazines, and papers we have seen displayed where we have stopped. The dominant publication has been the comic book. There have been local papers and I've bought and read them. There have been racks of paperbacks with some great and good titles but overwhelmingly outnumbered by the volumes of sex, sadism, and homicide. The big-city papers cast their shadows over large areas around them, the *New York Times* as far as the Great Lakes, the *Chicago Tribune* all the way here to North Dakota. Here, Charley, I give you a warning, should you be drawn to generalities. If this people has so atrophied its taste buds as to find tasteless food not only acceptable but desirable, what of the emotional life of the nation? Do they find their emotional fare so bland that it must be spiced with sex and sadism through the medium of the paperback? And if this is so, why are there no condiments save ketchup and mustard to enhance their foods?

"We've listened to local radio all across the country. And apart from a few reportings of football games, the mental fare has been as generalized, as packaged, and as undistinguished as the food." I stirred Charley with my foot to keep him awake.

I had been keen to hear what people thought politically. Those whom I had met did not talk about the subject, didn't seem to want to talk about it. It seemed to me partly caution and partly a lack of interest, but strong opinions were just not stated. One storekeeper did admit to me that he had to do business with both sides and could not permit himself the luxury of an opinion. He was a graying man in a little gray store, a crossroads place where I stopped for a box of dog biscuits and a can of pipe tobacco. This man, this store might have been anywhere in the nation, but actually it was back in Minnesota. The man had

a kind of gray wistful twinkle in his eyes as though he remembered humor when it was not against the law, so that I dared go
out on a limb. I said, "It looks then as though the natural con-
tentiousness of people had died. But I don't believe that. It'll
just take another channel. Can you think, sir, of what that channel might be?"

"You mean where will they bust out?"

"Where do they bust out?"

I was not wrong, the twinkle was there, the precious, humor-
ous twinkle. "Well, sir," he said, "we've got a murder now and
then, or we can read about them. Then we've got the World
Series. You can raise a wind any time over the Pirates or the
Yankees, but I guess the best of all is we've got the Russians."

"Feelings pretty strong there?"

"Oh, sure! Hardly a day goes by somebody doesn't take a
belt at the Russians." For some reason he was getting a little
easier, even permitted himself a chuckle that could have turned
to throat-clearing if he saw a bad reaction from me.

I asked, "Anybody know any Russians around here?"

And now he went all out and laughed. "Course not. That's
why they're valuable. Nobody can find fault with you if you
take out after the Russians."

"Because we're not doing business with them?"

He picked up a cheese knife from the counter and carefully
ran his thumb along the edge and laid the knife down. "Maybe
that's it. By George, maybe that's it. We're not doing business."

"You think then we might be using the Russians as an outlet
for something else, for other things."

"I didn't think that at all, sir, but I bet I'm going to. Why, I
remember when people took everything out on Mr. Roosevelt.
Andy Larsen got red in the face about Roosevelt one time when
his hens got the croup. Yes, sir," he said with growing enthusiasm, "those Russians got quite a load to carry. Man has a fight
with his wife, he belts the Russians."

"Maybe everybody needs Russians. I'll bet even in Russia they
need Russians. Maybe they call it Americans."

He cut a sliver of cheese from a wheel and held it out to me
on the knife blade. "You've give me something to think about
in a sneaking kind of way."

"I thought you gave it to me."

"How?"

"About business and opinions."

"Well, maybe so. Know what I'm going to do? Next time Andy Larsen comes in red in the face, I'm going to see if the Russians are bothering his hens. It was a great loss to Andy when Mr. Roosevelt died."

Now I don't say that an awful lot of people have this man's sense of things. Maybe they don't, but maybe they do—also in their privacy or in non-business areas.

Charley raised his head and roared a warning without bothering to get to his feet. Then I heard a motor approaching, and trying to get up found my feet were long gone in sleep in the cold water. I couldn't feel them at all. While I rubbed and massaged them and they awakened to painful pins and needles, a vintage sedan pulling a short coupled trailer like a box turtle lumbered down from the road and took a position on the water about fifty yards away. I felt annoyance at this invasion of my privacy, but Charley was delighted. He moved on stiff legs with little delicate mincing steps to investigate the newcomer and in the manner of dogs and people did not look directly at the object of his interest. If I seem to be ridiculing Charley, look you at what I was doing in the next half hour and also what my neighbor was doing. Each of us went about our business, with slow deliberateness, each being very careful not to stare at the other and at the same time sneaking glances, appraising, evaluating. I saw a man, not young, not old, but with a jaunty springy step. He was dressed in olive-drab trousers and a leather jacket, and he wore a cowboy hat but with a flat crown and the brim curled and held to a peak by the chin strap. He had a classic profile, and even in the distance I could see that he wore a beard that tied into his sideburns and so found his hair. My own beard is restricted to my chin. The air had grown quickly chill. And I don't know whether my head was cold or that I didn't want to remain uncovered in the presence of a stranger. At any rate, I put on my old naval cap, made a pot of coffee, and sat on my back steps glancing with great interest at everything except my neighbor, who swept out his trailer and threw out a dishpan of soapy water while he pointedly unwatched me. Charley's interest was captured and held by various growlings and barkings that came from inside the trailer.

There must be in everyone a sense of proper and civil timing, for I had just resolved to speak to my neighbor, in fact had just stood up to move toward him, when he strolled toward me. He too had felt that the period of waiting was over. He moved with a strange gait reminiscent to me of something I couldn't place. There was a seedy grandeur about the man. In the time of chivalric myth this would be the beggar who turns out to be a king's son. As he came near I stood up from my iron back stoop to greet him.

He did not give me a sweeping bow, but I had the impression that he might have—either that or a full regimental salute.

"Good afternoon," he said. "I see you are of the profession."

I guess my mouth fell open. It's years since I have heard the term. "Well, no. No, I'm not."

Now it was his turn to look puzzled. "Not? But—my dear chap, if you're not, how do you know the expression?"

"I guess I've been on the fringes."

"Ah! Fringes. Of course. Backstage no doubt—direction, stage manager?"

"Flops," I said. "Would you like a cup of coffee?"

"Delighted." He never let down. That's one nice thing about those of the profession—they rarely do. He folded himself on the divan seat behind my table with a grace I never achieved in all my traveling. And I set out two plastic mugs and two glasses, poured coffee, and set a bottle of whisky within easy reach. It seemed to me a mist of tears came into his eyes, but it might be that they were in mine.

"Flops," he said. "Who hasn't known them hasn't played."

"Shall I pour for you?"

"Please do—no, no water." He cleared his palate with black coffee and then munched delicately on the whisky while his eye swept my abode. "Nice place you have here, very nice."

"Tell me, please, what made you think I was in the theater?"

He chuckled dryly. "Very simple, Watson. You know I've played that. Both parts. Well, first I saw your poodle, and then I observed your beard. Then on approaching I saw that you wore a naval cap with the British Royal Arms."

"Was that what broadened your *a*'s?"

"That might be, old chap. That certainly might be. I fall into such things, hardly knowing I'm doing it." Now, close up, I saw that he was not young. His movements were pure youth but there was that about his skin texture and the edges of his lips that was middle-aged or past it. And his eyes, large warm brown irises set on whites that were turning yellow, corroborated this.

"Your health," I said. We emptied our plastic glasses, chased with coffee, and I refilled.

"If it isn't too personal or too painful—what did you do in the theater?"

"I wrote a couple of plays."

"Produced?"

"Yes. They flopped."

"Would I know your name?"

"I doubt it. Nobody else did."

He sighed. "It's a hard business. But if you're hooked, you're hooked. I was hooked by my granddaddy and my daddy set the hook."

"Both actors?"

"And my mother and grandmother."

"Lord. That *is* show business. Are you"—I searched for the old word—"resting now?"

"Not at all. I'm playing."

"What, for God's sake, and where?"

"Wherever I can trap an audience. Schools, churches, service clubs. I bring culture, give readings. I guess you can hear my partner over there complaining. He's very good too. Part Airedale and part coyote. Steals the show when he feels like it."

I began to feel delighted with this man. "I didn't know such things went on."

"They don't, some of the time."

"Been at it long?"

"Three years less two months."

"All over the country?"

"Wherever two or three are gathered together. I hadn't worked for over a year—just tramped the agencies and casting calls and lived up my benefits. With me there's no question of doing something else. It's all I know—all I ever have known.

Once long ago there was a community of theater people on Nantucket island. My daddy bought a nice lot there and put up a frame house. Well, I sold that and bought my outfit there and I've been moving ever since, and I like it. I don't think I'll ever go back to the grind. Of course, if there should be a part—but hell, who'd remember me for a part—any part?"

"You're striking close to home there."

"Yes, it's a hard business."

"I hope you won't think I'm inquisitive even if I am. I'd like to know how you go about it. What happens? How do people treat you?"

"They treat me very well. And I don't know how I go about it. Sometimes I even have to rent a hall and advertise, sometimes I speak to the principal of the high school."

"But aren't people scared of gypsies, vagabonds, and actors?"

"I guess they are at first. At the beginning they take me for a kind of harmless freak. But I'm honest and I don't charge much, and after a little the material takes over and gets into them. You see, I respect the material. That makes the difference. I'm not a charlatan, I'm an actor—good or bad, an actor." His color had deepened with whisky and vehemence, and perhaps at being able to talk to someone with a little likeness of experience. I poured more into his glass this time and watched with pleasure his enjoyment of it. He drank and sighed. "Don't get something like this very often," he said. "I hope I haven't given you the impression that I'm rolling in receipts. Sometimes it's a little rough."

"Go on about it. Tell more."

"Where was I?"

"You were saying you respected your material and that you were an actor."

"Oh, yes. Well, there's one more thing. You know when show people come into what they call the sticks, they have a contempt for the yokels. It took me a little time, but when I learned that there aren't any yokels I began to get on fine. I learned respect for my audience. They feel that and they work with me, and not against me. Once you respect them, they can understand anything you can tell them."

"Tell about your material. What do you use?"

He looked down at his hands and I saw that they were well-kept and very white, as though he wore gloves most of the time. "I hope you won't think I'm stealing material," he said. "I admire the delivery of Sir John Gielgud. I heard him do his monologue of Shakespeare—*The Ages of Man.* And then I bought a record of it to study. What he can do with words, with tones, and inflections!"

"You use that?"

"Yes, but I don't steal it. I tell about hearing Sir John, and what it did to me, and then I say I'm going to try to give an impression of how he did it."

"Clever."

"Well, it does help, because it gives authority to the performance, and Shakespeare doesn't need billing, and that way I'm not stealing his material. It's like I'm celebrating him, which I do."

"How do they respond?"

"Well, I guess I'm pretty much at home with it now, because I can watch the words sink in, and they forget about me and their eyes kind of turn inward and I'm not a freak to them any more. Well—what do you think?"

"I think Gielgud would be pleased."

"Oh! I wrote to him and told him what I was doing and how I was doing it, a long letter." He brought a lumpy wallet from his hip pocket and extracted a carefully folded piece of aluminum foil, opened it, and with careful fingers unfolded a small sheet of notepaper with the name engraved at the top. The message was typed. It said, "Dear . . . : Thank you for your kind and interesting letter. I would not be an actor if I were not aware of the sincere flattery implied in your work. Good luck and God bless you. John Gielgud."

I sighed, and I watched his reverent fingers fold the note and close it in its armor of foil and put it away. "I never show that to anyone to get a show," he said. "I wouldn't think of doing that."

And I'm sure he wouldn't.

He whirled his plastic glass in his hand and regarded the rinse

of whisky left in it, a gesture often designed to draw emptiness
to the attention of a host. I uncorked the bottle.

"No," he said. "No more for me. I learned long ago that the
most important and valuable of acting techniques is the exit."

"But I'd like to ask more questions."

"All the more reason for the exit." He drained the last drop.
"Keep them asking," he said, "and exit clean and sharp. Thank
you and good afternoon."

I watched him swing lightly toward his trailer and I knew I
would be haunted by one question. I called out,—"Wait a
moment."

He paused and turned back to me.

"What does the dog do?"

"Oh, a couple of silly tricks," he said. "He keeps the performance simple. He picks it up when it goes stale." And he
continued on to his home.

So it went on—a profession older than writing and one that
will probably survive when the written word has disappeared.
And all the sterile wonders of movies and television and radio
will fail to wipe it out—a living man in communication with a
living audience. But how did he live? Who were his companions?
What was his hidden life? He was right. His exit whetted the
questions.

The night was loaded with omens. The grieving sky turned the little water to a dangerous metal and then the wind got up—not the gusty, rabbity wind of the seacoasts I know but a great bursting sweep of wind with nothing to inhibit it for a thousand miles in any direction. Because it was a wind strange to me, and therefore mysterious, it set up mysterious responses in me. In terms of reason, it was strange only because I found it so. But a goodly part of our experience which we find inexplicable must be like that. To my certain knowledge, many people conceal experiences for fear of ridicule. How many people have seen or heard or felt something which so outraged their sense of what should be that the whole thing was brushed quickly away like dirt under a rug?

For myself, I try to keep the line open even for things I can't understand or explain, but it is difficult in this frightened time. At this moment in North Dakota I had a reluctance to drive on that amounted to fear. At the same time, Charley wanted to go—in fact, made such a commotion about going that I tried to reason with him.

"Listen to me, dog. I have a strong impulse to stay amounting to celestial command. If I should overcome it and go and a great snow should close in on us, I would recognize it as a warning disregarded. If we stay and a big snow should come I would be certain I had a pipeline to prophecy."

Charley sneezed and paced restlessly. "All right, *mon cur,* let's take your side of it. You want to go on. Suppose we do, and in the night a tree should crash down right where we are presently standing. It would be you who have the attention of the gods. And there is always that chance. I could tell you many stories about faithful animals who saved their masters, but I think you are just bored and I'm not going to flatter you." Charley leveled at me his most cynical eye. I think he is neither a romantic nor a mystic. "I know what you mean. If we go, and no tree crashes down, or stay and no snow falls—what then? I'll tell you what then. We forget the whole episode and the field of prophecy is in no way injured. I vote to stay. You vote to go. But being nearer the pinnacle of creation than you, and also president, I cast the deciding vote."

We stayed and it didn't snow and no tree fell, so naturally we forgot the whole thing and are wide open for more mystic feelings when they come. And in the early morning swept clean of clouds and telescopically clear, we crunched around on the thick white ground cover of frost and got under way. The caravan of the arts was dark but the dog barked as we ground up to the highway.

Someone must have told me about the Missouri River at Bismarck, North Dakota, or I must have read about it. In either case, I hadn't paid attention. I came on it in amazement. Here is where the map should fold. Here is the boundary between east and west. On the Bismarck side it is eastern landscape, eastern grass, with the look and smell of eastern America. Across the Missouri on the Mandan side, it is pure west, with brown grass and water scorings and small outcrops. The two sides of the river might well be a thousand miles apart. As I was not prepared for the Missouri boundary, so I was not prepared for the Bad Lands. They deserve this name. They are like the work of an evil child. Such a place the Fallen Angels might have built as a spite to Heaven, dry and sharp, desolate and dangerous, and for me filled with foreboding. A sense comes from it that it does not like or welcome humans. But humans being what they are, and I being human, I turned off the highway on a shaley road and headed in among the buttes, but with a shyness as though I crashed a party. The road surface tore viciously at my tires and made Rocinante's overloaded springs cry with anguish. What a place for a colony of troglodytes, or better, of trolls. And here's an odd thing. Just as I felt unwanted in this land, so do I feel a reluctance in writing about it.

Presently I saw a man leaning on a two-strand barbed-wire fence, the wires fixed not to posts but to crooked tree limbs stuck in the ground. The man wore a dark hat, and jeans and long jacket washed palest blue with lighter places at knees and elbows. His pale eyes were frosted with sun glare and his lips scaly as snakeskin. A .22 rifle leaned against the fence beside him and on the ground lay a little heap of fur and feathers—rabbits and small birds. I pulled up to speak to him, saw his eyes wash over Rocinante, sweep up the details, and then retire into their sockets. And I found I had nothing to say to him. The "Looks like an early winter," or "Any good fishing hereabouts?" didn't seem to apply. And so we simply brooded at each other.

"Afternoon!"

"Yes, sir," he said.

"Any place nearby where I can buy some eggs?"

"Not real close by 'less you want to go as far as Galva or up to Beach."

"I was set for some scratch-hen eggs."

"Powdered," he said. "My Mrs. gets powdered."

"Lived here long?"

"Yep."

I waited for him to ask something or to say something so we could go on, but he didn't. And as the silence continued, it became more and more impossible to think of something to say. I made one more try. "Does it get very cold here winters?"

"Fairly."

"You talk too much."

He grinned. "That's what my Mrs. says."

"So long," I said, and put the car in gear and moved along. And in my rear-view mirror I couldn't see that he looked after me. He may not be a typical Badlander, but he's one of the few I caught.

A little farther along I stopped at a small house, a section of war-surplus barracks, it looked, but painted white with yellow trim, and with the dying vestiges of a garden, frosted-down geraniums and a few clusters of chrysanthemums, little button things yellow and red-brown. I walked up the path with the certainty that I was being regarded from behind the white window curtains. An old woman answered my knock and gave me the drink of water I asked for and nearly talked my arm off. She was hungry to talk, frantic to talk, about her relatives, her friends, and how she wasn't used to this. For she was not a native and she didn't rightly belong here. Her native clime was a land of milk and honey and had its share of apes and ivory and peacocks. Her voice rattled on as though she was terrified of the silence that would settle when I was gone. As she talked it came to me that she was afraid of this place and, further, that so was I. I felt I wouldn't like to have the night catch me here.

I went into a state of flight, running to get away from the unearthly landscape. And then the late afternoon changed everything. As the sun angled, the buttes and coulees, the cliffs and sculptured hills and ravines lost their burned and dreadful look and glowed with yellow and rich browns and a hundred variations of red and silver gray, all picked out by streaks of coal black. It was so beautiful that I stopped near a thicket of dwarfed and wind-warped cedars and junipers, and once stopped I was caught, trapped in color and dazzled by the clarity of the light. Against the descending sun the battlements were dark and clean-lined, while to the east, where the uninhibited light poured slant-wise, the strange landscape shouted with color. And the night, far from being frightful, was lovely beyond thought, for the stars were close, and although there was no moon the starlight made a silver glow in the sky. The air cut the nostrils with dry frost. And for pure pleasure I collected a pile of dry dead cedar branches and built a small fire just to smell the perfume of the burning wood and to hear the excited crackle of the branches. My fire made a dome of yellow light over me, and nearby I heard a screech owl hunting and a barking of coyotes, not howling but the short chuckling bark of the dark of the moon. This is one of the few places I have ever seen where the night was friendlier than the day. And I can easily see how people are driven back to the Bad Lands.

Before I slept I spread a map on my bed, a Charley-tromped map. Beach was not far away, and that would be the end of North Dakota. And coming up would be Montana, where I had never been. That night was so cold that I put on my insulated underwear for pajamas, and when Charley had done his duties and had his biscuits and consumed his usual gallon of water and finally curled up in his place under the bed, I dug out an extra blanket and covered him—all except the tip of his nose—and he sighed and wriggled and gave a great groan of pure ecstatic comfort. And I thought how every safe generality I gathered in my travels was canceled by another. In the night the Bad Lands had become Good Lands. I can't explain it. That's how it was.

The next passage in my journey is a love affair. I am in love with Montana. For other states I have admiration, respect, recognition, even some affection, but with Montana it is love, and it's difficult to analyze love when you're in it. Once, when I raptured in a violet glow given off by the Queen of the World, my father asked me why, and I thought he was crazy not to see. Of course I know now she was a mouse-haired, freckle-nosed, scabby-kneed little girl with a voice like a bat and the loving kindness of a gila monster, but then she lighted up the landscape and me. It seems to me that Montana is a great splash of grandeur. The scale is huge but not overpowering. The land is rich with grass and color, and the mountains are the kind I would create if mountains were ever put on my agenda. Montana seems to me to be what a small boy would think Texas is like from hearing Texans. Here for the first time I heard a definite regional accent unaffected by TV-ese, a slow-paced warm speech. It seemed to me that the frantic bustle of America was not in Montana. Its people did not seem afraid of shadows in a John Birch Society sense. The calm of the mountains and the rolling grasslands had got into the inhabitants. It was hunting season when I drove through the state. The men I talked to seemed to me not moved to a riot of seasonal slaughter but simply to be going out to kill edible meat. Again my attitude may be informed by love, but it seemed to me that the towns were places to live in rather than nervous hives. People had time to pause in their occupations to undertake the passing art of neighborliness.

I found I did not rush through the towns to get them over with. I even found things I had to buy to make myself linger. In Billings I bought a hat, in Livingston a jacket, in Butte a rifle I didn't particularly need, a Remington bolt-action .222, secondhand but in beautiful condition. Then I found a telescope sight I had to have, and waited while it was mounted on the rifle, and in the process got to know everyone in the shop and any customers who entered. With the gun in a vise and the bolt out, we zeroed the new sight on a chimney three blocks away, and later when I got to shooting the little gun I found no reason to change it. I spent a good part of a morning at this, mostly because I wanted to stay. But I see that, as usual, love is inarticulate. Montana has a spell on me. It is grandeur and warmth. If Montana had a seacoast, or if I could live away from the sea, I would instantly move there and petition for admission. Of all the states it is my favorite and my love.

At Custer we made a side trip south to pay our respects to General Custer and Sitting Bull on the battlefield of Little Big Horn. I don't suppose there is an American who doesn't carry Remington's painting of the last defense of the center column of the 7th Cavalry in his head. I removed my hat in memory of brave men, and Charley saluted in his own manner but I thought with great respect.

The whole of eastern Montana and the western Dakotas is memory-marked as Injun country, and the memories are not very old either. Some years ago my neighbor was Charles Erskine Scott Wood, who wrote *Heavenly Discourse*. He was a very old man when I knew him, but as a young lieutenant just out of military academy he had been assigned to General Miles and he served in the Chief Joseph campaign. His memory of it was very clear and very sad. He said it was one of the most gallant retreats in all history. Chief Joseph and the Nez Percés with squaws and children, dogs, and all their possessions, retreated under heavy fire for over a thousand miles, trying to escape to Canada. Wood said they fought every step of the way against odds until finally they were surrounded by the cavalry under General Miles and the large part of them wiped out. It was the saddest duty he had ever performed, Wood said, and he had never lost his respect for the fighting qualities of the Nez Percés. "If they hadn't had their families with them we could never have caught them," he said. "And if we had been evenly matched in men and weapons, we couldn't have beaten them. They were men," he said, "Real men."

I must confess to a laxness in the matter of National Parks. I haven't visited many of them. Perhaps this is because they enclose the unique, the spectacular, the astounding—the greatest waterfall, the deepest canyon, the highest cliff, the most stupendous works of man or nature. And I would rather see a good Brady photograph than Mount Rushmore. For it is my opinion that we enclose and celebrate the freaks of our nation and of our civilization. Yellowstone National Park is no more representative of America than is Disneyland.

This being my natural attitude, I don't know what made me turn sharply south and cross a state line to take a look at Yellowstone. Perhaps it was a fear of my neighbors. I could hear them say, "You mean you were that near to Yellowstone and didn't go? You must be crazy." Again it might have been the American tendency in travel. One goes, not so much to see but to tell afterward. Whatever my purpose in going to Yellowstone, I'm glad I went because I discovered something about Charley I might never have known.

A pleasant-looking National Park man checked me in and then he said, "How about that dog? They aren't permitted in except on leash."

"Why?" I asked.

"Because of the bears."

"Sir," I said, "this is an unique dog. He does not live by tooth or fang. He respects the right of cats to be cats although he doesn't admire them. He turns his steps rather than disturb an earnest caterpillar. His greatest fear is that someone will point out a rabbit and suggest that he chase it. This is a dog of peace and tranquility. I suggest that the greatest danger to your bears will be pique at being ignored by Charley."

The young man laughed. "I wasn't so much worried about the bears," he said. "But our bears have developed an intolerance for dogs. One of them might demonstrate his prejudice with a clip on the chin, and then—no dog."

"I'll lock him in the back, sir. I promise you Charley will cause no ripple in the bear world, and as an old bear-looker, neither will I."

"I just have to warn you," he said. "I have no doubt your dog has the best of intentions. On the other hand, our bears have the worst. Don't leave food about. Not only do they steal but they are critical of anyone who tries to reform them. In a word, don't believe their sweet faces or you might get clobbered. And don't let the dog wander. Bears don't argue."

We went on our way into the wonderland of nature gone nuts, and you will have to believe what happened. The only way I can prove it would be to get a bear.

Less than a mile from the entrance I saw a bear beside the road, and it ambled out as though to flag me down. Instantly a change came over Charley. He shrieked with rage. His lips flared, showing wicked teeth that have some trouble with a dog biscuit. He screeched insults at the bear, which hearing, the bear reared up and seemed to me to overtop Rocinante. Frantically I rolled the windows shut and, swinging quickly to the left, grazed the animal, then scuttled on while Charley raved and ranted beside me, describing in detail what he would do to that bear if he could get at him. I was never so astonished in my life. To the best of my knowledge Charley had never seen a bear, and in his whole history had showed great tolerance for every living thing. Besides all this, Charley is a coward, so deep-seated a coward that he has developed a technique for concealing it. And yet he showed every evidence of wanting to get out and murder a bear that outweighed him a thousand to one. I don't understand it.

A little farther along two bears showed up, and the effect was doubled. Charley became a maniac. He leaped all over me, he cursed and growled, snarled and screamed. I didn't know he had the ability to snarl. Where did he learn it? Bears were in good supply, and the road became a nightmare. For the first time in his life Charley resisted reason, even resisted a cuff on the ear. He became a primitive killer lusting for the blood of his enemy, and up to this moment he had had no enemies. In a bearless stretch, I opened the cab, took Charley by the collar, and locked him in the house. But that did no good. When we passed other bears he leaped on the table and scratched at the windows trying to get out at them. I could hear canned goods crashing as he struggled in his mania. Bears simply brought out the Hyde in my Jekyll-headed dog. What could have caused it? Was it a pre-breed memory of a time when the wolf was in him? I know him well. Once in a while he tries a bluff, but it is a palpable lie. I swear that this was no lie. I am certain that if he were released he would have charged every bear we passed and found victory or death.

It was too nerve-wracking, a shocking spectacle, like seeing an old, calm friend go insane. No amount of natural wonders, of rigid cliffs and belching waters, of smoking springs could even engage my attention while that pandemonium went on. After about the fifth encounter I gave up, turned Rocinante about, and retraced my way. If I had stopped the night and bears had gathered to my cooking, I dare not think what would have happened.

At the gate the park guard checked me out. "You didn't stay long. Where's the dog?"

"Locked up back there. And I owe you an apology. That dog has the heart and soul of a bear-killer and I didn't know it. Heretofore he has been a little tender-hearted toward an underdone steak."

"Yeah!" he said. "That happens sometimes. That's why I warned you. A bear dog would know his chances, but I've seen a Pomeranian go up like a puff of smoke. You know, a well-favored bear can bat a dog like a tennis ball."

I moved fast, back the way I had come, and I was reluctant to camp for fear there might be some unofficial non-government bears about. That night I spent in a pretty auto court near Livingston. I had my dinner in a restaurant, and when I had settled in with a drink and a comfortable chair and my bathed bare feet on a carpet with red roses, I inspected Charley. He was dazed. His eyes held a faraway look and he was totally exhausted, emotionally no doubt. Mostly he reminded me of a man coming out of a long, hard drunk—worn out, depleted, collapsed. He couldn't eat his dinner, he refused the evening walk, and once we were in he collapsed on the floor and went to sleep. In the night I heard him whining and yapping, and when I turned on the light his feet were making running gestures and his body jerked and his eyes were wide open, but it was only a night bear. I awakened him and gave him some water. This time he went to sleep and didn't stir all night. In the morning he was still tired. I wonder why we think the thoughts and emotions of animals are simple.

I remember as a child reading or hearing the words "The Great Divide" and being stunned by the glorious sound, a proper sound for the granite backbone of a continent. I saw in my mind escarpments rising into the clouds, a kind of natural Great Wall of China. The Rocky Mountains are too big, too long, too important to have to be imposing. In Montana to which I had returned, the rise is gradual, and were it not for a painted sign I never would have known when I crossed it. It wasn't very high as elevations go. I passed it as I saw the sign, but I stopped and backed up and got out and straddled it. As I stood over it facing south it had a strange impact on me that rain falling on my right foot must fall into the Pacific Ocean, while that on my left foot would eventually find its way after uncountable miles to the Atlantic. The place wasn't impressive enough to carry a stupendous fact like that.

It is impossible to be in this high spinal country without giving thought to the first men who crossed it, the French explorers, the Lewis and Clark men. We fly it in five hours, drive it in a week, dawdle it as I was doing in a month or six weeks. But Lewis and Clark and their party started in St. Louis in 1804 and returned in 1806. And if we get to thinking we are men, we might remember that in the two and a half years of pushing through wild and unknown country to the Pacific Ocean and then back, only one man died and only one deserted. And we get sick if the milk delivery is late and nearly die of heart failure if there is an elevator strike. What must these men have thought as a really new world unrolled—or was the progress so slow that the impact was lost? I can't believe they were unimpressed. Certainly their report to the government is an excited and an exciting document. They were not confused. They knew what they had found.

I drove across the upraised thumb of Idaho and through real mountains that climbed straight up, tufted with pines and deep-dusted with snow. My radio went dead and I thought it was broken, but it was only that the high ridges cut off the radio waves. The snow started to fall, but my luck held, for it was only a light gay snow. The air was softer than it had been on the other side of the Great Divide and I seemed to remember reading that the warm airs from over the Japanese current penetrate deep inland. The underbrush was thick and very green, and everywhere was a rush of waters. The roads were deserted except for an occasional hunting party in red hats and yellow jackets, and sometimes with a deer or an elk draped over the hood of the car. A few mountain cabins were incised into the steep slopes, but not many.

I was having to make many stops for Charley's sake. Charley was having increasing difficulty in evacuating his bladder, which is Nellie talk for the sad symptoms of not being able to pee. This sometimes caused him pain and always caused him embarrassment. Consider this dog of great *élan*, of impeccable manner, of *ton, enfin* of a certain majesty. Not only did he hurt, but his feelings were hurt. I would stop beside the road and let him wander, and turn my back on him in kindness. It took him a very long time. If it had happened to a human male I would have thought it was prostatitis. Charley is an elderly gentleman of the French persuasion. The only two ailments the French will admit to are that and a bad liver.

And so, while waiting for him and pretending to inspect plants and small water courses, I tried to reconstruct my trip as a single piece and not as a series of incidents. What was I doing wrong? Was it going as I wished? Before I left, I was briefed, instructed, directed, and brain-washed by many of my friends. One among them is a well-known and highly respected political reporter. He had been grass-rooting with the presidential candidates, and when I saw him he was not happy, because he loves his country, and he felt a sickness in it. I might say further that he is a completely honest man.

He said bitterly, "If anywhere in your travels you come on a man with guts, mark the place. I want to go to see him. I haven't seen anything but cowardice and expediency. This used to be a nation of giants. Where have they gone? You can't defend a nation with a board of directors. That takes men. Where are they?"

"Must be somewhere," I said.

"Well, you try to root a few out. We need them. I swear to God the only people in this country with any guts seem to be Negroes. Mind you," he said, "I don't want to keep Negroes out of the hero business, but I'm damned if I want them to corner the market. You dig me up ten white, able-bodied Americans who aren't afraid to have a conviction, an idea, or an opinion in an unpopular field, and I'll have the major part of a standing army."

His obvious worry in this matter impressed me, so I did listen and look along the way. And it is true I didn't hear many convictions. I saw only two real-man fights, with bare fists and enthusiastic inaccuracy, and both of those were over women.

Charley came back apologizing for needing more time. I wished I could help him but he wanted to be alone. And I remembered another thing my friend said.

"There used to be a thing or a commodity we put great store by. It was called the People. Find out where the People have gone. I don't mean the square-eyed toothpaste-and-hair-dye people or the new-car-or-bust people, or the success-and-coronary people. Maybe they never existed, but if there ever were the People, that's the commodity the Declaration was talking about, and Mr. Lincoln. Come to think of it, I've known a few, but not many. Wouldn't it be silly if the Constitution had been talking about a young man whose life centers around a whistle, a wink, and Wildroot?"

I remember retorting, "Maybe the People are always those who used to live the generation before last."

Charley was pretty stiff. I had to help him into the cab of Rocinante. And we proceeded up the mountain. A very light dry snow blew like white dust on the highway, and the evening was coming earlier now, I thought. Just under the ridge of a pass I stopped for gasoline in a little put-together, do-it-yourself group of cabins, square boxes, each with a stoop, a door, and one window, and no vestige of a garden or gravel paths. The small combined store, repair shop, and lunch room behind the gas pumps was as unprepossessing as any I have ever seen. The blue restaurant signs were old and autographed by the flies of many past summers. "Pies like mother would of made if mother could of cooked." "We don't look in your mouth. Don't look in our kitchen." "No checks cashed unless accompanied by fingerprints." The standard old ones. There would be no cellophane on the food here.

No one came to the gas pump, so I went into the lunch room. A sound of a quarrel came from the back room, which was probably the kitchen—a deep voice and a lighter male voice yammering back and forth. I called, "Anybody home?" and the voices stopped. Then a burly man came through the door, still scowling from the fracas.

"Want something?"

"Fill-up of gas. But if you have a cabin, I might stay the night."

"Take your pick. Ain't a soul here."

"Can I have a bath?"

"I'll bring you a bucket of hot water. Winter rate's two dollars."

"Good. Can I get something to eat?"

"Baked ham and beans, ice cream."

"Okay. I've got a dog."

"It's a free country. The cabins are all open. Take your pick. Sing out if you need something."

No effort had been spared to make the cabins uncomfortable and ugly. The bed was lumpy, the walls dirty yellow, the curtains like the underskirts of a slattern. And the close room had a mixed aroma of mice and moisture, mold and the smell of old, old dust, but the sheets were clean and a little airing got rid of the memories of old inhabitants. A naked globe hung from the ceiling and the room was heated by kerosene stove.

There was a knock on the door, and I admitted a young man of about twenty, dressed in gray flannel slacks, two-tone shoes, a polka-dotted ascot, and a blazer with the badge of a Spokane high school. His dark, shining hair was a masterpiece of overcombing, the top hair laid back and criss-crossed with long side strands that just cleared the ears. He was a shock to me after the ogre of the lunch counter.

"Here's your hot water," he said, and his was the voice of the other quarreler. The door was open, and I saw his eyes go over Rocinante and linger on the license plate.

"You really from New York?"

"Yep."

"I want to go there sometime."

"Everybody there wants to come out here."

"What for? There's nothing here. You can just rot here."

"If it's rotting you want, you can do it any place."

"I mean there's no chance for advancing yourself."

"What do you want to advance toward?"

"Well, you know, there's no theater and no music, no one to—talk to. Why it's even hard to get late magazines unless you subscribe."

"So you read *The New Yorker?*"

"How did you know? I subscribe."

"And *Time* magazine?"

"Of course."

"You don't have to go anywhere."

"Beg pardon?"

"You've got the world at your fingertips, the world of fashion, of art, and the world of thought right in your own back yard. Going would only confuse you further."

"One likes to see for one's self," he said. I swear he said it.

"That your father?"

"Yes, but I'm more like an orphan. All he likes is fishing and hunting and drinking."

"And what do you like?"

"I want to get ahead in the world. I'm twenty years old. I've got to think of my future. There he is yelling for me. He can't say anything without yelling. You going to eat with us?"

"Sure."

I bathed slowly in the crusted galvanized bucket. For a moment I thought of digging out New York clothes and putting on a puff for the boy, but I dropped that one and settled for clean chino slacks and a knitted shirt.

The burly proprietor's face was red as a ripe raspberry when I went into the lunch counter. He thrust his jaw at me. "As if I ain't carrying enough trouble, you got to be from New York."

"Is that bad?"

"For me it is. I just got that kid quieted down and you put burrs under his blanket."

"I didn't give New York a good name."

"No, but you come from there and now he's all riled up again. Oh, hell, what's the use? He's no damn good around here. Come on, you might as well eat with us out back."

Out back was kitchen, larder, pantry, dining room—and the cot covered with army blankets made it bedroom too. A great gothic wood stove clicked and purred. We were to eat at a square table covered with white, knife-scarred oilcloth. The keyed-up boy dished up bowls of bubbling navy beans and fat-back.

"I wonder if you could rig me a reading light?"

"Hell, I turn off the generator when we go to bed. I can give you a coal-oil lamp. Pull up. Got a canned baked ham in the oven."

The moody boy served the beans listlessly.

The red-faced man spoke up. "I thought he'd just finish high school and that would be the end of it, but not him, not Robbie. He took a night course—now get this—not in high school. He paid for it. Don't know where he got the money."

"Sounds pretty ambitious."

"Ambitious my big fat foot. You don't know what the course was—hairdressing. Not barbering—hairdressing—for women. Now maybe you see why I got worries."

Robbie turned from carving the ham. The slender knife was held rigidly in his right hand. He searched my face for the look of contempt he expected.

I strove to look stern, thoughtful, and noncommittal all at once. I pulled at my beard, which is said to indicate concentration. "Whatever I say, one or the other of you is going to sic the dog on me. You've got me in the middle."

Papa took a deep breath and let it out slowly. "By God, you're right," he said, and then he chuckled and the tension went out of the room.

Robbie brought the plates of ham to the table and he smiled at me, I think in gratitude.

"Now that we got our hackles down, what do you think of this hairdressing beautician stuff?" Papa said.

"You're not going to like what I think."

"How do I know if you don't say it?"

"Well, okay, but I'm going to eat fast in case I have to run for it."

I went through my beans and half my ham before I answered him.

"All right," I said. "You've hit on a subject I've given a lot of thought to. I know quite a few women and girls—all ages, all kinds, all shapes—no two alike except in one thing—the hairdresser. It is my considered opinion that the hairdresser is the most influential man in any community."

"You're making a joke."

"I am not. I've made a deep study of this. When women go to the hairdresser, and they all do if they can afford it, something happens to them. They feel safe, they relax. They don't have to keep up any kind of pretense. The hairdresser knows what their skin is like under the make-up, he knows their age, their face-liftings. This being so, women tell a hairdresser things they wouldn't dare confess to a priest, and they are open about matters they'd try to conceal from a doctor."

"You don't say."

"I do say. I tell you I'm a student of this. When women place their secret lives in the hairdresser's hands, he gains an authority few other men ever attain. I have heard hairdressers quoted with complete conviction in art, literature, politics, economics, child care, and morals."

"I think you're kidding but on the level."

"I'm not smiling when I say it. I tell you that a clever, thoughtful, ambitious hairdresser wields a power beyond the comprehension of most men."

"Jesus Christ! You hear that, Robbie? Did you know all that?"

"Some of it. Why, in the course I took there was a whole section on psychology."

"I never would of thought of it," Papa said. "Say, how about a little drink?"

"Thanks, not tonight. My dog's not well. I'm going to push on early and try to find a vet."

"Tell you what—Robbie will rig up a reading light for you. I'll leave the generator on. Will you want some breakfast?"

"I don't think so. I'm going to get an early start."

When I came to my cabin after trying to help Charley in his travail, Robbie was tying a trouble light to the iron frame of my sad bed.

He said quietly, "Mister, I don't know if you believe all that you said, but you sure gave me a hand up."

"You know, I think most of it might be true. If it is, that's a lot of responsibility, isn't it, Robbie?"

"It sure is," he said solemnly.

It was a restless night for me. I had rented a cabin not nearly as comfortable as the one I carried with me, and once installed I had interfered in a matter that was none of my business. And while it is true that people rarely take action on advice of others unless they were going to do it anyway, there was the small chance that in my enthusiasm for my hairdressing thesis I might have raised up a monster.

In the middle of the night Charley awakened me with a soft apologetic whining, and since he is not a whining dog I got up immediately. He was in trouble, his abdomen distended and his nose and ears hot. I took him out and stayed with him, but he could not relieve the pressure.

I wish I knew something of veterinary medicine. There's a feeling of helplessness with a sick animal. It can't explain how it feels, though on the other hand it can't lie, build up its symptoms, or indulge in the pleasures of hypochondria. I don't mean they are incapable of faking. Even Charley, who is as honest as they come, is prone to limp when his feelings are hurt. I wish someone would write a good, comprehensive book of home dog medicine. I would do it myself if I were qualified.

Charley was a really sick dog, and due to get sicker unless I could find some way to relieve the growing pressure. A catheter would do it, but who has one in the mountains in the middle of the night? I had a plastic tube for siphoning gasoline, but the diameter was too great. Then I remembered something about pressure causing muscular tension which increases the pressure, etc., so that the first step is to relax the muscles. My medicine chest was not designed for general practice, but I did have a bottle of sleeping pills—seconal, one and a half grains. But how about dosage? That is where the home medicine book would be helpful. I took a capsule apart and unloaded half of it and fitted it together again. I slipped the capsule back beyond the bow in Charley's tongue where he could not push it out, then held up his head and massaged it down his throat. Then I lifted him on the bed and covered him. At the end of an hour there was no change in him, so I opened a second capsule and gave him another half. I think that, for his weight, one and a half grains is a pretty heavy dose, but Charley must have a high tolerance. He resisted it for three quarters of an hour before his breathing slowed and he went to sleep. I must have dozed off too. The next thing I knew, he hit the floor. In his drugged condition his legs buckled under him. He got up, stumbled, and got up again. I opened the door and let him out. Well, the method worked all right, but I don't see how one medium-sized dog's body could have held that much fluid. Finally he staggered in and collapsed on a piece of carpet and was asleep immediately. He was so completely out that I worried over the dosage. But his temperature had dropped and his breathing was normal and his heart beat was strong and steady. My sleep was restless, and when dawn came I saw that Charley had not moved. I awakened him and he was quite agreeable when I got his attention. He smiled, yawned, and went back to sleep.

I lifted him into the cab and drove hell for leather for Spokane. I don't remember a thing about the country on the way. On the outskirts I looked up a veterinary in the phone book, asked directions, and rushed Charley into the examination room as an emergency. I shall not mention the doctor's name, but he is one more reason for a good home book on dog medicine. The doctor was, if not elderly, pushing his luck, but who am I to say he had a hangover? He raised Charley's lip with a shaking hand, then turned up an eyelid and let it fall back.

"What's the matter with him?" he asked, with no interest whatever.

"That's why I'm here—to find out."

"Kind of dopey. Old dog. Maybe he had a stroke."

"He had a distended bladder. If he's dopey, it's because I gave him one and a half grains of seconal."

"What for?"

"To relax him."

"Well, he's relaxed."

"Was the dosage too big?"

"I don't know."

"Well, how much would you give?"

"I wouldn't give it at all."

"Let's start fresh—what's wrong with him?"

"Probably a cold."

"Would that cause bladder symptoms?"

"If the cold was there—yes, sir."

"Well, look—I'm on the move. I'd like a little closer diagnosis."

He snorted. "Look here. He's an old dog. Old dogs get aches and pains. That's just the way it is."

I must have been snappish from the night. "So do old men," I said. "That doesn't keep them from doing something about it." And I think for the first time I got through to him.

"Give you something to flush out his kidneys," he said. "Just a cold."

I took the little pills and paid my bill and got out of there. It wasn't that this veterinary didn't like animals. I think he didn't like himself, and when that is so the subject usually must find an area for dislike outside himself. Else he would have to admit his self-contempt.

On the other hand, I yield to no one in my distaste for the self-styled dog-lover, the kind who heaps up his frustrations and makes a dog carry them around. Such a dog-lover talks baby talk to mature and thoughtful animals, and attributes his own sloppy characteristics to them until the dog becomes in his mind an alter ego. Such people, it seems to me, in what they imagine to be kindness, are capable of inflicting long and lasting tortures on an animal, denying it any of its natural desires and fulfillments until a dog of weak character breaks down and becomes the fat, asthmatic, befurred bundle of neuroses. When a stranger addresses Charley in baby talk, Charley avoids him. For Charley is not a human; he's a dog, and he likes it that way. He feels that he is a first-rate dog and has no wish to be a second-rate human. When the alcoholic vet touched him with his unsteady, inept hand, I saw the look of veiled contempt in Charley's eyes. He knew about the man, I thought, and perhaps the doctor knew he knew. And maybe that was the man's trouble. It would be very painful to know that your patients had no faith in you.

After Spokane, the danger of early snows had passed, for the air was changed and mulsed by the strong breath of the Pacific. The actual time on the way from Chicago was short, but the overwhelming size and variety of the land, the many incidents and people along the way, had stretched time out of all bearing. For it is not true that an uneventful time in the past is remembered as fast. On the contrary, it takes the time-stones of events to give a memory past dimension. Eventlessness collapses time.

The Pacific is my home ocean; I knew it first, grew up on its shore, collected marine animals along the coast. I know its moods, its color, its nature. It was very far inland that I caught the first smell of the Pacific. When one has been long at sea, the smell of land reaches far out to greet one. And the same is true when one has been long inland. I believe I smelled the sea rocks and the kelp and the excitement of churning sea water, the sharpness of iodine and the under odor of washed and ground calcareous shells. Such a far-off and remembered odor comes subtly so that one does not consciously smell it, but rather an electric excitement is released—a kind of boisterous joy. I found myself plunging over the roads of Washington, as dedicated to the sea as any migrating lemming.

I remembered lush and lovely eastern Washington very well and the noble Columbia River, which left its mark on Lewis and Clark. And, while there were dams and power lines I hadn't seen, it was not greatly changed from what I remembered. It was only as I approached Seattle that the unbelievable change became apparent.

Of course, I had been reading about the population explosion on the West Coast, but for West Coast most people substitute

California. People swarming in, cities doubling and trebling in numbers of inhabitants, while the fiscal guardians groan over the increasing weight of improvements and the need to care for a large new spate of indigents. It was here in Washington that I saw it first. I remembered Seattle as a town sitting on hills beside a matchless harborage—a little city of space and trees and gardens, its houses matched to such a background. It is no longer so. The tops of hills are shaved off to make level warrens for the rabbits of the present. The highways eight lanes wide cut like glaciers through the uneasy land. This Seattle had no relation to the one I remembered. The traffic rushed with murderous intensity. On the outskirts of this place I once knew well I could not find my way. Along what had been country lanes rich with berries, high wire fences and mile-long factories stretched, and the yellow smoke of progress hung over all, fighting the sea winds' efforts to drive them off.

This sounds as though I bemoan an older time, which is the preoccupation of the old, or cultivate an opposition to change, which is the currency of the rich and stupid. It is not so. This Seattle was not something changed that I once knew. It was a new thing. Set down there not knowing it was Seattle, I could not have told where I was. Everywhere frantic growth, a carcinomatous growth. Bulldozers rolled up the green forests and heaped the resulting trash for burning. The torn white lumber from concrete forms was piled beside gray walls. I wonder why progress looks so much like destruction.

Next day I walked in the old port of Seattle, where the fish and crabs and shrimps lay beautifully on white beds of shaved ice and where the washed and shining vegetables were arranged in pictures. I drank clam juice and ate the sharp crab cocktails at stands along the waterfront. It was not much changed—a little more run-down and dingy than it was twenty years ago. And here a generality concerning the growth of American cities, seemingly true of all of them I know. When a city begins to grow and spread outward, from the edges, the center which was once its glory is in a sense abandoned to time. Then the buildings grow dark and a kind of decay sets in; poorer people move in as the rents fall, and small fringe businesses take the place of once flowering establishments. The district is still too good to tear down and too outmoded to be desirable. Besides, all the energy has flowed out to the new developments, to the semi-rural supermarkets, the outdoor movies, new houses with wide lawns and stucco schools where children are confirmed in their illiteracy. The old port with narrow streets and cobbled surfaces, smoke-grimed, goes into a period of desolation inhabited at night by the vague ruins of men, the lotus eaters who struggle daily toward unconsciousness by way of raw alcohol. Nearly every city I know has such a dying mother of violence and despair where at night the brightness of the street lamps is sucked away and policemen walk in pairs. And then one day perhaps the city returns and rips out the sore and builds a monument to its past.

The rest during my stay in Seattle had improved Charley's condition. I wondered whether in his advancing age the constant vibration of the truck might not have been the cause of his trouble.

Quite naturally, as we moved down the beautiful coast my method of travel was changed. Each evening I found a pleasant auto court to rest in, beautiful new places that have sprung up in recent years. Now I began to experience a tendency in the West that perhaps I am too old to accept. It is the principle of do it yourself. At breakfast a toaster is on your table. You make your own toast. When I drew into one of these gems of comfort and convenience, registered, and was shown to my comfortable room after paying in advance, of course, that was the end of any contact with the management. There were no waiters, no bell boys. The chambermaids crept in and out invisibly. If I wanted ice, there was a machine near the office. I got my own ice, my own papers. Everything was convenient, centrally located, and lonesome. I lived in the utmost luxury. Other guests came and went silently. If one confronted them with "Good evening," they looked a little confused and then responded, "Good evening." It seemed to me that they looked at me for a place to insert a coin.

Somewhere in Oregon, on a rainy Sunday, the gallant Rocinante bespoke my attention. I have not spoken of my faithful vehicle except in formal terms of passing praise. Is it not always so? We value virtue but do not discuss it. The honest book-keeper, the faithful wife, the earnest scholar get little of our attention compared to the embezzler, the tramp, the cheat. If Rocinante has been neglected in this account, it is because she performed perfectly. Neglect did not extend to the mechanical, however. Meticulously I had changed the oil and attended to the greasing. I hate to see a motor neglected or mistreated or worked beyond its capacity.

Rocinante responded to my kindness as she must, with purring motor and perfect performance. In only one thing was I thoughtless, or perhaps overzealous. I carried too much of everything—too much food, too many books, tools enough to assemble a submarine. If I found sweet-tasting water I filled her tank, and thirty gallons of water weigh three hundred pounds. A spare container of butane gas for safety's sake weighs seventy-five pounds. Her springs were deeply depressed but seemingly safe, and on hard-pitching roads I slowed and eased her through, and because of her ready goodness I treated her like the honest bookkeeper, the faithful wife: I ignored her. And in Oregon on a rainy Sunday, moving through an endless muddy puddle, a right rear tire blew out with a damp explosion. I have known and owned mean, ugly-natured cars which would have done this thing out of pure evil and malice, but not Rocinante.

All in the day's work, I thought; that's the way the ball bounces. Well, this ball had bounced in eight inches of muddy water, and the spare tire, under the cab, had been let down into the mud. The changing tools had been put away under the floor under the table, so that my total load had to be unpacked. The new jack, never used and bright with factory paint, was stiff and unruly, and it was not designed for the overhang of Rocinante. I lay on my stomach and edged my way, swam my way under the truck, holding my nostrils clear of the surface of the water. The jack handle was slippery with greasy mud. Mud balls formed in my beard. I lay panting like a wounded duck, quietly cursing as I inched the jack forward under an axle that I had to find by feel, since it was under water. Then, with superhuman gruntings and bubblings, my eyes starting from their sockets, I levered the great weight. I could feel my muscles tearing apart and separating from their anchoring bones. In actual time, not over an hour elapsed before I had the spare tire on. I was unrecognizable under many layers of yellow mud. My hands were cut and bleeding. I rolled the bad tire to a high place and inspected it. The whole side wall had blown out. Then I looked at the left rear tire, and to my horror saw a great rubber bubble on its side and, farther along, another. It was obvious that the other tire might go at any moment, and it was Sunday and it was raining and it was Oregon. If the other tire blew, there we were, on a wet and lonesome road, having no recourse except to burst into tears and wait for death. And perhaps some kind birds might cover us with leaves. I peeled off mud and clothes together and changed to new finery, which got muddy in the process.

No car has ever had such obsequious treatment as did Rocinante as we moved slowly on. Every irregularity in the road hurt me clear through. We crawled along at not more than five miles an hour. And that ancient law went into effect which says that when you need towns they are very far apart. I needed more than a town. I needed two new heavy-duty rear tires. The men who had designed my truck had not anticipated the load I would carry.

After forty years in the painful wet desert with no cloud by day nor pillar of fire by night to guide us, we came to a damp little shut-up town whose name escapes me because I never learned it. Everything was closed—everything but one small service station. The owner was a giant with a scarred face and an evil white eye. If he were a horse I wouldn't buy him. He was a mostly silent man. "You got trouble," he said.

"You're telling me. Don't you sell tires?"

"Not your size. Have to send to Portland for those. Could phone tomorrow and get them maybe the next day."

"Isn't there any place in town that might have them?"

"There's two. Both closed. I don't think they got that size. You going to need bigger tires." He scratched his beard, peered long at the bubbles on the left rear, and poked them with a forefinger like a file. Finally he went into his little office, pushed a litter of brake linings and fan belts and catalogues aside, and from underneath dug out a telephone. And if ever my faith in the essential saintliness of humans becomes tattered, I shall think of that evil-looking man.

After three calls he found a dealer who had one of the kind and size required, but this man was tied up with a wedding and couldn't tear himself away. Three calls later, he turned up a rumor of another tire, but it was eight miles away. The rain continued to fall. The process was endless because between each call there was a line of cars waiting to be filled with gas and oil, and all this had to be done with a stately slowness.

A brother-in-law was finally aroused. He had a farm up the road a piece. He didn't want to get out in the rain, but my evil saint exerted some kind of pressure on him. That brother-in-law drove to the two places far apart where the tires might be, found them, and brought them to me. In a little less than four hours I was equipped, riding on big heavy-duty tires of a kind that should have been there in the first place. I could have knelt in the mud and kissed the man's hands, but I didn't. I tipped him rather royally and he said, "You didn't ought to do that. Jus' remember one thing," he said. "Them new tires is bigger. They're gonna change your speedometer reading. You'll be goin' faster'n the needle says and you get some itchy cop, why, he might pick you up."

I was so full of humble gratefulness, I could hardly speak. That happened on Sunday in Oregon in the rain, and I hope that evil-looking service-station man may live a thousand years and people the earth with his offspring.

Now, there is not any question that Charley was rapidly becoming a tree expert of enormous background. He could probably get a job as a consultant with the Davies people. But from the first I had withheld from him any information about the giant redwoods. It seemed to me that a Long Island poodle who had made his devoirs to *Sequoia sempervirens* or *Sequoia gigantea* might be set apart from other dogs—might even be like that Galahad who saw the Grail. The concept is staggering. After this experience he might be translated mystically to another plane of existence, to another dimension, just as the redwoods seem to be out of time and out of our ordinary thinking. The experience might even drive him mad. I had thought of that. On the other hand, it might make of him a consummate bore. A dog with an experience like that could become a pariah in the truest sense of the word.

The redwoods, once seen, leave a mark or create a vision that stays with you always. No one has ever successfully painted or photographed a redwood tree. The feeling they produce is not transferable. From them comes silence and awe. It's not only their unbelievable stature, nor the color which seems to shift and vary under your eyes, no, they are not like any trees we know, they are ambassadors from another time. They have the mystery of ferns that disappeared a million years ago into the coal of the carboniferous era. They carry their own light and shade. The vainest, most slap-happy and irreverent of men, in the presence of redwoods, goes under a spell of wonder and respect. Respect—that's the word. One feels the need to bow to un-questioned sovereigns. I have known these great ones since my earliest childhood, have lived among them, camped and slept against their warm monster bodies, and no amount of association has bred contempt in me. And the feeling is not limited to me.

A number of years ago, a newcomer, a stranger, moved to my country near Monterey. His senses must have been blunted and atrophied with money and the getting of it. He bought a grove of sempervirens in a deep valley near the coast, and then, as was his right by ownership, he cut them down and sold the lumber, and left on the ground the wreckage of his slaughter. Shock and numb outrage filled the town. This was not only murder but sacrilege. We looked on that man with loathing, and he was marked to the day of his death.

Of course, many of the ancient groves have been lumbered off, but many of the stately monuments remain and will remain, for a good and interesting reason. States and governments could not buy and protect these holy trees. This being so, clubs, organizations, even individuals, bought them and dedicated them to the future. I don't know any other similar case. Such is the impact of the sequoias on the human mind. But what would it be on Charley?

Approaching the redwood country, in southern Oregon, I kept him in the back of Rocinante, hooded as it were. I passed several groves and let them go as not quite adequate—and then on a level meadow by a stream we saw the grandfather, standing alone, three hundred feet high and with the girth of a small apartment house. The branches with their flat, bright green leaves did not start below a hundred and fifty feet up. Under that was the straight, slightly tapering column with its red to purple to blue. Its top was noble and lightning-riven by some ancient storm. I coasted off the road and pulled to within fifty feet of the godlike thing, so close that I had to throw back my head and raise my eyes to vertical to see its branches. This was the time I had waited for. I opened the back door and let Charley out and stood silently watching, for this could be dog's dream of heaven in the highest.

Charley sniffed and shook his collar. He sauntered to a weed, collaborated with a sapling, went to the stream and drank, then looked about for new things to do.

"Charley," I called. "Look!" I pointed at the grandfather. He wagged his tail and took another drink. I said, "Of course. He doesn't raise his head high enough to see the branches to prove it's a tree." I strolled to him and raised his muzzle straight up. "Look, Charley. It's the tree of all trees. It's the end of the Quest."

Charley got a sneezing fit, as all dogs do when the nose is elevated too high. I felt the rage and hatred one has toward non-appreciators, toward those who through ignorance destroy a treasured plan. I dragged him to the trunk and rubbed his nose against it. He looked coldly at me and forgave me and sauntered away to a hazlenut bush.

"If I thought he did it out of spite or to make a joke," I said to myself, "I'd kill him out of hand. I can't live without knowing." I opened my pocket knife and moved to the creekside, where I cut a branch from a small willow tree, a Y-branch well tufted with leaves. I trimmed the branch ends neatly and finally sharpened the butt end, then went to the serene grandfather of Titans and stuck the little willow in the earth so that its greenery rested against the shaggy redwood bark. Then I whistled to Charley and he responded amiably enough. I pointedly did not look at him. He cruised casually about until he saw the willow with a start of surprise. He sniffed its new-cut leaves delicately and then, after turning this way and that to get range and trajectory, he fired.

I stayed two days close to the bodies of the giants, and there were no trippers, no chattering troupes with cameras. There's a cathedral hush here. Perhaps the thick soft bark absorbs sound and creates a silence. The trees rise straight up to zenith; there is no horizon. The dawn comes early and remains dawn until the sun is high. Then the green fernlike foliage so far up strains the sunlight to a green gold and distributes it in shafts or rather in stripes of light and shade. After the sun passes zenith it is afternoon and quickly evening with a whispering dusk as long as was the morning.

Thus time and the ordinary divisions of the day are changed. To me dawn and dusk are quiet times, and here in the redwoods nearly the whole of daylight is a quiet time. Birds move in the dim light or flash like sparks through the stripes of sun, but they make little sound. Underfoot is a mattress of needles deposited for over two thousand years. No sound of footsteps can be heard on this thick blanket. To me there's a remote and cloistered feeling here. One holds back speech for fear of disturbing something—what? From my earliest childhood I've felt that something was going on in the groves, something of which I was not a part. And if I had forgotten the feeling, I soon got it back.

At night, the darkness is black—only straight up a patch of gray and an occasional star. And there's a breathing in the black, for these huge things that control the day and inhabit the night are living things and have presence, and perhaps feeling, and, somewhere in deep-down perception, perhaps communication. I have had lifelong association with these things. (Odd that the word "trees" does not apply.) I can accept them and their power and their age because I was early exposed to them. On the other hand, people lacking such experience begin to have a feeling of uneasiness here, of danger, of being shut in, enclosed and over-whelmed. It is not only the size of these redwoods but their strangeness that frightens them. And why not? For these are the last remaining members of a race that flourished over four continents as far back in geologic time as the upper Jurassic period. Fossils of these ancients have been found dating from the Cretaceous era while in the Eocene and Miocene they were spread over England and Europe and America. And then the glaciers moved down and wiped the Titans out beyond recovery. And only these few are left—a stunning memory of what the world was like once long ago. Can it be that we do not love to be reminded that we are very young and callow in a world that was old when we came into it? And could there be a strong resistance to the certainty that a living world will continue its stately way when we no longer inhabit it?

I find it difficult to write about my native place, northern California. It should be the easiest, because I knew that strip angled against the Pacific better than any place in the world. But I find it not one thing but many—one printed over another until the whole thing blurs. What it is is warped with memory of what it was and that with what happened there to me, the whole bundle wracked until objectiveness is nigh impossible. This four-lane concrete highway slashed with speeding cars I remember as a narrow, twisting mountain road where the wood teams moved, drawn by steady mules. They signaled their coming with the high, sweet jangle of hame bells. This was a little little town, a general store under a tree and a blacksmith shop and a bench in front on which to sit and listen to the clang of hammer on anvil. Now little houses, each one like the next, particularly since they try to be different, spread for a mile in all directions. That was a woody hill with live oaks dark green against the parched grass where the coyotes sang on moonlit nights. The top is shaved off and a television relay station lunges at the sky and feeds a nervous picture to thousands of tiny houses clustered like aphids beside the roads.

And isn't this the typical complaint? I have never resisted change, even when it has been called progress, and yet I felt resentment toward the strangers swamping what I thought of as my country with noise and clutter and the inevitable rings of junk. And of course these new people will resent the newer people. I remember how when I was a child we responded to the natural dislike of the stranger. We who were born here and our parents also felt a strange superiority over newcomers, barbarians, *forestieri*, and they, the foreigners, resented us and even made a rude poem about us:

> The miner came in forty-nine,
> The whores in fifty-one.

And when they got together,
They made a Native Son.

And we were an outrage to the Spanish-Mexicans and they in their turn on the Indians. Could that be why the sequoias make folks nervous? Those natives were grown trees when a political execution took place on Golgotha. They were well toward middle age when Caesar destroyed the Roman republic in the process of saving it. To the sequoias everyone is a stranger, a barbarian.

Sometimes the view of change is distorted by a change in oneself. The room which seemed so large is shrunk, the mountain has become a hill. But this is no illusion in this case. I remember Salinas, the town of my birth, when it proudly announced four thousand citizens. Now it is eighty thousand and leaping pell mell on in a mathematical progression—a hundred thousand in three years and perhaps two hundred thousand in ten, with no end in sight. Even those people who joy in numbers and are impressed with bigness are beginning to worry, gradually becoming aware that there must be a saturation point and the progress may be a progression toward strangulation. And no solution has been found. You can't forbid people to be born—at least not yet.

I spoke earlier of the emergence of the trailer home, the mobile unit, and of certain advantages to their owners. I had thought there were many of them in the East and the Middle West, but California spawns them like herrings. The trailer courts are everywhere, lapping up the sides of hills, spilling into river beds. And they bring with them a new problem. These people partake of all the local facilities, the hospitals, the schools, police protection, welfare programs, and so far they do not pay taxes. Local facilities are supported by real-estate taxes, from which the mobile home is immune. It is true that the state imposes a license fee, but that fee does not come to the counties or the towns except for road maintenance and extension. Thus the owners of immovable property find themselves supporting swarms of guests, and they are getting pretty angry about it. But our tax laws and the way we think about them were long developing.

The mind shies away from a head tax, a facility tax. The concept of real property is deeply implanted in us as the source and symbol of wealth. And now a vast number of people have found a way to bypass it. This might be applauded, since we generally admire those who can escape taxes, were it not that the burden of this freedom falls with increasing weight on others. It is obvious that within a very short time a whole new method of taxation will have to be devised, else the burden on real estate will be so great that no one will be able to afford it; far from being a source of profit, ownership will be a penalty, and this will be the apex of a pyramid of paradoxes. We have in the past been forced into reluctant change by weather, calamity, and plague. Now the pressure comes from our biologic success as a species. We have overcome all enemies but ourselves.

When I was a child growing up in Salinas we called San Francisco "the City." Of course it was the only city we knew, but I still think of it as the City, and so does everyone else who has ever associated with it. A strange and exclusive word is "city." Besides San Francisco, only small sections of London and Rome stay in the mind as the City. New Yorkers say they are going to town. Paris has no title but Paris. Mexico City is the Capital.

Once I knew the City very well, spent my attic days there, while others were being a lost generation in Paris. I fledged in San Francisco, climbed its hills, slept in its parks, worked on its docks, marched and shouted in its revolts. In a way I felt I owned the City as much as it owned me.

San Francisco put on a show for me. I saw her across the bay, from the great road that bypasses Sausalito and enters the Golden Gate Bridge. The afternoon sun painted her white and gold—rising on her hills like a noble city in a happy dream. A city on hills has it over flat-land places. New York makes its own hills with craning buildings, but this gold and white acropolis rising wave on wave against the blue of the Pacific sky was a stunning thing, a painted thing like a picture of a medieval Italian city which can never have existed. I stopped in a parking place to look at her and the necklace bridge over the entrance from the sea that led to her. Over the green higher hills to the south, the evening fog rolled like herds of sheep coming to cote in the golden city. I've never seen her more lovely. When I was a child and we were going to the City, I couldn't sleep for several nights before, out of bursting excitement. She leaves a mark.

Then I crossed the great arch hung from filaments and I was in the city I knew so well.

It remained the City I remembered, so confident of its greatness that it can afford to be kind. It had been kind to me in the days of my poverty and it did not resent my temporary solvency. I might have stayed indefinitely, but I had to go to Monterey to send off my absentee ballot.

In my young days in Monterey County, a hundred miles south of San Francisco, everyone was a Republican. My family was Republican. I might still be one if I had stayed there. President Harding stirred me toward the Democratic party and President Hoover cemented me there. If I indulge in personal political history, it is because I think my experience may not be unique.

I arrived in Monterey and the fight began. My sisters are still Republicans. Civil war is supposed to be the bitterest of wars, and surely family politics are the most vehement and venomous. I can discuss politics coldly and analytically with strangers. That was not possible with my sisters. We ended each session panting and spent with rage. On no point was there any compromise. No quarter was asked or given.

Each evening we promised, "Let's just be friendly and loving. No politics tonight." And ten minutes later we would be screaming at each other. "John Kennedy was a so-and-so—"

"Well, if that's your attitude, how can you reconcile Dick Nixon?"

"Now let's be calm. We're reasonable people. Let's explore this."

"I have explored it. How about the scotch whisky?"

"Oh, if you take that line, how about the grocery in Santa Ana? How about Checkers, my beauty?"

"Father would turn in his grave if he heard you."

"No, don't bring him in, because he would be a Democrat today."

"Listen to you. Bobby Kennedy is out buying sacks full of votes."

"You mean no Republican ever bought a vote? Don't make me laugh."

It was bitter and it was endless. We dug up obsolete convention weapons and insults to hurl back and forth.

"You talk like a Communist."

"Well, you sound suspiciously like Genghis Khan."

It was awful. A stranger hearing us would have called the police to prevent bloodshed. And I don't think we were the only ones. I believe this was going on all over the country in private. It must have been only publicly that the nation was tongue-tied.

The main purpose of this homecoming seemed to be fighting over politics, but in between I visited old places. There was a touching reunion in Johnny Garcia's bar in Monterey, with tears and embraces, speeches and endearments in the *poco* Spanish of my youth. There were Jolón Indians I remembered as shirttail *chamacos*. The years rolled away. We danced formally, hands locked behind us. And we sang the southern county anthem, "There wass a jung guy from Jolón—got seek from leeving ha-lone. He wan to Keeng Ceety to gat sometheeng pretty—*Puta chingada cabrón.*" I hadn't heard it in years. It was old home week. The years crawled back in their holes. It was the Monterey where they used to put a wild bull and a grizzly bear in the ring together, a place of sweet and sentimental violence, and a wise innocence as yet unknown and therefore undirtied by un-diapered minds.

We sat at the bar, and Johnny Garcia regarded us with his tear-blown Gallego eyes. His shirt was open and a gold medal on a chain hung at his throat. He leaned close over the bar and said to the nearest man, "Look at it! Juanito here gave it to me years ago, brought it from Mexico—la Morena, La Virgincita de Guadalupe, and look!" He turned the gold oval. "My name and his."

I said, "Scratched with a pin."

"I have never taken it off," said Johnny.

A big dark *paisano* I didn't know stood on the rail and leaned over the bar. "*Favor?*" he asked, and without looking Johnny extended the medal. The man kissed it, said *"Gracias,"* and went quickly out through the swinging doors.

Johnny's chest swelled with emotion and his eyes were wet. "Juanito," he said. "Come home! Come back to your friends. We love you. We need you. This is your seat, *compadre,* do not leave it vacant."

I must admit I felt the old surge of love and oratory and I haven't a drop of Galician blood. *"Cuñado mio,"* I said sadly, "I live in New York now."

"I don't like New York," Johnny said.

"You've never been there."

"I know. That's why I don't like it. You have to come back. You belong here."

I drank deeply, and darned if I didn't find myself making a speech. The old words unused for so long came rattling back to me. "Let your heart have ears, my uncle, my friend. We are not baby skunks, you and I. Time has settled some of our problems."

"Silence," he said. "I will not hear it. It is not true. You still love wine, you still love girls. What has changed? I know you. *No me cagas, niño.*"

"Te cago nunca. There was a great man named Thomas Wolfe and he wrote a book called *You Can't Go Home Again.* And that is true."

"Liar," said Johnny. "This is your cradle, your home." Suddenly he hit the bar with the oaken indoor ball bat he used in arguments to keep the peace. "In the fullness of time—maybe a hundred years—this should be your grave." The bat fell from his hand and he wept at the prospect of my future demise. I puddled up at the prospect myself.

I gazed at my empty glass. "These Gallegos have no manners."

"Oh, for God's sake," Johnny said. "Oh, forgive me!" and he filled us up.

The line-up at the bar was silent now, dark faces with a courteous lack of expression.

"To your home-coming, *compadre,*" Johnny said. "John the Baptist, get the hell out of those potato chips."

"*Conejo de mi Alma,*" I said. "Rabbit of my soul, hear me out."

The big dark one came in from the street, leaned over the bar and kissed Johnny's medal, and went out again.

I said irritably, "There was a time when a man could be listened to. Must I buy a ticket? Must I make a reservation to tell a story?"

Johnny turned to the silent bar. "Silence!" he said fiercely, and took up his indoor ball bat.

"I will now tell you true things, brother-in-law. Step into the street—strangers, foreigners, thousands of them. Look to the hills, a pigeon loft. Today I walked the length of Alvarado Street and back by the Calle Principál and I saw nothing but strangers. This afternoon I got lost in Peter's Gate. I went to the Field of Love back of Joe Duckworth's house by the Ball Park. It's a used-car lot. My nerves are jangled by traffic lights. Even the police are strangers, foreigners. I went to the Carmel Valley where once we could shoot a thirty-thirty in any direction. Now you couldn't shoot a marble knuckles down without wounding a foreigner. And Johnny, I don't mind people, you know that. But these are rich people. They plant geraniums in big pots. Swimming pools where frogs and crayfish used to wait for us. No, my goatly friend. If this were my home, would I get lost in it? If this were my home could I walk the streets and hear no blessing?"

Johnny was slumped casually over the bar. "But here, Juanito, it's the same. We don't let them in."

I looked down the line of faces. "Yes, here it is better. But can I live on a bar stool? Let us not fool ourselves. What we knew is dead, and maybe the greatest part of what we were is dead. What's out there is new and perhaps good, but it's nothing we know."

Johnny held his temples between his cupped hands and his eyes were bloodshot.

"Where are the great ones? Tell me, where's Willie Trip?"

"Dead," Johnny said hollowly.

"Where is Pilon, Johnny, Pom Pom, Miz Gragg, Stevie Field?"

"Dead, dead, dead," he echoed.

"Ed Ricketts, Whitey's Number One and Two, where's Sonny Boy, Ankle Varney, Jesús María Corcoran, Joe Portagee, Shorty Lee, Flora Wood, and that girl who kept spiders in her hat?"

"Dead—all dead," Johnny moaned.

"It's like we was in a bucket of ghosts," said Johnny.

"No. They're not true ghosts. We're the ghosts."

The big dark one came in and Johnny held out his medal for kissing without being asked.

Johnny turned and walked with widespread legs back to the bar mirror. He studied his face for a moment, picked up a bottle, took out the cork, smelled it, tasted it. Then he looked at his fingernails. There was a stir of restlessness along the bar, shoulders hunched, legs were uncrossed.

There's going to be trouble, I said to myself.

Johnny came back and delicately set the bottle on the bar between us. His eyes were wide and dreamy.

Johnny shook his head. "I guess you don't like us any more. I guess maybe you're too good for us." His fingertips played slow chords on an invisible keyboard on the bar.

For just a moment I was tempted. I heard the wail of trumpets and the clash of arms. But hell, I'm too old for it. I made the door in two steps. I turned. "Why does he kiss your medal?"

"He's placing bets."

"Okay. See you tomorrow, Johnny."

The double door swung to behind me. I was on Alvarado Street, slashed with neon light—and around me it was nothing but strangers.

In my flurry of nostalgic spite, I have done the Monterey Peninsula a disservice. It is a beautiful place, clean, well run, and progressive. The beaches are clean where once they festered with fish guts and flies. The canneries which once put up a sickening stench are gone, their places filled with restaurants, antique shops, and the like. They fish for tourists now, not pilchards, and that species they are not likely to wipe out. And Carmel, begun by starveling writers and unwanted painters, is now a community of the well-to-do and the retired. If Carmel's founders should return, they could not afford to live there, but it wouldn't go that far. They would be instantly picked up as suspicious characters and deported over the city line.

The place of my origin had changed, and having gone away I had not changed with it. In my memory it stood as it once did and its outward appearance confused and angered me.

What I am about to tell must be the experience of very many in this nation where so many wander and come back. I called on old and valued friends. I thought their hair had receded a little more than mine. The greetings were enthusiastic. The memories flooded up. Old crimes and old triumphs were brought out and dusted. And suddenly my attention wandered, and looking at my ancient friend, I saw that his wandered also. And it was true what I had said to Johnny Garcia—I was the ghost. My town had grown and changed and my friend along with it. Now returning, as changed to my friend as my town was to me, I distorted his picture, muddied his memory. When I went away I had died, and so became fixed and unchangeable. My return caused only confusion and uneasiness. Although they could not say it, my old friends wanted me gone so that I could take my proper place in the pattern of remembrance—and I wanted to go for the same reason. Tom Wolfe was right. You can't go home again because home has ceased to exist except in the mothballs of memory.

My departure was flight. But I did do one formal and senti-mental thing before I turned my back. I drove up to Fremont's Peak, the highest point for many miles around. I climbed the last spiky rocks to the top. Here among these blackened granite outcrops General Frémont made his stand against a Mexican army, and defeated it. When I was a boy we occasionally found cannon balls and rusted bayonets in the area. This solitary stone peak overlooks the whole of my childhood and youth, the great Salinas Valley stretching south for nearly a hundred miles, the town of Salinas where I was born now spreading like crab grass toward the foothills. Mount Toro, on the brother range to the west, was a rounded benign mountain, and to the north Mon-terey Bay shone like a blue platter. I felt and smelled and heard the wind blow up from the long valley. It smelled of the brown hills of wild oats.

I remembered how once, in that part of youth that is deeply concerned with death, I wanted to be buried on this peak where without eyes I could see everything I knew and loved, for in those days there was no world beyond the mountains. And I remembered how intensely I felt about my interment. It is strange and perhaps fortunate that when one's time grows nearer one's interest in it flags as death becomes a fact rather than a pageantry. Here on these high rocks my memory myth repaired itself. Charley, having explored the area, sat at my feet, his fringed ears blowing like laundry on a line. His nose, moist with curiosity, sniffed the wind-borne pattern of a hundred miles.

"You wouldn't know, my Charley, that right down there, in that little valley, I fished for trout with your namesake, my Uncle Charley. And over there—see where I'm pointing—my mother shot a wildcat. Straight down there, forty miles away, our family ranch was—old starvation ranch. Can you see that darker place there? Well, that's a tiny canyon with a clear and lovely stream bordered with wild azaleas and fringed with big oaks. And on one of those oaks my father burned his name with a hot iron together with the name of the girl he loved. In the long years the bark grew over the burn and covered it. And just a little while ago, a man cut that oak for firewood and his split-ting wedge uncovered my father's name and the man sent it to me. In the spring, Charley, when the valley is carpeted with blue lupines like a flowery sea, there's the smell of heaven up here, the smell of heaven."

I printed it once more on my eyes, south, west, and north, and then we hurried away from the permanent and changeless past where my mother is always shooting a wildcat and my father is always burning his name with his love.

It would be pleasant to be able to say of my travels with Charley, "I went out to find the truth about my country and I found it." And then it would be such a simple matter to set down my findings and lean back comfortably with a fine sense of having discovered truths and taught them to my readers. I wish it were that easy. But what I carried in my head and deeper in my perceptions was a barrel of worms. I discovered long ago in collecting and classifying marine animals that what I found was closely intermeshed with how I felt at the moment. External reality has a way of being not so external after all.

This monster of a land, this mightiest of nations, this spawn of the future, turns out to be the macrocosm of microcosm me. If an Englishman or a Frenchman or an Italian should travel my route, see what I saw, hear what I heard, their stored pictures would be not only different from mine but equally different from one another. If other Americans reading this account should feel it true, that agreement would only mean that we are alike in our Americanness.

From start to finish I found no strangers. If I had, I might be able to report them more objectively. But these are my people and this my country. If I found matters to criticize and to deplore, they were tendencies equally present in myself. If I were to prepare one immaculately inspected generality it would be this: For all of our enormous geographic range, for all of our sectionalism, for all of our interwoven breeds drawn from every part of the ethnic world, we are a nation, a new breed. Americans are much more American than they are Northerners, Southerners, Westerners, or Easterners. And descendants of English, Irish, Italian, Jewish, German, Polish are essentially American. This is not patriotic whoop-de-do; it is carefully observed fact. California Chinese, Boston Irish, Wisconsin German, yes, and Alabama Negroes, have more in common than they have apart. And this is the more remarkable because it has happened so quickly. It is a fact that Americans from all sections and of all racial extractions are more alike than the Welsh are like the English, the Lancashireman like the Cockney, or for that matter the Lowland Scot like the Highlander. It is astonishing that this has happened in less than two hundred years and most of it in the last fifty. The American identity is an exact and provable thing.

Starting on my return journey, I realized by now that I could not see everything. My impressionable gelatin plate was getting muddled. I determined to inspect two more sections and then call it a day—Texas and a sampling of the Deep South. From my reading, it seemed to me that Texas is emerging as a separate force and that the South is in the pain of labor with the nature of its future child still unknown. And I have thought that such is the bitterness of the labor that the child has been forgotten.

This journey had been like a full dinner of many courses, set before a starving man. At first he tries to eat all of everything, but as the meal progresses he finds he must forgo some things to keep his appetite and his taste buds functioning.

I bucketed Rocinante out of California by the shortest possible route—one I knew well from the old days of the 1930s. From Salinas to Los Banos, through Fresno and Bakersfield, then over the pass and into the Mojave Desert, a burned and burning desert even this late in the year, its hills like piles of black cinders in the distance, and the rutted floor sucked dry by the hungry sun. It's easy enough now, on the high-speed road in a dependable and comfortable car, with stopping places for shade and every service station vaunting its refrigeration. But I can remember when we came to it with prayer, listening for trouble in our laboring old motors, drawing a plume of steam from our boiling radiators. Then the broken-down wreck by the side of the road was in real trouble unless someone stopped to offer help. And I have never crossed it without sharing something with those early families foot-dragging through this terrestrial hell, leaving the white skeletons of horses and cattle which still mark the way.

The Mojave is a big desert and a frightening one. It's as though nature tested a man for endurance and constancy to prove whether he was good enough to get to California. The shimmering dry heat made visions of water on the flat plain. And even when you drive at high speed, the hills that mark the boundaries recede before you. Charley, always a dog for water, panted asthmatically, jarring his whole body with the effort, and a good eight inches of his tongue hung out flat as a leaf and dripping. I pulled off the road into a small gulley to give him water from my thirty-gallon tank. But before I let him drink I poured water all over him and on my hair and shoulders and shirt. The air is so dry that evaporation makes you feel suddenly cold.

I opened a can of beer from my refrigerator and sat well inside the shade of Rocinante, looking out at the sun-pounded plain, dotted here and there with clumps of sagebrush.

About fifty yards away two coyotes stood watching me, their tawny coats blending with sand and sun. I knew that with any quick or suspicious movement of mine they could drift into invisibility. With the most casual slowness I reached down my new rifle from its sling over my bed—the .222 with its bitter little high-speed, long-range stings. Very slowly I brought the rifle up. Perhaps in the shade of my house I was half hidden by the blinding light outside. The little rifle has a beautiful telescope sight with a wide field. The coyotes had not moved.

I got both of them in the field of my telescope, and the glass brought them very close. Their tongues lolled out so that they seemed to smile mockingly. They were favored animals, not starved, but well furred, the golden hair tempered with black guard hairs. Their little lemon-yellow eyes were plainly visible in the glass. I moved the cross hairs to the breast of the right-hand animal, and pushed the safety. My elbows on the table steadied the gun. The cross hairs lay unmoving on the brisket. And then the coyote sat down like a dog and its right rear paw came up to scratch the right shoulder.

My finger was reluctant to touch the trigger. I must be getting very old and my ancient conditioning worn thin. Coyotes are vermin. They steal chickens. They thin the ranks of quail and all other game birds. They must be killed. They are the enemy. My first shot would drop the sitting beast, and the other would whirl to fade away. I might very well pull him down with a running shot because I am a good rifleman.

And I did not fire. My training said, "Shoot!" and my age

replied, "There isn't a chicken within thirty miles, and if there are any they aren't my chickens. And this waterless place is not quail country. No, these boys are keeping their figures with kangaroo rats and jackrabbits, and that's vermin eat vermin. Why should I interfere?"

"Kill them," my training said. "Everyone kills them. It's a public service." My finger moved to the trigger. The cross was steady on the breast just below the panting tongue. I could imagine the splash and jar of angry steel, the leap and struggle until the torn heart failed, and then, not too long later, the shadow of a buzzard, and another. By that time I would be long gone—out of the desert and across the Colorado River. And beside the sagebush there would be a naked, eyeless skull, a few picked bones, a spot of black dried blood and a few rags of golden fur.

I guess I'm too old and too lazy to be a good citizen. The second coyote stood sidewise to my rifle. I moved the cross hairs to his shoulder and held steady. There was no question of missing with that rifle at that range. I owned both animals. Their lives were mine. I put the safety on and laid the rifle on the table. Without the telescope they were not so intimately close. The hot blast of light tousled the air to shimmering.

Then I remembered something I heard long ago that I hope is true. It was unwritten law in China, so my informant told me, that when one man saved another's life he became responsible for that life to the end of its existence. For, having interfered with a course of events, the savior could not escape his responsibility. And that has always made good sense to me.

Now I had a token responsibility for two live and healthy coyotes. In the delicate world of relationships, we are tied together for all time. I opened two cans of dog food and left them as a votive.

I have driven through the Southwest many times, and even more often have flown over it—a great and mysterious wasteland, a sun-punished place. It is a mystery, something concealed and waiting. It seems deserted, free of parasitic man, but this is not entirely so. Follow the double line of wheel tracks through sand and rock and you will find a habitation somewhere huddled in a protected place, with a few trees pointing their roots at under-earth water, a patch of starveling corn and squash, and strips of jerky hanging on a string. There is a breed of desert men, not hiding exactly but gone to sanctuary from the sins of confusion.

At night in this waterless air the stars come down just out of reach of your fingers. In such a place lived the hermits of the early church piercing to infinity with unlittered minds. The great concepts of oneness and of majestic order seem always to be born in the desert. The quiet counting of the stars, and observation of their movements, came first from desert places. I have known desert men who chose their places with quiet and slow passion, rejecting the nervousness of a watered world. These men have not changed with the exploding times except to die and be replaced by others like them.

And always there are mysteries in the desert, stories told and retold of secret places in the desert mountains where surviving clans from an older era wait to re-emerge. Usually these groups guard treasures hidden from the waves of conquest, the golden artifacts of an archaic Montezuma, or a mine so rich that its discovery would change the world. If a stranger discovers their existence, he is killed or so absorbed that he is never seen again. These stories have an inevitable pattern untroubled by the question, If none return, how is it known what is there? Oh, it's there all right, but if you find it you will never be found.

And there is another monolithic tale which never changes. Two prospectors in partnership discover a mine of preternatural richness—of gold or diamonds or rubies. They load themselves with samples, as much as they can carry, and they mark the place in their minds by landmarks all around. Then, on the way out to the other world, one dies of thirst and exhaustion, but the other crawls on, discarding most of the treasure he has grown too weak to carry. He comes at last to a settlement, or perhaps is found by other prospecting men. They examine his samples with great excitement. Sometimes in the story the survivor dies after leaving directions with his rescuers, or again he is nursed back to strength. Then a well-equipped party sets out to find the treasure, and it can never be found again. That is the invariable end of the story—it is never found again. I have heard this story many times, and it never changes. There is nourishment in the desert for myth, but myth must somewhere have its roots in reality.

And there are true secrets in the desert. In the war of sun and dryness against living things, life has its secrets of survival. Life, no matter on what level, must be moist or it will disappear. I find most interesting the conspiracy of life in the desert to circumvent the death rays of the all-conquering sun. The beaten earth appears defeated and dead, but it only appears so. A vast and inventive organization of living matter survives by seeming to have lost. The gray and dusty sage wears oily armor to protect its inward small moistness. Some plants engorge themselves with water in the rare rainfall and store it for future use. Animal life wears a hard, dry skin or an outer skeleton to defy the desiccation. And every living thing has developed techniques for finding or creating shade. Small reptiles and rodents burrow or slide below the surface or cling to the shaded side of an outcropping. Movement is slow to preserve energy, and it is a rare animal which can or will defy the sun for long. A rattlesnake will die in an hour of full sun. Some insects of bolder inventiveness have devised personal refrigeration systems. Those animals which must drink moisture get it at second hand—a rabbit from a leaf, a coyote from the blood of a rabbit.

One may look in vain for living creatures in the daytime, but when the sun goes and the night gives consent, a world of creatures awakens and takes up its intricate pattern. Then the hunted come out and the hunters, and hunters of the hunters. The night awakes to buzzing and to cries and barks.

When, very late in the history of our planet, the incredible accident of life occurred, a balance of chemical factors, combined with temperature, in quantities and in kinds so delicate as to be unlikely, all came together in the retort of time and a new thing emerged, soft and helpless and unprotected in the savage world of unlife. Then processes of change and variation took place in the organisms, so that one kind became different from all others. But one ingredient, perhaps the most important of all, is planted in every life form—the factor of survival. No living thing is without it, nor could life exist without this magic formula. Of course, each form developed its own machinery for survival, and some failed and disappeared while others peopled the earth. The first life might easily have been snuffed out and the accident may never have happened again—but, once it existed, its first quality, its duty, preoccupation, direction, and end, shared by every living thing, is to go on living. And so it does and so it will until some other accident cancels it. And the desert, the dry and sun-lashed desert, is a good school in which to observe the cleverness and the infinite variety of techniques of survival under pitiless opposition. Life could not change the sun or water the desert, so it changed itself.

The desert, being an unwanted place, might well be the last stand of life against unlife. For in the rich and moist and wanted areas of the world, life pyramids against itself and in its confusion has finally allied itself with the enemy non-life. And what the scorching, searing, freezing, poisoning weapons of non-life have failed to do may be accomplished to the end of its destruction and extinction by the tactics of survival gone sour. If the most versatile of living forms, the human, now fights for survival as it always has, it can eliminate not only itself but all other life. And if that should transpire, unwanted places like the desert might be the harsh mother of repopulation. For the inhabitants of the desert are well trained and well armed against desolation. Even our own misguided species might re-emerge from the desert. The lone man and his sun-toughened wife who cling to the shade in an unfruitful and uncoveted place might, with their brothers in arms—the coyote, the jackrabbit, the horned toad, the rattlesnake, together with a host of armored insects—these trained and tested fragments of life might well be the last hope of life against non-life. The desert has mothered magic things before this.

Much earlier I spoke of the changes at state lines, changes in Highway English, in prose forms on the signs, changes in permitted speeds. The states' rights guaranteed under the Constitution seem to be passionately and gleefully exercised. California searches vehicles for vegetables and fruits which might carry pernicious insects and diseases, and regulations of these are enforced with almost religious intensity.

Some years ago I knew a gay and inventive family from Idaho. Planning to visit relatives in California, they took a truckload of potatoes to sell along the way to help pay expenses. They had disposed of over half their cargo when they were stopped at the California line and their potatoes refused entrance. They were not financially able to abandon their potatoes, so they cheerfully set up camp right on the state line, where they ate potatoes, sold potatoes, bartered potatoes. At the end of two weeks the truck was empty. Then they went through the inspector's station in good standing and continued on their way.

The separateness of the states, which has been bitterly called Balkanization, creates many problems. Rarely do two states have the same gasoline tax, and these taxes largely support the building and maintenance of highways. The enormous interstate trucks make use of the roads and by their very weight and speed increase the maintenance costs. Thus the states have weighing stations for trucks where the loads are assessed and taxed. And if there is a differential in gasoline tax, the tanks are measured and the tax applied. The signs say, "All trucks stop." Being a truck, I stopped, only to be waved on over the scales. They were not looking for such as I. But sometimes I stopped and talked to the inspectors when they were not too busy. And this brings me to the subject of state police. Like most Americans I am no lover of cops, and the consistent investigation of city forces for bribery, brutality, and a long and picturesque list of malfeasances is not designed to reassure me. However, my hostility does not extend to the state troopers now maintained in most parts of the country. By the simple expedient of recruiting intelligent and educated men, paying them adequately, and setting them beyond political coercion, many states have succeeded in creating elite corps of men, secure in their dignity and proud of their service. Eventually our cities may find it necessary to reorganize their police on the pattern of the state police. But this will never happen while political organizations retain the slightest power to reward or to punish.

Across the Colorado River from Needles, the dark and jagged ramparts of Arizona stood up against the sky, and behind them the huge tilted plain rising toward the backbone of the continent again. I know this way so well from many crossings—Kingman, Ash Fork, Flagstaff with its mountain peak behind it, then Winslow, Holbrook, Sanders, down hill and up again, and then Arizona passed. The towns were a little larger and more brightly lighted than I remembered them, the motels bigger and more luxurious.

I crossed into New Mexico, rushed past Gallup in the night, and camped on the Continental Divide—and much more spectacular it is here than in the north. The night was very cold and dry, and the stars were cut glass. I drove into a little canyon out of the wind and parked by a mound of broken bottles—whisky and gin bottles, thousands of them. I don't know why they were there.

And I sat in the seat and faced what I had concealed from myself. I was driving myself, pounding out the miles because I was no longer hearing or seeing. I had passed my limit of taking in or, like a man who goes on stuffing in food after he is filled, I felt helpless to assimilate what was fed in through my eyes. Each hill looked like the one just passed. I have felt this way in the Prado in Madrid after looking at a hundred paintings—the stuffed and helpless inability to see more.

This would be a time to find a sheltered place beside a stream to rest and refurbish. Charley, in the dark seat beside me, mentioned a difficulty with a little moaning sigh. I had even forgotten him. I let him out and he staggered to the hill of broken bottles, sniffed at them, and took another way.

The night air was very cold, shivery cold, so that I lighted the cabin and turned up the gas to warm the air. The cabin was not neat. My bed was unmade and breakfast dishes lay desolate in the sink. I sat on the bed and stared into gray dreariness. Why had I thought I could learn anything about the land? For the last hundreds of miles I had avoided people. Even at necessary stops for gasoline I had answered in monosyllables and retained no picture. My eye and brain had welshed on me. I was fooling myself that this was important or even instructive. There was a ready remedy, of course. I reached out the whisky bottle without getting up, poured half a tumbler, smelled it, and poured it back in the bottle. No remedy was there.

Charley had not returned. I opened the door and whistled him and got no response. That shook me out of it. I grabbed my searchlight and turned its spearing beam up the canyon. The light flashed on two eyes about fifty yards away. I ran up the trail and found him standing staring into space, just as I had been.

"What's the matter, Charley, aren't you well?"

His tail slowly waved his replies. "Oh, yes. Quite well, I guess."

"Why didn't you come when I whistled?"

"I didn't hear you whistle."

"What are you staring at?"

"I don't know. Nothing I guess."

"Well, don't you want your dinner?"

"I'm really not hungry. But I'll go through the motions."

Back in the cabin he flopped down on the floor and put his chin down on his paws.

"Come on up on the bed, Charley. Let's be miserable together." He complied but without enthusiasm and I riffled my fingers in his topknot and behind his ears the way he likes it. "How's that?"

He shifted his head. "A little more to the left. There. That's the place."

"We'd be lousy explorers. A few days out and we get the mullygrubs. The first white man through here—I think he was named Narváez and I'm under the impression his little jaunt took six years. Move over. I'll look it up. Nope, it was eight years—1528 to 1536. And Narváez himself didn't make it this far. Four of his men did, though. I wonder if they ever got the mullygrubs. We're soft, Charley. Maybe it's time for a little gallantry. When's your birthday?"

"I don't know. Maybe it's like horses, the first of January."

"Think it might be today?"

"Who knows?"

"I could make you a cake. Have to be hotcake mix because that's what I have. Plenty of syrup and a candle on top."

Charley watched the operation with some interest. His silly tail made delicate conversation. "Anybody saw you make a birthday cake for a dog that he don't even know when's his birthday would think you were nuts."

"If you can't manage any better grammar than that with your tail, maybe it's a good thing you can't talk."

It turned out pretty well—four layers of hotcakes with maple syrup between and a stub of a miner's candle on top. I drank Charley's health in straight whisky as he ate and licked up the syrup. And then we both felt better. But there was Narváez' party—eight years. There were men in those days.

Charley licked the syrup from his whiskers. "What makes you so moony?"

"It's because I've stopped seeing. When that happens you think you'll never see again."

He stood up and stretched himself, first fore and then aft. "Let's take a stroll up the hill," he suggested. "Maybe you've started again."

We inspected the pile of broken whisky bottles and then continued up the trail. The dry, frozen air came out of us in plumes of steam. Some fairly large animal went leaping up the broken stone hill, or maybe a small animal and a big little avalanche.

"What does your nose say that was?"

"Nothing I recognize. Kind of a musky smell. Nothing I'm going to chase, either."

So dark was the night that it was prickled with fiery dots. My light brought an answering flash up the steep rocky bank. I climbed up, slipping and floundering, lost the echoed light and found it again, a good little new-split stone with a piece of mica in it—not a fortune but a good thing to have. I put it in my pocket and we went to bed.

PART FOUR

When I started this narrative, I knew that sooner or later I would have to have a go at Texas, and I dreaded it. I could have bypassed Texas about as easily as a space traveler can avoid the Milky Way. It sticks its big old Panhandle up north and it slops and slouches along the Rio Grande. Once you are in Texas it seems to take forever to get out, and some people never make it.

Let me say in the beginning that even if I wanted to avoid Texas I could not, for I am wived in Texas and mother-in-lawed and uncled and aunted and cousined within an inch of my life. Staying away from Texas geographically is no help whatever, for Texas moves through our house in New York, our fishing cottage at Sag Harbor, and when we had a flat in Paris, Texas was there too. It permeates the world to a ridiculous degree. Once, in Florence, on seeing a lovely little Italian princess, I said to her father, "But she doesn't look Italian. It may seem strange, but she looks like an American Indian." To which her father replied, "Why shouldn't she? Her grandfather married a Cherokee in Texas."

Writers facing the problem of Texas find themselves floundering in generalities, and I am no exception. Texas is a state of mind. Texas is an obsession. Above all, Texas is a nation in every sense of the word. And there's an opening covey of generalities. A Texan outside of Texas is a foreigner. My wife refers to herself as the Texan that got away, but that is only partly true. She has virtually no accent until she talks to a Texan, when she instantly reverts. You would not have to scratch deep to find her origin. She says such words as yes, air, hair, guess, with two syllables —yayus, ayer, hayer, gayus. And sometimes in a weary moment the word ink becomes ank. Our daughter, after a stretch in Austin, was visiting New York friends. She said, "Do you have a pin?"

"Certainly, dear," said her host. "Do you want a straight pin or a safety pin?"

"Aont a fountain pin," she said.

I've studied the Texas problem from many angles and for many years. And of course one of my truths is inevitably canceled by another. Outside their state I think Texans are a little frightened and very tender in their feelings, and these qualities cause boasting, arrogance, and noisy complacency—the outlets of shy children. At home Texans are none of these things. The ones I know are gracious, friendly, generous, and quiet. In New York we hear them so often bring up their treasured uniqueness. Texas is the only state that came into the Union by treaty. It retains the right to secede at will. We have heard them threaten to secede so often that I formed an enthusiastic organization—The American Friends for Texas Secession. This stops the subject cold. They want to be able to secede but they don't want anyone to want them to.

Like most passionate nations Texas has its own private history based on, but not limited by, facts. The tradition of the tough and versatile frontiersman is true but not exclusive. It is for the few to know that in the great old days of Virginia there were three punishments for high crimes—death, exile to Texas, and imprisonment, in that order. And some of the deportees must have descendants.

Again—the glorious defense to the death of the Alamo against the hordes of Santa Anna is a fact. The brave bands of Texans did indeed wrest their liberty from Mexico, and freedom, liberty, are holy words. One must go to contemporary observers in Europe for a non-Texan opinion as to the nature of the tyranny that raised need for revolt. Outside observers say the pressure was twofold. The Texans, they say, didn't want to pay taxes and, second, Mexico had abolished slavery in 1829, and Texas, being part of Mexico, was required to free its slaves. Of course there were other causes of revolt, but these two are spectacular to a European, and rarely mentioned here.

I have said that Texas is a state of mind, but I think it is more than that. It is a mystique closely approximating a religion. And this is true to the extent that people either passionately love Texas or passionately hate it and, as in other religions, few people dare to inspect it for fear of losing their bearings in mystery and paradox. Any observations of mine can be quickly canceled by opinion or counter-observation. But I think there will be little quarrel with my feeling that Texas is one thing. For all its enormous range of space, climate, and physical appearance, and for all the internal squabbles, contentions, and strivings, Texas has a tight cohesiveness perhaps stronger than any other section of America. Rich, poor, Panhandle, Gulf, city, country, Texas is the obsession, the proper study and the passionate possession of all Texans. Some years ago, Edna Ferber wrote a book about a very tiny group of very rich Texans. Her description was accurate, so far as my knowledge extends, but the emphasis was one of disparagement. And instantly the book was attacked by Texans of all groups, classes, and possessions. To attack one Texan is to draw fire from all Texans. The Texas joke, on the other hand, is a revered institution, beloved and in many cases originating in Texas.

The tradition of the frontier cattleman is as tenderly nurtured in Texas as is the hint of Norman blood in England. And while it is true that many families are descended from contract colonists not unlike the present-day braceros, all hold to the dream of the longhorn steer and the unfenced horizon. When a man makes his fortune in oil or government contracts, in chemicals or wholesale groceries, his first act is to buy a ranch, the largest he can afford, and to run some cattle. A candidate for public office who does not own a ranch is said to have little chance of election. The tradition of the land is deep fixed in the Texas psyche. Businessmen wear heeled boots that never feel a stirrup, and men of great wealth who have houses in Paris and regularly shoot grouse in Scotland refer to themselves as little old country boys. It would be easy to make sport of their attitude if one did not know that in this way they try to keep their association with the strength and simplicity of the land. Instinctively they feel that this is the source not only of wealth but of energy. And the energy of Texans is boundless and explosive. The successful man with his traditional ranch, at least in my experience, is no absentee owner. He works at it, oversees his herd and adds to it. The energy, in a climate so hot as to be staggering, is also staggering. And the tradition of hard work is maintained whatever the fortune or lack of it.

The power of an attitude is amazing. Among other tendencies

to be noted, Texas is a military nation. The armed forces of the
United States are loaded with Texans and often dominated by
Texans. Even the dearly loved spectacular sports are run almost
like military operations. Nowhere are there larger bands or more
marching organizations, with corps of costumed girls whirling
glittering batons. Sectional football games have the glory and the
despair of war, and when a Texas team takes the field against a
foreign state, it is an army with banners.

If I keep coming back to the energy of Texas, it is because I
am so aware of it. It seems to me like that thrust of dynamism
which caused and permitted whole peoples to migrate and to
conquer in earlier ages. The land mass of Texas is rich in recov-
erable spoil. If this had not been so, I think I believe the relentless energy of Texans would have moved out and conquered new
lands. This conviction is somewhat borne out in the restless
movement of Texas capital. But now, so far, the conquest has
been by purchase rather than by warfare. The oil deserts of the
Near East, the opening lands of South America have felt the
thrust. Then there are new islands of capital conquest: factories
in the Middle West, food-processing plants, tool and die works,
lumber and pulp. Even publishing houses have been added to
the legitimate twentieth-century Texas spoil. There is no moral
in these observations, nor any warning. Energy must have an
outlet and will seek one.

In all ages, rich, energetic, and successful nations, when they
have carved their place in the world, have felt hunger for art, for
culture, even for learning and beauty. The Texas cities shoot
upward and outward. The colleges are heavy with gifts and en-
dowments. Theaters and symphony orchestras sprout overnight.
In any huge and boisterous surge of energy and enthusiasm there
must be errors and miscalculations, even breach of judgment and
taste. And there is always the non-productive brotherhood of
critics to disparage and to satirize, to view with horror and contempt. My own interest is attracted to the fact that these things
are done at all. There will doubtless be thousands of ribald failures, but in the world's history artists have always been drawn
where they are welcome and well treated.

By its nature and its size Texas invites generalities, and the
generalities usually end up as paradox—the "little ol' country

boy" at a symphony, the booted and blue-jeaned ranchman in Neiman-Marcus, buying Chinese jades.

Politically Texas continues its paradox. Traditionally and nostalgically it is Old South Democrat, but this does not prevent its voting conservative Republican in national elections while electing liberals to city and county posts. My opening statement still holds—everything in Texas is likely to be canceled by something else.

Most areas in the world may be placed in latitude and longitude, described chemically in their earth, sky and water, rooted and fuzzed over with identified flora and peopled with known fauna, and there's an end to it. Then there are others where fable, myth, preconception, love, longing, or prejudice step in and so distort a cool, clear appraisal that a kind of high-colored magical confusion takes permanent hold. Greece is such an area, and those parts of England where King Arthur walked. One quality of such places as I am trying to define is that a very large part of them is personal and subjective. And surely Texas is such a place.

I have moved over a great part of Texas and I know that within its borders I have seen just about as many kinds of country, contour, climate, and conformation as there are in the world saving only the Arctic, and a good north wind can even bring the icy breath down. The stern horizon-fenced plains of the Panhandle are foreign to the little wooded hills and sweet streams in the Davis Mountains. The rich citrus orchards of the Rio Grande valley do not relate to the sagebrush grazing of South Texas. The hot and humid air of the Gulf Coast has no likeness in the cool crystal in the northwest of the Panhandle. And Austin on its hills among the bordered lakes might be across the world from Dallas.

What I am trying to say is that there is no physical or geographical unity in Texas. Its unity lies in the mind. And this is not only in Texans. The word Texas becomes a symbol to everyone in the world. There's no question that this Texas-of-the-mind fable is often synthetic, sometimes untruthful, and frequently romantic, but that in no way diminishes its strength as a symbol.

The foregoing investigation into the nature of the idea of

Texas is put down as a prelude to my journeying across Texas with Charley in Rocinante. It soon became apparent that this stretch had to be different from the rest of the trip. In the first place I knew the countryside, and in the second I had friends and relatives by marriage, and such a situation makes objectivity practically impossible, for I know no place where hospitality is practiced so fervently as in Texas.

But before that most pleasant and sometimes exhausting human trait took hold, I had three days of namelessness in a beautiful motor hotel in the middle of Amarillo. A passing car on a gravel road had thrown up pebbles and broken out the large front window of Rocinante and it had to be replaced. But, more important, Charley had been taken with his old ailment again, and this time he was in bad trouble and great pain. I remembered the poor incompetent veterinary in the Northwest, who did not know and did not care. And I remembered how Charley had looked at him with pained wonder and contempt.

In Amarillo the doctor I summoned turned out to be a young man. He drove up in a medium-priced convertible. He leaned over Charley. "What's his problem?" he asked. I explained Charley's difficulty. Then the young vet's hands went down and moved over hips and distended abdomen—trained and knowing hands. Charley sighed a great sigh and his tail wagged slowly up from the floor and down again. Charley put himself in this man's care, completely confident. I've seen this instant rapport before, and it is good to see.

The strong fingers probed and investigated and then the vet straightened up. "It can happen to any little old boy," he said.

"Is it what I think it is?"

"Yep. Prostatitis."

"Can you treat it?"

"Sure. I'll have to relax him first, and then I can give him medication for it. Can you leave him for maybe four days?"

"Whether I can or not, I will."

He lifted Charley in his arms and carried him out and laid him in the front seat of the convertible, and the tufted tail twittered against the leather. He was content and confident, and so was I. And that is how I happened to stay around Amarillo for a while. To complete the episode, I picked up Charley four days later, completely well. The doctor gave me pills to give at intervals while traveling so that the ailment never came back. There's absolutely nothing to take the place of a good man.

I do not intend to dwell long on Texas. Since the death of Hollywood the Lone Star State has taken its place at the top for being interviewed, inspected, and discussed. But no account of Texas would be complete without a Texas orgy, showing men of great wealth squandering their millions on tasteless and impassioned exhibitionism. My wife had come from New York to join me, and we were invited to a Texas ranch for Thanksgiving. It is owned by a friend who sometimes comes to New York, where we give him an orgy. I shall not name him, following the tradition of letting the reader guess. I presume that he is rich, although I have never asked him about it. As invited, we arrived at the ranch on the afternoon before the Thanksgiving orgy. It is a beautiful ranch, rich in water and trees and grazing land. Everywhere bulldozers had pushed up earth dams to hold back the water, making a series of life-giving lakes down the center of the ranch. On well-grassed flats the blooded Herefords grazed, only looking up as we drove by in a cloud of dust. I don't know how big the ranch is. I didn't ask my host.

The house, a one-story brick structure, stood in a grove of cottonwoods on a little eminence over a pool made by a dammed-up spring. The dark surface of the water was disturbed by trout that had been planted there. The house was comfortable, had three bedrooms, each room with a bath—both tub and shower. The living room, paneled in stained pine, served also as a dining room, with a fireplace at one end and a glass-fronted gun case against the side. Through the open kitchen door the staff could be seen—a large dark lady and a giggleful girl. Our host met us and helped carry our bags in.

The orgy began at once. We had a bath and on emerging were given scotch and soda, which we drank thirstily. After that we inspected the barn across the way, the kennels in which there were three pointers, one of them not feeling so well. Then to the corral, where the daughter of the house was working on the training of a quarter horse, an animal of parts named Specklebottom. After that we inspected two new dams with water building slowly behind them, and at several drinking stations communed with a small herd of recently purchased cattle. This violence exhausted us and we went back to the house for a short nap.

We awakened from this to find neighboring friends arriving; they brought a large pot of chili con carne, made from a family recipe, the best I have ever tasted. Now other rich people began to arrive, concealing their status in blue jeans and riding boots. Drinks were passed and a gay conversation ensued having to do with hunting, riding, and cattle-breeding, with many bursts of laughter. I reclined on a window seat and in the gathering dusk watched the wild turkeys come in to roost in the cottonwood trees. They fly up clumsily and distribute themselves and then suddenly they blend with the tree and disappear. At least thirty of them came in to roost.

As the darkness came the window became a mirror in which I could watch my host and his guests without their knowledge. They sat about the little paneled room, some in rocking chairs and three of the ladies on a couch. And the subtlety of their ostentation drew my attention. One of the ladies was making a sweater while another worked a puzzle, tapping her teeth with the eraser of a yellow pencil. The men talked casually of grass and water, of So-and-So who had bought a new champion bull in England and flown it home. They were dressed in jeans of that light blue, lighter and a little frayed at the seams, that can be achieved only by a hundred washings.

But the studied detail did not stop there. Boots were scuffed on the inside and salted with horse sweat, and the heels run over. The open collars of the men's shirts showed dark red lines of sunburn on their throats, and one guest had gone to the trouble and expense of breaking his forefinger, which was splinted and covered with laced leather cut from a glove. My host went to the extreme of serving his guests from a bar which consisted of a tub of ice, quart bottles of soda, two bottles of whisky and a case of pop.

The smell of money was everywhere. The daughter of the house, for example, sat on the floor cleaning a .22 rifle, telling a sophisticated and ribald story of how Specklebottom, her stallion, had leaped a five-bar corral gate and visited a mare in the next county. She thought she had property rights in the foal, Specklebottom's blood line being what it was. The scene verified what we have all heard about fabulous Texas millionaires.

I was reminded of a time in Pacific Grove when I was painting the inside of a cottage my father had built there before I was born. My hired helper worked beside me, and neither of us being expert we were well splattered. Suddenly we found ourselves out of paint. I said, "Neal, run up to Holman's and get a half-gallon of paint and a quart of thinner."

"I'll have to clean up and change my clothes," he said.

"Nuts! Go as you are."

"I can't do it."

"Why not? I would."

Then he said a wise and memorable thing. "You got to be awful rich to dress as bad as you do," he said.

And this isn't funny. It's true. And it was true at the orgy. How unthinkably rich these Texans must be to live as simply as they were.

I took a walk with my wife, around the trout pool and over against the hill. The air was chill and the wind blowing from the north had winter in it. We listened for frogs, but they had shacked up for the winter. But we heard a coyote howl upwind and we heard a cow bawling for her late weaned bairn. The pointers came to the wire mesh of the kennel, wriggling like happy snakes and sneezing with enthusiasm, and even the sickly one came out of his house and fleered at us. Then we stood in the high entrance of the great barn and smelled at the sweetness of alfalfa and the bready odor of rolled barley. At the corral the stock horses snorted at us and rubbed their heads against the bars, and Specklebottom took a kick at a gelded friend just to keep in practice. Owls were flying this night, shrieking to start their prey, and a nighthawk made soft rhythmic whoops in the distance. I wished that Able Baker Charley Dog could have been with us. He would have admired this night. But he was resting under sedatives in Amarillo curing his prostatitis. The sharp north wind clashed the naked branches of the cottonwoods. It seemed to me that winter, which had been on my tail during the whole trip, had finally caught up with me. Somewhere in our, or at least my, recent zoologic past, hibernation must have been a fact of being. Else why does cold night air make me so sleepy? It does and it did, and we went in to the house where the ghosts had already retired and we went to bed.

I awakened early. I had seen two trout rods leaning against the screen outside our room. I went down the grassed hill, slipping in the frost to the edge of the dark pool. A fly was ready fastened on the line, a black gnat, a little frayed but still hairy enough. And as it touched the surface of the pool the water boiled and churned. I brought in a ten-inch rainbow trout and skidded him up on the grass and knocked him on the head. I cast four times and had four trout. I cleaned them and threw the innards to their friends.

In the kitchen the cook gave me coffee and I sat in an alcove while she dipped my fish in corn meal and fried them crisp in bacon fat and served them to me under a coverlet of bacon that crumbled in my mouth. It was a long time since I had eaten trout like that, five minutes from water to pan. You take him in your fingers delicately by head and tail and nibble him from off his backbone, and finally you eat the tail, crisp as a potato chip. Coffee has a special taste of a frosty morning, and the third cup is as good as the first. I would have lingered in the kitchen discussing nothing with the staff, but she cleared me out because she had to stuff two turkeys for the Thanksgiving orgy.

In the mid-morning sunshine we went quail-hunting, I with my old and shiny 12-bore with the dented barrel, which I carried in Rocinante. That gun was no great shakes when I bought it second-hand fifteen years ago, and it has never got any better. But I suppose it is as good as I am. If I can hit them the gun will pull them down. But before we started I looked with a certain longing through the glass door at a Luigi Franchi 12-gauge double with a Purdy lock so beautiful that I was filled with covetousness. The carving on the steel had the pearly gleam of a Damascus blade, while the stock flowed into lock and lock into barrels as though they had grown that way from a magic planted seed. I'm sure that if my host had seen my envy he would have loaned me the beauty, but I didn't ask. Suppose I tripped and fell, or dropped it, or knocked its lovely tubes against a rock? No, it would be like carrying the crown jewels through a mine field. My old beat-up gun is no bargain, but at least anything that can happen to it has, and there's no worrying.

For a week our host had noted where the coveys were gathering. We spread out and moved through brush and thicket, down into water, out, and up, while the spring-steel pointers worked ahead of us and a fat old bitch pointer named Duchess with flame in her eyes outworked them all, and us too. We found quail tracks in the dust, quail tracks in the sand and mud of stream beds, bits of quail-feather fluff in the dry tips of the sage. We walked for miles, slowly, guns up and ready to throw shot at a drumming flight. And we never saw a quail. The dogs never saw or smelled a quail. We told stories and some lies about previous quail hunts, but it did no good. The quail had gone, really gone. I am only a reasonable quail shot but the men with me were excellent, the dogs were professional, keen, hard, and hardworking. No quail. But there's one nice thing about hunting. Even with no birds, you'd rather go then not.

My host thought my heart was breaking. He said, "Look. You take that little .222 of yours this afternoon and shoot yourself a wild turkey."

"How many are there?" I asked.

"Well, two years ago I planted thirty. I think there are about eighty now."

"I counted thirty in the band that flew up near the house last night."

"There's two other bands," he said.

I really didn't want a turkey. What would I do with it in Rocinante? I said, "Wait a year. When they top a hundred birds, I'll come down and hunt with you."

We came back to the house and showered and shaved, and because it was Thanksgiving we put on white shirts and jackets and ties. The orgy came off on schedule at two o'clock. I'll skip through the details quickly in order not to shock the readers, and also I see no reason to hold these people up to scorn. After two good drinks of whisky, the two brown and glazed turkeys were brought in, carved by our host and served by us. We said grace and afterward drank a toast all around and ate ourselves into a proper insensibility. Then, like decadent Romans at Petronius's board, we took a walk and retired for the necessary and inevitable nap. And that was my Thanksgiving orgy in Texas.

Of course I don't think they do it every day. They couldn't. And somewhat the same thing happens when they visit us in New York. Of course they want to see shows and go to night clubs. And at the end of a few days of this they say, "We just don't see how you can live like this." To which we reply, "We don't. And when you go home, we won't."

And now I feel better for having exposed to the light of scrutiny the decadent practices of the rich Texans I know. But I don't for one moment think they eat chili con carne or roast turkey every day.

When I laid the ground plan of my journey, there were definite questions to which I wanted matching answers. It didn't seem to me that they were impossible questions. I suppose they could all be lumped into the single question: "What are Americans like today?"

In Europe it is a popular sport to describe what the Americans are like. Everyone seems to know. And we are equally happy in this game. How many times have I not heard one of my fellow countrymen, after a three-week tour of Europe, describe with certainty the nature of the French, the British, the Italians, the Germans, and above all the Russians? Traveling about, I early learned the difference between an American and the Americans. They are so far apart that they might be opposites. Often when a European has described the Americans with hostility and scorn he has turned to me and said, "Of course, I don't mean you. I am speaking of those others." It boils down to this: the Americans, the British are that faceless clot you don't know, but a Frenchman or an Italian is your acquaintance and your friend. He has none of the qualities your ignorance causes you to hate.

I had always considered this a kind of semantic deadfall, but moving about in my own country I am not at all sure that is so. Americans as I saw them and talked to them were indeed individuals, each one different from the others, but gradually I began to feel that the Americans exist, that they really do have generalized characteristics regardless of their states, their social and financial status, their education, their religious, and their political convictions. But if there is indeed an American image built of truth rather than reflecting either hostility or wishful thinking, what is this image? What does it look like? What does it do? If the same song, the same joke, the same style sweeps through all parts of the country at once, it must be that all Americans are alike in something. The fact that the same joke, the same style, has no effect in France or England or Italy makes this contention valid. But the more I inspected this American image, the less sure I became of what it is. It appeared to me increasingly paradoxical, and it has been my experience that when paradox crops up too often for comfort, it means that certain factors are missing in the equation.

Now I had moved through a galaxy of states, each with its own character, and through clouds and myriads of people, and ahead of me lay an area, the South, that I dreaded to see and yet knew I must see and hear. I am not drawn to pain and violence. I never gaze at accidents unless I can help, or attend street fights for kicks. I faced the South with dread. Here, I knew, were pain and confusion and all the manic results of bewilderment and fear. And the South being a limb of the nation, its pain spreads out to all America.

I knew, as everyone knows, the true but incomplete statement of the problem—that an original sin of the fathers was being visited on the children of succeeding generations. I have many Southern friends, both Negro and white, many of them of superb minds and characters, and often, when not the problem but the mere suggestion of the Negro-white subject has come up, I have seen and felt them go into a room of experience into which I cannot enter.

Perhaps I, more than most people from the so-called North, am kept out of real and emotional understanding of the agony not because I, a white, have no experience with Negroes but because of the nature of my experience.

In Salinas in California, where I was born and grew and went to school gathering the impressions that formed me, there was only one Negro family. The name was Cooper and the father and mother were there when I was born, but they had three sons, one a little older than I, one my age, and one a year younger, so that in grade school and high school there was always a Cooper in the grade ahead, one in my class, and one in the class below. In a word, I was bracketed with Coopers. The father, universally called Mr. Cooper, ran a little trucking business—ran it well and made a good living. His wife was a warm and friendly woman who was good for a piece of gingerbread any time we wanted to put the hustle on her.

If there was any color prejudice in Salinas I never heard or felt a breath of it. The Coopers were respected, and their self-respect was in no way forced. Ulysses, the oldest, was one of the best pole-vaulters our town every developed, a tall, quiet boy. I remember the lean grace of his movements in a track suit and I remember envying his smooth and perfect timing. He died in his third year in high school and I was one of his pallbearers, and I think I was guilty of the sin of pride at being chosen. The second son, Ignatius, my classmate, was not my favorite, I discover now, because he was far and away the best student. In arithmetic and later in mathematics he topped our grades, and in Latin he not only was a better student but he didn't cheat. And who can like a classmate like that? The youngest Cooper —the baby—was all smiles. It's odd that I do not remember his first name. He was a musician from the start, and when I last saw him he was deep in composition which seemed, to my partially instructed ear, bold and original and good. But beyond this giftedness, the Cooper boys were my friends.

Now, these were the only Negroes I knew or had contact with in the days of my flypaper childhood, and you can see how little I was prepared for the great world. When I heard, for example, that Negroes were an inferior race, I thought the authority was misinformed. When I heard that Negroes were dirty I remembered Mrs. Cooper's shining kitchen. Lazy? The drone and clop of Mr. Cooper's horse-drawn dray in the street outside used to awaken us in the dawn. Dishonest? Mr. Cooper was one of the very few Salinians who never let a debt cross the fifteenth of the month.

I realize now that there was something else about the Coopers that set them apart from other Negroes I have seen and met since. Because they were not hurt or insulted, they were not defensive or combative. Because their dignity was intact, they had no need to be overbearing, and because the Cooper boys had never heard that they were inferior, their minds could grow to their true limits.

That was my Negro experience until I was well grown, perhaps too far grown to reform the inflexible habits of childhood. Oh, I have seen plenty since and have felt the shattering waves of violence and despair and confusion. I have seen Negro children who really cannot learn, particularly those who in their gelatin plate of babyness have been told they were inferior. And, remembering the Coopers and how we felt about them, I think my main feeling is sorrow at the curtain of fear and anger drawn down between us. And I've just thought of an amusing possibility. If in Salinas anyone from a wiser and more sophisticated world had asked, "How would you like your sister to marry a Cooper?" I think we would have laughed. For it might have occurred to us that a Cooper might not have wanted to marry our sister, good friends though we all were.

Thus it remains that I am basically unfitted to take sides in the racial conflict. I must admit that cruelty and force exerted against weakness turn me sick with rage, but this would be equally true in the treatment of any weak by any strong.

Beyond my failings as a racist, I knew I was not wanted in the South. When people are engaged in something they are not proud of, they do not welcome witnesses. In fact, they come to believe the witness causes the trouble.

In all this discussion of the South I have been speaking only about the violence set loose by the desegregation movements—the children going to school, the young Negroes demanding the questionable privilege of lunch counters, buses, and toilets. But I am particularly interested in the school business, because it seems to me that the blight can disappear only when there are millions of Coopers.

Recently a dear Southern friend instructed me passionately in the theory of "equal but separate." "It just happens," he said, "that in my town there are three new Negro schools not equal but superior to the white schools. Now wouldn't you think they would be satisfied with that? And in the bus station the washrooms are exactly the same. What's your answer to that?"

I said, "Maybe it's a matter of ignorance. You could solve it and really put them in their places if you switched schools and toilets. The moment they realized that your schools weren't as good as theirs, they would realize their error."

And do you know what he said? He said, "You troublemaking son of a bitch." But he said it smiling.

While I was still in Texas, late in 1960, the incident most reported and pictured in the newspapers was the matriculation of a couple of tiny Negro children in a New Orleans school. Behind these small dark mites were the law's majesty and the law's power to enforce—both the scales and the sword were allied with the infants—while against them were three hundred years of fear and anger and terror of change in a changing world. I had seen photographs in the papers every day and motion pictures on the television screen. What made the newsmen love the story was a group of stout middle-aged women who, by some curious definition of the word "mother," gathered every day to scream invectives at children. Further, a small group of them had become so expert that they were known as the Cheerleaders, and a crowd gathered every day to enjoy and to applaud their performance.

This strange drama seemed so improbable that I felt I had to see it. It had the same draw as a five-legged calf or a two-headed foetus at a sideshow, a distortion of normal life we have always found so interesting that we will pay to see it, perhaps to prove to ourselves that we have the proper number of legs or heads. In the New Orleans show, I felt all the amusement of the improbable abnormal, but also a kind of horror that it could be so.

At this time the winter which had been following my track ever since I left home suddenly struck with a black norther. It brought ice and freezing sleet and sheeted the highways with dark ice. I gathered Charley from the good doctor. He looked half his age and felt wonderful, and to prove it he ran and jumped and rolled and laughed and gave little yips of pure joy. It felt very good to have him with me again, sitting up right in the seat beside me, peering ahead at the unrolling road, or curling up to sleep with his head in my lap and his silly ears available for fondling. That dog can sleep through any amount of judicious caresses.

Now we stopped dawdling and laid our wheels to the road and went. We could not go fast because of the ice, but we drove relentlessly, hardly glancing at the passing of Texas beside us. And Texas was achingly endless—Sweetwater and Balinger and Austin. We bypassed Houston. We stopped for gasoline and coffee and slabs of pie. Charley had his meals and his walks in gas stations. Night did not stop us, and when my eyes ached and burned from peering too long and my shoulders were side hills of pain, I pulled into a turnout and crawled like a mole into my bed, only to see the highway writhe along behind my closed lids. No more than two hours could I sleep, and then out into the bitter cold night and on and on. Water beside the road was frozen solid, and people moved about with shawls and sweaters wrapped around their ears.

Other times I have come to Beaumont dripping with sweat and lusting for ice and air-conditioning. Now Beaumont with all its glare of neon signs was what they called froze up. I went through Beaumont at night, or rather in the dark well after midnight. The blue-fingered man who filled my gas tank looked in at Charley and said, "Hey, it's a dog! I thought you had a nigger in there." And he laughed delightedly. It was the first of many repetitions. At least twenty times I heard it—"Thought you had a nigger in there." It was an unusual joke—always fresh—and never Negro or even Nigra, always Nigger or rather Niggah. That word seemed terribly important, a kind of safety word to cling to lest some structure collapse.

And then I was in Louisiana, with Lake Charles away to the side in the dark, but my lights glittered on ice and glinted on diamond frost, and those people who forever trudge the roads at night were mounded over with cloth against the cold. I dogged it on through La Fayette and Morgan City and came in the early dawn to Houma, which is pronounced Homer and is in my memory one of the pleasantest places in the world. There lives my old friend Doctor St. Martin, a gentle, learned man, a Cajun who has lifted babies and cured colic among the shell-heap Cajuns for miles around. I guess he knows more about Cajuns than anyone living, but I remembered with longing other gifts of Doctor St. Martin. He makes the best and most subtle martini in the world by a process approximating magic. The only part of his formula I know is that he uses distilled water for his ice and distills it himself to be sure. I have eaten black duck at his table—two St. Martin martinis and a brace of black duck with a burgundy delivered from the bottle as a baby might be delivered, and this in a darkened house where the shades have been closed at dawn and the cool night air preserved. At that table with its silver soft and dull, shining as pewter, I remember the raised glass of the grape's holy blood, the stem caressed by the doctor's strong artist fingers, and even now I can hear the sweet little health and welcome in the singing language of Acadia which once was French and now is itself. This picture filled my frosty windshield, and if there had been traffic would have made me a dangerous driver. But it was pale yellow frozen dawn in Houma and I knew that if I stopped to pay my respects, my will and my determination would drift away on the particular lotus St. Martin purveys and we would be speaking of timeless matters when the evening came, and another evening. And so I only bowed in the direction of my friend and scudded on toward New Orleans, for I wanted to catch a show of the Cheerleaders.

Even I know better than to drive a car near trouble, particularly Rocinante, with New York license plates. Only yesterday a reporter had been beaten and his camera smashed, for even convinced voters are reluctant to have their moment of history recorded and preserved.

So, well on the edge of town I drove into a parking lot. The attendant came to my window. "Man, oh man, I thought you had a nigger in there. Man, oh man, it's a dog. I see that big old black face and I think it's a big old nigger."

"His face is blue-gray when he's clean," I said coldly.

"Well I see some blue-gray niggers and they wasn't clean. New York, eh?"

It seemed to me a chill like the morning air came into his voice. "Just driving through," I said. "I want to park for a couple of hours. Think you can get me a taxi?"

"Tell you what I bet. I bet you're going to see the Cheerleaders."

"That's right."

"Well, I hope you're not one of those trouble-makers or reporters."

"I just want to see it."

"Man, oh man, you going to see something. Ain't those Cheerleaders something? Man, oh man, you never heard nothing like it when they get going."

I locked Charley in Rocinante's house after giving the attendant a tour of the premises, a drink of whisky, and a dollar. "Be kind of careful about opening the door when I'm away," I said. "Charley takes his job pretty seriously. You might lose a hand." This was an outrageous lie, of course, but the man said, "Yes, sir. You don't catch me fooling around with no strange dog."

The taxi driver, a sallow, yellowish man, shriveled like a chickpea with the cold, said, "I wouldn't take you more than a couple of blocks near. I don't go to have my cab wrecked."

"Is it that bad?"

"It ain't is it. It's can it get. And it can get that bad."

"When do they get going?"

He looked at his watch. "Except it's cold, they been coming in since dawn. It's quarter to. You get along and you won't miss nothing except it's cold."

I had camouflaged myself in an old blue jacket and my British navy cap on the supposition that in a seaport no one ever looks at a sailor any more than a waiter is inspected in a restaurant. In his natural haunts a sailor has no face and certainly no plans beyond getting drunk and maybe in jail for fighting. At least that's the general feeling about sailors. I've tested it. The most that happens is a kindly voice of authority saying, "Why don't you go back to your ship, sailor? You wouldn't want to sit in the tank and miss your tide, now would you, sailor?" And the speaker wouldn't recognize you five minutes later. And the Lion and Unicorn on my cap made me even more anonymous. But I must warn anyone testing my theory, never try it away from a shipping port.

"Where you from?" the driver asked with a complete lack of interest.

"Liverpool."

"Limey, huh? Well, you'll be all right. It's the goddamn New York Jews cause all the trouble."

I found myself with a British inflection and by no means one of Liverpool. "Jews—what? How do they cause trouble?"

"Why, hell, mister. We know how to take care of this. Everybody's happy and getting along fine. Why, I *like* niggers. And them goddamn New York Jews come in and stir the niggers up. They just stay in New York there wouldn't be no trouble. Ought to take them out."

"You mean lynch them?"

"I don't mean nothing else, mister."

He let me out and I started to walk away. "Don't try to get too close, mister," he called after me. "Just you enjoy it but don't mix in."

"Thanks," I said, and killed the "awfully" that came to my tongue.

As I walked toward the school I was in a stream of people all white and all going in my direction. They walked intently like people going to a fire after it has been burning for some time. They beat their hands against their hips or hugged them under coats, and many men had scarves under their hats and covering their ears.

Across the street from the school the police had set up wooden barriers to keep the crowd back, and they paraded back and forth, ignoring the jokes called to them. The front of the school was deserted but along the curb United States marshals were spaced, not in uniform but wearing armbands to identify them. Their guns bulged decently under their coats but their eyes darted about nervously, inspecting faces. It seemed to me that they inspected me to see if I was a regular, and then abandoned me as unimportant.

It was apparent where the Cheerleaders were, because people shoved forward to try to get near them. They had a favored place at the barricade directly across from the school entrance, and in that area a concentration of police stamped their feet and slapped their hands together in unaccustomed gloves.

Suddenly I was pushed violently and a cry went up: "Here she comes. Let her through. . . . Come on, move back. Let her through. Where you been? You're late for school. Where you been, Nellie?"

The name was not Nellie. I forget what it was. But she shoved through the dense crowd quite near enough to me so that I could see her coat of imitation fleece and her gold earrings. She was not tall, but her body was ample and full-busted. I judge she was about fifty. She was heavily powdered, which made the line of her double chin look very dark.

She wore a ferocious smile and pushed her way through the milling people, holding a fistful of clippings high in her hand to keep them from being crushed. Since it was her left hand I looked particularly for a wedding ring, and saw that there was none. I slipped in behind her to get carried along by her wave, but the crush was dense and I was given a warning too. "Watch it, sailor. Everybody wants to hear."

Nellie was received with shouts of greeting. I don't know how many Cheerleaders there were. There was no fixed line between the Cheerleaders and the crowd behind them. What I could see was that a group was passing newspaper clippings back and forth and reading them aloud with little squeals of delight.

Now the crowd grew restless, as an audience does when the clock goes past curtain time. Men all around me looked at their watches; I looked at mine. It was three minutes to nine.

The show opened on time. Sound of sirens. Motorcycle cops. Then two big black cars filled with big men in blond felt hats pulled up in front of the school. The crowd seemed to hold its breath. Four big marshals got out of each car and from somewhere in the automobiles they extracted the littlest Negro girl you ever saw, dressed in shining starchy white, with new white shoes on feet so little they were almost round. Her face and little legs were very black against the white.

The big marshals stood her on the curb and a jangle of jeering shrieks went up from behind the barricades. The little girl did not look at the howling crowd but from the side the whites of her eyes showed like those of a frightened fawn. The men turned her around like a doll, and then the strange procession moved up the broad walk toward the school, and the child was even more a mite because the men were so big. Then the girl made a curious hop, and I think I know what it was. I think in her whole life she had not gone ten steps without skipping, but now in the middle of her first skip the weight bore her down and her little round feet took measured, reluctant steps between the tall guards. Slowly they climbed the steps and entered the school.

The papers had printed that the jibes and jeers were cruel and sometimes obscene, and so they were, but this was not the big show. The crowd was waiting for the white man who dared to bring his white child to school. And here he came along the guarded walk, a tall man dressed in light gray, leading his frightened child by the hand. His body was tensed as a strong leaf spring drawn to the breaking strain; his face was grave and gray, and his eyes were on the ground immediately ahead of him. The muscles of his cheeks stood out from clenched jaws, a man afraid who by his will held his fears in check as a great rider directs a panicked horse.

A shrill, grating voice rang out. The yelling was not in chorus. Each took a turn and at the end of each the crowd broke into howls and roars and whistles of applause. This is what they had come to see and hear.

No newspaper had printed the words these women shouted. It was indicated that they were indelicate, some even said obscene. On television the sound track was made to blur or had crowd noises cut in to cover. But now I heard the words, bestial and filthy and degenerate. In a long and unprotected life I have seen and heard the vomitings of demoniac humans before. Why then did these screams fill me with a shocked and sickened sorrow?

The words written down are dirty, carefully and selectedly filthy. But there was something far worse here than dirt, a kind of frightening witches' Sabbath. Here was no spontaneous cry of anger, of insane rage.

Perhaps that is what made me sick with weary nausea. Here was no principle good or bad, no direction. These blowzy women with their little hats and their clippings hungered for attention. They wanted to be admired. They simpered in happy, almost innocent triumph when they were applauded. Their was the demented cruelty of egocentric children, and somehow this made their insensate beastliness much more heartbreaking. These were not mothers, not even women. They were crazy actors playing to a crazy audience.

The crowd behind the barrier roared and cheered and

pounded one another with joy. The nervous strolling police watched for any break over the barrier. Their lips were tight but a few of them smiled and quickly unsmiled. Across the street the U.S. marshals stood unmoving. The gray-clothed man's legs had speeded for a second, but he reined them down with his will and walked up the school pavement.

The crowd quieted and the next cheer lady had her turn. Her voice was the bellow of a bull, a deep and powerful shout with flat edges like a circus barker's voice. There is no need to set down her words. The pattern was the same; only the rhythm and tonal quality were different. Anyone who has been near the theater would know that these speeches were not spontaneous. They were tried and memorized and carefully rehearsed. This was theater. I watched the intent faces of the listening crowd and they were the faces of an audience. When there was applause, it was for a performer.

My body churned with weary nausea, but I could not let an illness blind me after I had come so far to look and to hear. And suddenly I knew something was wrong and distorted and out of drawing. I knew New Orleans, I have over the years had many friends there, thoughtful, gentle people, with a tradition of kindness and courtesy. I remembered Lyle Saxon, a huge man of soft laughter. How many days I have spent with Roark Bradford, who took Louisiana sounds and sights and created God and the Green Pastures to which He leadeth us. I looked in the crowd for such faces of such people and they were not there. I've seen this kind bellow for blood at a prize fight, have orgasms when a man is gored in the bull ring, stare with vicarious lust at a highway accident, stand patiently in line for the privilege of watching any pain or any agony. But where were the others—the ones who would be proud they were of a species with the gray man—the ones whose arms would ache to gather up the small, scared black mite?

I don't know where they were. Perhaps they felt as helpless as I did, but they left New Orleans misrepresented to the world. The crowd, no doubt, rushed home to see themselves on television, and what they saw went out all over the world, unchallenged by the other things I know are there.

The show was over and the river of us began to move away. Second show would be when school-closing bell rang and the little black face had to look out at her accusers again. I was in New Orleans of the great restaurants. I know them all and most of them know me. And I could no more have gone to Gallatoir's for an omelet and champagne than I could have danced on a grave. Even setting this down on paper has raised the weary, hopeless nausea in me again. It is not written to amuse. It does not amuse me.

I bought a poor-boy sandwich and got out of town. Not too far along I found a pleasant resting place where I could sit and munch and contemplate and stare out over the stately brown, slow-moving Father of Waters as my spirit required. Charley did not wander about but sat close and pressed his shoulder against my knee, and he does that only when I am ill, so I suppose I was ill with a kind of sorrow.

I lost track of time, but a while after the sun had passed top a man came walking and we exchanged good afternoons. He was a neatly dressed man well along in years, with a Greco face and fine wind-lifted white hair and a clipped white mustache. I asked him to join me, and when he accepted I went into my house and set coffee to cooking and, remembering how Roark Bradford liked it, I doubled the dosage, two heaping tablespoons of coffee to each cup and two heaping for the pot. I cracked an egg and cupped out the yolk and dropped white and shells into the pot, for I know nothing that polishes coffee and makes it shine like that. The air was still very cold and a cold night was coming, so that the brew, rising from cold water to a rolling boil, gave the good smell that competes successfully with other good smells.

My guest was satisfied, and he warmed his hands against the plastic cup. "By your license, you're a stranger here," he said. "How do you come to know about coffee?"

"I learned on Bourbon Street from giants in the earth," I said.

"But they would have asked the bean of a darker roast and they would have liked a little chicory for bite."

"You do know," he said. "You're not a stranger after all. And can you make diablo?"

"For parties, yes. You come from here?"

"More generations than I can prove beyond doubt, except classified under *ci gît* in St. Louis."

"I see. You're of that breed. I'm glad you stopped by. I used to know St. Louis, even collected epitaphs."

"Did you, sir? You'll remember the queer one, then."

"If it's the same one, I tried to memorize it. You mean that one that starts, 'Alas that one whose darnthly joy . . .' ?"

"That's it. Robert John Cresswell, died 1845 aged twenty-six."

"I wish I could remember it."

"Have you a paper? You can write it down."

And when I had a pad on my knee he said, "Alas that one whose darnthly joy had often to trust in heaven should canty thus sudden to from all its hopes benivens and though thy love for off remore that dealt the dog pest thou left to prove thy sufferings while below."

"It's wonderful," I said. "Lewis Carroll could have written it. I almost know what it means."

"Everyone does. Are you traveling for pleasure?"

"I was until today. I saw the Cheerleaders."

"Oh, yes, I see," he said, and a weight and a darkness fell on him.

"What's going to happen?"

"I don't know. I just don't know. I don't dare think about it. Why do I have to think about it? I'm too old. Let the others take care of it."

"Can you see an end?"

"Oh, certainly an end. It's the means—it's the means. But you're from the North. This isn't your problem."

"I guess it's everybody's problem. It isn't local. Would you have another cup of coffee and talk to me about it? I don't have a position. I mean I want to hear."

"There's nothing to learn," he said. "It seems to change its face with who you are and where you've been and how you feel—not think, but feel. You didn't like what you saw?"

"Would you?"

"Maybe less than you because I know all of its aching past and some of its stinking future. That's an ugly word, sir, but there's no other."

"The Negroes want to be people. Are you against that?"

"Bless you, no, sir. But to get to be people they must fight those who aren't satisfied to be people."

"You mean the Negroes won't be satisfied with any gain?"

"Are you? Is anyone you know?"

"Would you be content to let them be people?"

"Content enough, but I wouldn't understand it. I've got too many *ci gîts* here. How can I tell you? Well, suppose your dog here, he looks a very intelligent dog—"

"He is."

"Well, suppose he could talk and stand on his hind legs. Maybe he could do very well in every way. Perhaps you could invite him to dinner, but could you think of him as people?"

"Do you mean, how would I like my sister to marry him?"

He laughed. "I'm only telling you how hard it is to change a feeling about things. And will you believe that it will be just as hard for Negroes to change their feeling about us as it is for us to change about them? This isn't new. It's been going on a long time."

"Anyway, the subject skims the joy off a pan of conversation."

"That it does, sir. I think I'm what you might call an enlightened Southerner mistaking an insult for a compliment. As such a new-born hybrid, I know what will happen over the ages. It's starting now in Africa and in Asia."

"You mean absorption—the Negroes will disappear?"

"If they outnumber us, we will disappear, or more likely both will disappear into something new."

"And meanwhile?"

"It's the meanwhile frightens me, sir. The ancients placed love and war in the hands of closely related gods. That was no accident. That, sir, was a profound knowledge of man."

"You reason well."

"The ones you saw today do not reason at all. They're the ones who may alert the god."

"Then you do think it can't happen in peace?"

"I don't know," he cried. "I guess that's the worst. I just don't know. Sometimes I long to assume my rightful title Ci Gît."

"I wish you would ride along with me. Are you on the move?"

"No. I have a little place just off there below that grove. I spend a lot of time there, mostly reading—old things—mostly looking at—old things. It's my intentional method of avoiding the issue because I'm afraid of it."

"I guess we all do some of that."

He smiled. "I have an old Negro couple as old as I am to take care of me. And sometimes in the evening we forget. They forget to envy me and I forget they might, and we are just three pleasant . . . things living together and smelling the flowers."

"Things," I repeated. "That's interesting—not man and beast, not black and white, but pleasant things. My wife told me of an old old man who said, 'I remember a time when Negroes had no souls. It was much better and easier then. Now it's confusing.' "

"I don't remember, but it must be so. It is my guess that we can cut and divide our inherited guilt like a birthday cake," he said, and save for the mustache he looked like the Greco San Pablo who holds the closed book in his hands. "Surely my ancestors had slaves, but it is possible that yours caught them and sold them to us."

"I have a puritan strain that might well have done so."

"If by force you make a creature live and work like a beast, you must think of him as a beast, else empathy would drive you mad. Once you have classified him in your mind, your feelings are safe." He stared at the river, and the breeze stirred his hair like white smoke. "And if your heart has human vestiges of courage and anger, which in a man are virtues, then you have fear of a dangerous beast, and since your heart has intelligence and inventiveness and the ability to conceal them, you live with terror. Then you must crush his manlike tendencies and make of him the docile beast you want. And if you can teach your child from the beginning about the beast, he will not share your bewilderment."

"I've been told the good old-time Negro sang and danced and was content."

"He also ran away. The fugitive laws suggest how often."

"You're not what the North thinks of as a Southerner."

"Perhaps not. But I'm not alone." He stood up and dusted his trousers with his fingers. "No—not alone. I'll go along to my pleasant things now."

"I have not asked your name, sir, nor offered mine."

"Ci Gît," he said. "Monsieur Ci Gît—a big family, a common name."

When he went away I felt a sweetness like music, if music could pleasure the skin with a little chill.

To me, it had been a day larger than a day, not to be measured against other days with any chance of matching. With little sleep the night before I knew I should stop. I was very tired, but sometimes fatigue can be a stimulant and a compulsion. It forced me to fill my gas tank and compelled me to stop and offer a ride to an old Negro who trudged with heavy heels in the grass-grown verge beside the concrete road. He was reluctant to accept and did so only as though helpless to resist. He wore the battered clothes of a field hand and an ancient broadcloth coat highly polished by age and wear. His face was coffee-colored and cross-hatched with a million tiny wrinkles, and his lower lids showed red rims like a bloodhound's eyes. He clasped his hands in his lap, knotted and lumpy as cherry twigs, and all of him seemed to shrink in the seat as though he sucked in his outline to make it smaller.

He never looked at me. I could not see that he looked at anything. But first he asked, "Dog bite, captain, sir?"

"No. He's friendly."

After a long silent while I asked, "How are things going with you?"

"Fine, just fine, captain, sir."

"How do you feel about what's going on?"

He didn't answer.

"I mean about the schools and the sit-ins."

"I don't know nothing about that, captain, sir."

"Work on a farm?"

"Crop a cotton lot, sir."

"Make a living at it?"

"I get along fine, captain, sir."

We went in silence for a stretch upriver. The trees and the tropic grass were burned and sad from the ferocious northern freeze. After a time I said, more to myself than to him, "After all, why should you trust me? A question is a trap and an answer is your foot in it." I remembered a scene—something that happened in New York—and was moved to tell him about it, but I quickly abandoned the impulse because out of the corner of my eye I could see that he had drawn away and squeezed himself against the far side of the cab. But the memory was strong.

I lived then in a small brick house in Manhattan, and, being for the moment solvent, employed a Negro. Across the street and on the corner there was a bar and restaurant. One winter dusk when the sidewalks were iced I stood in my window looking out and saw a tipsy woman come out of the bar, slip on the ice, and fall flat. She tried to struggle up but slipped and fell again and lay there screaming maudlinly. At that moment the Negro who worked for me came around the corner, saw the woman, and instantly crossed the street, keeping as far from her as possible.

When he came in I said, "I saw you duck. Why didn't you give that woman a hand?"

"Well, sir, she's drunk and I'm Negro. If I touched her she could easy scream rape, and then it's a crowd, and who believes me?"

"It took quick thinking to duck that fast."

"Oh, no sir!" he said. "I've been practicing to be a Negro a long time."

And now in Rocinante I was foolishly trying to destroy a lifetime of practice.

"I won't ask you any more questions," I said.

But he squirmed with restlessness. "Would you let me down here, please, captain? I live nearby."

I let him down and saw in the mirror how he took up his trudging beside the road. He didn't live nearby at all, but walking was safer than riding with me.

Weariness flagged me down and I stopped in a pleasant motel. The beds were good but I could not sleep. The gray man walked across my eyes, and the faces of the Cheerladies, but mostly I saw the old man squeezed as far away from me as he could get, as though I carried the infection, and perhaps I did. I came out to learn. What was I learning? I had not felt one moment free from the tension, a weight of savage fear. No doubt I felt it more being new-come, but it was there; I hadn't brought it. Everyone, white and black, lived in it and breathed it—all ages, all trades, all classes. To them it was a fact of existence. And it was building pressure like a boil. Could there be no relief until it burst?

I had seen so little of the whole. I didn't see a great deal of World War II—one landing out of a hundred, a few separated times of combat, a few thousand dead out of millions—but I saw enough /and felt enough to believe war was no stranger. So here—a little episode, a few people, but the breath of fear was everywhere. I wanted to get away—a cowardly attitude, perhaps, but more cowardly to deny. But the people around me lived here. They accepted it as a permanent way of life, had never known it otherwise nor expected it to stop. The Cockney children in London were restless when the bombing stopped and disturbed a pattern to which they had grown accustomed.

I tossed about until Charley grew angry with me and told me "Ftt" several times. But Charley doesn't have our problems. He doesn't belong to a species clever enough to split the atom but not clever enough to live in peace with itself. He doesn't even know about race, nor is he concerned with his sisters' marriage. It's quite the opposite. Once Charley fell in love with a dachshund, a romance racially unsuitable, physically ridiculous, and mechanically impossible. But all these problems Charley ignored. He loved deeply and tried dogfully. It would be difficult to explain to a dog the good and moral purpose of a thousand humans gathered to curse one tiny human. I've seen a look in dogs' eyes, a quickly vanishing look of amazed contempt, and I am convinced that basically dogs think humans are nuts.

I didn't choose my first customer the next day. He picked me. He sat on a stool next to me eating a hamburger whose twin I held in my hand. He was somewhere between thirty and thirty-five, long and stringy, and nice-looking. His long lank hair was nearly ash-blond, worn long and treasured since he whopped it with a pocket comb unconsciously and often. He wore a light gray suit that was travel-wrinkled and stained; he carried the jacket over his shoulder. His white shirt was open at the collar, permitted so by pulling down the knot of his pale paisley tie. His speech was the deepest south I had heard so far. He asked where I was going and, when I told him I aimed toward Jackson and Montgomery, begged a ride with me. When he saw Charley he thought at first I had a nigger in there. It had got to be a pattern.

We settled ourselves comfortably. He combed back his hair and complimented me on Rocinante. "Of course," he said, "I could tell right off you're from the North."

"You've got a good ear," I said, I thought facetiously.

"Oh, I get around," he admitted.

I think I was responsible for what happened. If I could have kept my mouth shut I might have learned something of value. There's the restless night to blame and the length of the journey and the nervousness. Then, too, Christmas was coming and I found myself thinking of getting home more often than was helpful.

We established that I was traveling for pleasure and that he was on the lookout for a job.

"You come up the river," he said. "Did you see the doings in New Orleans?"

"Yes, I did."

"Wasn't they something, especially that Nellie? She really ripped the roof off."

"Yes, she did."

"Does your heart good to see somebody do their duty."

I think it was there that I went haywire. I should have grunted and let him read what he wanted in it. But a nasty little worm of anger began to stir in me. "They doing it out of duty?"

"Sure, God bless them. Somebody got to keep the goddamn niggers out of our schools." The sublimity of self-sacrifice activating the Cheerleaders overwhelmed him. "Comes a time when a man's got to sit down and think, and that's the time you got to make up your mind to sell your life for something you believe in."

"Did you decide to do it?"

"I sure did, and a lot more like me."

"What do you believe in?"

"I'm not just about to allow my kids to go to school with no niggers. Yes, sir. I'll sell my life first but I aim to kill me a whole goddamn flock of niggers before I go."

"How many children do you have?"

He swung around toward me. "I don't have any but I aim to have some and I promise you they won't go to school with no niggers."

"Do you propose to sell your life before or after you have children?"

I had to watch the road so I only got a glimpse of his expression, and it wasn't pleasant. "You sound to me like a nigger-lover. I might of known it. Trouble-makers—come down here and tell us how to live. Well, you won't get away with it, mister. We got an eye on you Commie nigger-lovers."

"I just had a brave picture of you selling your life."

"By God, I was right. You are a nigger-lover."

"No, I'm not. And I'm not a white-lover either, if it includes those noble Cheerladies."

His face was very near to me. "You want to hear what I think of you?"

"No. I heard Nellie use the words yesterday." I put on the brake and pulled Rocinante off the road.

He looked puzzled. "What you stopping for?"

"Get out," I said.

"Oh, you want to go round."

"No. I want to get rid of you. Get out."

"You going to make me?"

I reached into the space between the seat and the door where there is nothing.

"Okay, okay," he said, and got out and slammed the door so hard that Charley wailed with annoyance.

I started instantly, but I heard him scream, and in the mirror saw his hating face and his open spit-ringed mouth. He shrilled

"Nigger-lover, nigger-lover, nigger-lover," as long as I could see him and I don't know how long after. It's true I goaded him, but I couldn't help it. I guess when they're drafting peacemakers they'd better pass me by.

I picked up one more passenger between Jackson and Montgomery, a young Negro student with a sharp face and the look and feel of impatient fierceness. He carried three fountain pens in his breast pocket, and his inner pocket bulged with papers. I knew he was a student because I asked him. He was alert. License plate and speech relaxed him as much as he is ever likely to relax.

We discussed the sit-ins. He had taken part in them, and in the bus boycott. I told him what I had seen in New Orleans. He had been there. He had expected what I was shocked at.

Finally we spoke of Martin Luther King and his teaching of passive but unrelenting resistance.

"It's too slow," he said. "It will take too long."

"There's improvement, there's constant improvement. Gandhi proved it's the only weapon that can win against violence."

"I know all that. I've studied it. The gains are drops of water and time is passing. I want it faster, I want action—action now."

"That might defeat the whole thing."

"I might be an old man before I'm a man at all. I might be dead before."

"That's true. And Gandhi's dead. Are there many like you who want action?"

"Yes. I mean, some—I mean, I don't know how many."

We talked of many things then. He was a passionate and articulate young man with anxiety and fierceness just below the surface. But when I dropped him in Montgomery he leaned through the window of the cab and he laughed. "I'm ashamed," he said. "It's just selfishness. But I want to see it—me—not dead. Here! Me! I want to see it—soon." And then he swung around and wiped his eyes with his hand and he walked quickly away.

With all the polls and opinion posts, with newspapers more opinion than news so that we no longer know one from the other, I want to be very clear about one thing. I have not intended to present, nor do I think I have presented, any kind of cross-section so that a reader can say, "He thinks he has presented a true picture of the South." I don't. I've only told what a few people said to me and what I saw. I don't know whether they were typical or whether any conclusion can be drawn. But I do know it is a troubled place and a people caught in a jam. And I know that the solution when it arrives will not be easy or simple. I feel with Monsieur Ci Gît that the end is not in question. It's the means—the dreadful uncertainty of the means.

In the beginning of this record I tried to explore the nature of journeys, how they are things in themselves, each one an individual and no two alike. I speculated with a kind of wonder on the strength of the individuality of journeys and stopped on the postulate that people don't take trips—trips take people. That discussion, however, did not go into the life span of journeys. This seems to be variable and unpredictable. Who has not known a journey to be over and dead before the traveler returns? The reverse is also true: many a trip continues long after movement in time and space have ceased. I remember a man in Salinas who in his middle years traveled to Honolulu and back, and that journey continued for the rest of his life. We could watch him in his rocking chair on his front porch, his eyes squinted, half-closed, endlessly traveling to Honolulu.

My own journey started long before I left, and was over before I returned. I know exactly where and when it was over. Near Abingdon, in the dog-leg of Virginia, at four o'clock of a windy afternoon, without warning or good-by or kiss my foot, my journey went away and left me stranded far from home. I tried to call it back, to catch it up—a foolish and hopeless matter, because it was definitely and permanently over and finished. The road became an endless stone ribbon, the hills obstructions, the trees green blurs, the people simply moving figures with heads but no faces. All the food along the way tasted like soup, even the soup. My bed was unmade. I slipped into it for naps at long uneven intervals. My stove was unlighted and a loaf of bread gathered mold in my cupboard. The miles rolled under me unacknowledged. I know it was cold, but I didn't feel it; I know the countryside must have been beautiful, but I didn't see it. I bulldozed blindly through West Virginia, plunged into Pennsylvania and grooved Rocinante to the great wide turnpike. There was no night, no day, no distance. I must have stopped to fill my gas tank, to walk and feed Charley, to eat, to telephone, but I don't remember any of it.

It is very strange. Up to Abingdon, Virginia, I can reel back the trip like film. I have almost total recall, every face is there, every hill and tree and color, and sound of speech and small scenes ready to replay themselves in my memory. After Abingdon—nothing. The way was a gray, timeless, eventless tunnel, but at the end of it was the one shining reality—my own wife, my own house in my own street, my own bed. It was all there, and I lumbered my way toward it. Rocinante could be fleet, but I had not driven her fast. Now she leaped under my heavy relentless foot, and the wind shrieked around the corners of the house. If you think I am indulging in fantasy about the trip, how can you explain that Charley knew it was over too? He at least is no dreamer, no coiner of moods. He went to sleep with his head in my lap, never looked out the window, never said "Ftt," never urged me to a turn-out. He carried out his functions like a sleepwalker, ignored whole rows of garbage cans. If that doesn't prove the truth of my statement, nothing can.

New Jersey was another turnpike. My body was in a nerveless, tireless vacuum. The increasing river of traffic for New York carried me along, and suddenly there was the welcoming maw of Holland Tunnel and at the other end home.

A policeman waved me out of the snake of traffic and flagged me to a stop. "You can't go through the tunnel with that butane," he said.

"But officer, it's turned off."

"Doesn't matter. It's the law. Can't take gas into the tunnel."

And suddenly I fell apart, collapsed into a jelly of weariness. "But I want to get home," I wailed. "How am I going to get home?"

He was very kind to me, and patient too. Maybe he had a home somewhere. "You can go up and take George Washington Bridge, or you can take a ferry."

It was rush hour, but the gentle-hearted policeman must have seen a potential maniac in me. He held back the savage traffic and got me through and directed me with great care. I think he was strongly tempted to drive me home.

Magically I was on the Hoboken ferry and then ashore, far downtown with the daily panic rush of commuters leaping and running and dodging in front, obeying no signals. Every evening is Pamplona in lower New York. I made a turn and then another, entered a one-way street the wrong way and had to back out, got boxed in the middle of a crossing by a swirling rapids of turning people.

Suddenly I pulled to the curb in a no-parking area, cut my motor, and leaned back in the seat and laughed, and I couldn't stop. My hands and arms and shoulders were shaking with road jitters.

An old-fashioned cop with a fine red face and a frosty blue eye leaned in toward me. "What's the matter with you, Mac, drunk?" he asked.

I said, "Officer, I've driven this thing all over the country—mountains, plains, deserts. And now I'm back in my own town, where I live—and I'm lost."

He grinned happily. "Think nothing of it, Mac," he said. "I got lost in Brooklyn only Saturday. Now where is it you were wanting to go?"

And that's how the traveler came home again.

APPENDIX: L'ENVOI

"L'Envoi," Steinbeck's original proposed ending for Travels with Charley, *was omitted from the first 1962 Viking Press edition of the book.*

This narrative opened with a storm, the hurricane Donna, far and away the greatest sendoff an expedition ever had and I thought at the time a little overboard. And by rights it should end with a storm, and it did. But again I am troubled by matters of proportion. My travels with Charley were a simple, almost humble undertaking. They caused no flurry and piled up a limited heap of information. Thinking back, I don't know what, if anything, I learned. Therefore the storm at the end may seem a very big stage, set for a very small drama. Of course I could whomp up a medium storm or a small earthquake in good taste and proper proportion, but in this account I have clung tenaciously, perhaps foolishly, to the truth. The storm I must use is the only storm I have.

My lady wife lowered the *New York Times* and gazed at me so long that I inspected any recent deeds and impulses.

"You've been invited to the inauguration," she said.

"You made the rule about no jokes in the morning."

"It says here you've been invited to the inauguration."

"By whom, for God's sakes?"

"By the President, who else?"

"But I don't know him. What is this?"

"Four painters, four poets and four novelists. You're one of the novelists."

"That's crazy," I said. "Everybody knows what the government thinks of artists. They're good for questioning about overcoming the government by force and violence. I'm not sure the invitation isn't unconstitutional. That new guy had better watch his step. Aren't westerns good enough for him? Who does he think he is?"

"I've never seen an inauguration," she said.

"Neither have I."

And there we were.

In one trait I am predictable. I dislike being late. I arrive at the theater while they are sweeping out from the matinee. I haunt a ship hours before it has any intention of sailing. Reluctantly accepting a cocktail invitation, I usually arrive before my hostess is out of the tub.

The historic snowstorm of the Kennedy inauguration caused endless trouble. Some heads of state were long late and some didn't get there at all. It was not so with us. We had arrived and were billeted in a lovely house in Georgetown and were having a tall cool drink when the first snow fell and we watched it flake by flake as it slowed, and finally brought the city to a standstill, covered stalled cars with a soft white blanket. It may have inconvenienced some charging bellowing officials but for us it made of Washington the most beautiful city in the world, a quiet place. In cities, the muffled under-sound of motors is so constant that we consider it silence. When it is removed the effect is startling, almost shocking. It was very well for us sitting comfortably watching through the window while the heavy businesslike flakes settled with every intention of remaining. And the depth built up. Every statue wore a tall white cap and every marble nose was tipped with a horn like that of a rhinoceros. The streets were tangles of abandoned cars and the sidewalks narrow paths between high shoveled walls. Men and women moved with high tiptoe leaps as though speed and posture might keep the snow from their shoes. I thought of the grand preparations, the hours of ladies in beauty parlors, the hundreds of thousands of new and delicate ball gowns, the spike-heeled satin shoes a passing out might sully. What despair there must be in thousands of feminine breasts. It is true the inauguration concerned only one man who by one short oath would renounce the world he knew and could never regain it. But it is also true that if the last judgment were announced, the first and proper thought of all ladies would be "What shall I wear?" And while the archangels are preparing the courtroom and the blessed tune their harps and certain others lie hunching under their fires, the ladies will be dashing hysterically in and out of fitting rooms.

And then, as the snow piled deeper and deeper and movement became impossible and then ridiculous—people changed. A kind of hell-for-leather gaiety invaded the city. Tragedy became a holiday. Even Republicans who had seen in the weather Divine wrath at a Democratic victory began to have fun.

Our blessings held. The cocktail parties to which we were assigned were all in easy walking distance.

The morning was like the Christmas song—"where the snow lay all about, deep and soft and even." And the sun turned it glittering. In the night the Army had been out plowing the main thoroughfares. And true to form, I got us to our seats below the rostrum at the Capitol long before the ceremony, so long before that we nearly froze. Mark Twain defined women as lovely creatures with a backache. I wonder how he omitted the only other safe generality—goddesses with cold feet. A warm-footed woman would be a monstrosity.

I think I was the only man there who heard the inauguration while holding his wife's feet in his lap, rubbing vigorously. With every sentence of the interminable prayers, I rubbed. And the prayers were interesting, if long. One sounded like general orders to the deity issued in a parade-ground voice. One prayer brought God up to date on current events with a view to their revision. In the midst of one prayer, smoke issued from the lectern and I thought we had gone too far but it turned out to be a short circuit.

How startling then to hear the simple stark oath of office offered and accepted. How moving. How deeply moving. I had never seen the ceremony before and it was good and I was glad.

Only one episode remains to be told and then my travels with Charley are finished. And we have never admitted this scene although we haven't out and out lied about it. Remember when you have visited some foreign area and some other traveler has asked. "Did you see such and such?" If you say no he screams, "What? Why that was the best. Don't see why you went at all if you didn't see such and such." We have learned to reply to the question, "Wonderful." Or "Remarkable!" That doesn't say we did or didn't see it and saves the argument.

Well, we were invited to the Inaugural Ball, the biggest and most desirable one where thousands of people would gather, where all the new dresses and satin shoes and hairdos would be. In the house of our hostess, other guests were ready, fingers moving restlessly in filmy cloth or tucking in hair that had never escaped, and every mirror was a place for sidelong glances. Dress ties were patted reassuringly every few seconds. The radio said that traffic conditions were impossible. Mobs of people, beautifully dressed, were floundering through snowdrifts and the great black official cars chugged through streets clanking chains. We drank together a last glass of champagne. And then everyone was gone and the house was quiet and the low lights were soft and the room a cushion of warm comfort. It was automatic. We didn't plan it. We drank another glass of wine looking out at the mountains of snow and then we crept up to our room and put on dressing gowns. In the kitchen we made sandwiches and arranged trays. Then I stood the great and important tickets of invitation to the ball on top of the television and turned on the set. We saw the President and his lady right up close and we saw the packed thousands below in crushed and snow-dabbled ball gowns. We nibbled our sandwiches and had a tall drink. And afterwards, when asked how we liked the Inaugural Ball, we have said, "Loved it. Remarkable. Wonderful!" And so it was. And we saw much more of it than the ones who were there. I guess it was the best ball I was ever invited to, and I enjoyed it the most, too.

And in the morning the snow was past and so was the journey.

I do know this—the big and mysterious America is bigger than I thought. And more mysterious.